BASEBALL CONTEST 1990

AMERICAN LEAGUE PLAYERS

By Jon Allison

LITTLE, BROWN AND COMPANY

Boston   Toronto   London

D1223639

Produced by
Cloverdale Press, Inc.
96 Morton Street
New York, New York 10014

First Edition

Library of Congress Catalog Card Number: 89-63982

ISBN 0-316-08309-7
10   9   8   7   6   5   4   3   2   1

*Published simultaneously in Canada
by Little, Brown & Company (Canada) Limited*

RRD OH

PRINTED IN THE UNITED STATES OF AMERICA

This book is neither endorsed nor authorized by the American League or by the
American League Baseball Association.

Statistics provided by Stats Inc.
7250 N. Cicero
Lincolnwood, IL 60646

INTRODUCTION

Does it get any better than baseball in 1989? How do you top the four down-to-the-wire pennant races, the strikeout magic of ageless Nolan Ryan, the season-long power surge by Kevin Mitchell, the amazing return to glory of the Baltimore Orioles, and the spectacular, never-to-be forgotten, earthquake-divided World Series sweep by the awesome Oakland A's?

Well, 1990 will be more exciting. We guarantee it. Because this time around, you can manage the champions—and collect *your* winning share, too! Welcome to *Baseball Contest 1990: American League Players*—your opportunity to match wits with tens of thousands of big-time fantasy-league managers all across the country. Best of all, you don't need to spend years of minor-league apprenticeship to manage in *Baseball Contest 1990*. In fact, everything you need is in your hands right now. If your team gets the job done on the field, you will win $10,000 in cash!

Let's start with the ground rules. You are going to pick 24 players from this book to fill out your roster:

- Six outfielders
- Six infielders—one first baseman, one second baseman, one third baseman, one shortstop, and two additional players from any of the infield positions
- Two catchers
- Ten pitchers

You can pick six left fielders if you wish, but not three shortstops or three third basemen.

You can pick a player who has played more than one position, but in our game he qualifies only at the position at which he's listed. The only eligible players are those listed in this book.

Lest you believe that one American League team will decimate its opponents, the rules also specify that at least 7 of the 12 American League clubs be represented on your roster. Like the baseball rule book, *Baseball Contest 1990* has its rule book, too. Please check it before sending in your entry. It begins on page 185.

How will the contest umpires make their calls? There are eight basic statistical measurements, four for hitters and four for pitchers.

First, the offensive categories:

- *Batting average:* You earn one point for each .001 in every player's average. Minnesota catcher Brian Harper hit .325 last season. That would produce 325 points for his manager.
- *Home Runs:* Each player's home run total is multiplied by 10. Fred McGriff's 36 homers in 1989 would have been worth 360 points for anyone who put him on their roster.
- *Runs Batted In:* A player's RBI total is multiplied by three. Don Mattingly knocked in 113 runs last season, which would be worth 339 points.
- *Runs Scored:* Like RBIs, a multiple of three is assigned to a player's runs scored. Cal Ripken scored 80 runs in 1989, for a total of 240 points.

Now, the pitching categories:

- *Earned Run Average:* One point for each .01 below 6.00. Subtract your pitcher's ERA from that number, then divide by .01. Dave Stewart's 1989 ERA was 3.32. That's a difference of 2.68 (6.00 − 3.32). Divided by .01, Stewart's performance earns 268 points.
- *Wins:* Every pitcher's victory total is multiplied by 25. Alan Anderson won 17 games last season, which would have been good for 425 points.

- *Losses:* There's jeopardy in a loss. The umpires will deduct 10 points for every defeat. Andy Hawkins, a 15-game winner for the Yankees in 1989, also lost 15 games. That would cost his manager 150 points.
- *Saves:* Ten points will be awarded for every save. Doug Jones saved 32 games for the Indians last season. In our game, that would be worth 320 points.

It would be a lead-pipe cinch to pick 24 superstars and pray that they stay healthy in 1990. "Nothing to it," you say? Sorry. To make this game a challenge, you'll have to build your roster with a salary cap. George Steinbrenner's budget director need not apply. Your cap is 75 points. Every eligible player has been rated on a scale of 1 to 5, with 5 being the highest. The rating is clearly displayed next to each player's profile.

The ratings were done after carefully evaluating each player's all-time record, with special emphasis on the most recent three years. (Only Nolan Ryan and Robin Yount seem to be playing as well today as they did 15 years ago!) For second-year players, this meant looking at their minor league numbers as well. The result is what professional scouts call a "projection evaluation"—a rating indicating the level at which the player can be expected to perform in 1990.

To simplify the ratings, consider a player rated 5 to be a superstar, one who will help you in most or all categories and dominate one or two; a 4 is an above-average player who will help you in two or three categories and stand out in one or two; a 3 is an average major league player, who will contribute in most categories, or will stand out in one or two; a 2 is a below-average major leaguer statistically; and a 1 is a player of little impact.

Each player was rated relative to his position. Therefore, a 5-rated catcher is not necessarily as good as a 5-rated outfielder—but he is the best of the catching corps. Likewise, a 5-rated reliever is not necessarily a better pitcher than a 5-rated starter. A 5-rated starter won't get any saves, while a 5-rated reliever may not pick up many wins.

The ratings have been carefully compiled by the author, in consultation with key baseball insiders. They represent the collective wisdom of the group. You may well disagree with them. Terrific! That's what makes baseball the great game it is. You may believe that one of our 3s should be a 5. Wonderful. Spend the 3 and save the other 2 points for help elsewhere. If we've given a 5 to a player you consider a 2, please take the opportunity to shop for a bargain elsewhere. That's what makes great managers and general managers great.

How should you build your roster? Think carefully. Study the rules. Try to get an edge if you can find one. You might look for players who can score for you in a variety of categories. A player who hits 30 homers but bats only .220 and, hence, doesn't get on base often (remember—runs scored count), might not be your best choice. Although stolen bases aren't included in the contest, you might look at those stats because runners who steal are more often in scoring position for a succeeding batter. We've even included notes on defense in our profiles. A guy who can get the job done defensively will get lots more playing time than another of equal offensive talent who doesn't know what to do with a baseball when it's hit to him.

Ponder your choice of pitchers with equal care. Should you go with a staff of starters who will produce a bunch of wins and a low ERA? Or should you stock up on relievers who'll get lots of saves and, quite probably, an even lower ERA? That's entirely up to you.

So grab a pencil and paper, go through the player evaluations, and start making notes. Then get your lineup card (entry form) ready for the season. Keep in mind, there are bonus points available for early entries.

If you've been hollering at your favorite team's general manager for not producing a winner every year, here's your opportunity to build your own championship franchise. It will be a great season. Enjoy! And good luck!

FIRST BASEMEN

Steve Balboni

Birth Date: 1/5/57
Bats: Right
Throws: Right
1989 Club:
Seattle Mariners &
New York Yankees
Contest Code #: 475

Rating: 2

Okay, he doesn't look pretty out there. Okay, he's a statuesque runner—with all of the mobility of a statue. Okay, with a glove on his hand he's hazardous to his team's health. But if the opponent's pitcher makes a mistake, grooves a fastball, hangs a curve ball, throws a slider that doesn't slide, Steve Balboni can hit it into the next county. At 6'3" and at least his listed 235 pounds, Bye-Bye Balboni remains an awesome offensive threat.

At age 33, the bald-headed first-sacker has lost whatever speed he may have had, and his defense is weak. But in any league that utilizes the designated hitter, he can certainly contribute.

The Yankees knew that when they retrieved him last season, six years after shipping him off to Kansas City. Balboni wound up with 17 homers in 300 at-bats with the Mariners and Yanks last season and his .237 average was a smidgen over his lifetime .231 mark.

Year	Team	G	AB	R	H	2B	3B	HR	RBI	BB	SB	AVG
1981	NYA....	4	7	2	2	1	1	0	2	1	0	.286
1982	NYA....	33	107	8	20	2	1	2	4	6	0	.187
1983	NYA....	32	86	8	20	2	0	5	17	8	0	.233
1984	KC.....	126	438	58	107	23	2	28	77	45	0	.244
1985	KC.....	160	600	74	146	28	2	36	88	52	1	.243
1986	KC.....	138	512	54	117	25	1	29	88	43	0	.229
1987	KC.....	121	386	44	80	11	1	24	60	34	0	.207
1988	KC.....	21	63	2	9	2	0	2	5	1	0	.143
1988	Sea	97	350	44	88	15	1	21	61	23	0	.251
1989	NYA....	110	300	33	71	12	2	17	59	25	0	.237
		842	2849	327	660	121	11	164	461	238	1	.232

Dave Bergman

Birth Date: 6/6/53
Bats: Left
Throws: Left
1989 Club:
Detroit Tigers
Contest Code #: 476

Rating: 3

At age 36, Dave Bergman remains one of the most useful players in the game. Versatility and reliability are his watchwords and, as long as he can hit and play several positions well, he'll be around the big leagues.

The Chicago-area native, who starred for Illinois State before signing with the Yankees in 1974, does an excellent job at first base, fills in admirably in the outfield, and remains a solid pick as a DH or pinch hitter. The scouts are impressed with Bergman's work habits, and they also like his aggressiveness, a trait that has kept less talented guys around for years beyond the expiration of their effectiveness.

The Tigers' leading hitter (at an unbelieveable .268) a year ago, Bergman still possesses occasional home run power. Though Dave has now spent six seasons in De-

troit, his previous major-league stops included San Francisco, Houston, and the Yankees.

Year	Team	G	AB	R	H	2B	3B	HR	RBI	BB	SB	AVG
1975	NYA....	7	17	0	0	0	0	0	0	2	0	.000
1977	NYN	5	4	1	1	0	0	0	1	0	0	.250
1978	Hou	104	186	15	43	5	1	0	12	39	2	.231
1979	Hou	13	15	4	6	0	0	1	2	0	0	.400
1980	Hou	90	78	12	20	6	1	0	3	10	1	.256
1981	Hou	6	6	1	1	0	0	1	1	0	0	.167
1981	SF	63	145	16	37	9	0	3	13	19	2	.255
1982	SF	100	121	22	33	3	1	4	14	18	3	.273
1983	SF	90	140	16	40	4	1	6	24	24	2	.286
1984	Det	120	271	42	74	8	5	7	44	33	3	.273
1985	Det	69	140	8	25	2	0	3	7	14	0	.179
1986	Det	65	130	14	30	6	1	1	9	21	0	.231
1987	Det	91	172	25	47	7	3	6	22	30	0	.273
1988	Det	116	289	37	85	14	0	5	35	38	0	.294
1989	Det	137	385	38	103	13	1	7	37	44	1	.268
		1076	2099	251	545	77	14	44	224	292	14	.260

George Brett

Birth Date: May 15, 1953
Bats: Left
Throws: Right
1989 Club:
Kansas City Royals
Contest Code #: 477

Rating: 5

At age 37 (this May), George Brett, long one of the game's premier hitters, has begun to show a little wear-and-tear. To the average fan, his slowing down is practically imperceptible. To the expert eye, however, it's especially noticeable on defense. The brother of former major-league pitcher Ken Brett has been a hitting machine through all of his sixteen years in the majors, and he'll probably be able to hit for another ten years—if he wants to.

That's another question. Injuries have cut short three of Brett's last four seasons, understandable for someone who has played more than 2,000 big-league games. Still, Brett keeps himself in amazing physical condition, which may be the secret of his long-term success. He hit .282 a year ago, with 12 homers and 80 RBI's. Probably most impressive were his 14 stolen bases.

His advancing years have moved Brett from third base to full-time duty at first, and he has mastered it nicely. The man's a winner and deserves another World Series shot before he's done.

Year	Team	G	AB	R	H	2B	3B	HR	RBI	BB	SB	AVG
1973	KC	13	40	2	5	2	0	0	0	0	0	.125
1974	KC	133	457	49	129	21	5	2	47	21	8	.282
1975	KC	159	634	84	195	35	13	11	89	46	13	.308
1976	KC	159	645	94	215	34	14	7	67	49	21	.333
1977	KC	139	564	105	176	32	13	22	88	55	14	.312
1978	KC	128	510	79	150	45	8	9	62	39	23	.294
1979	KC	154	645	119	212	42	20	23	107	51	17	.329
1980	KC	117	449	87	175	33	9	24	118	58	15	.390
1981	KC	89	347	42	109	27	7	6	43	27	14	.314
1982	KC	144	552	101	166	32	9	21	82	71	6	.301
1983	KC	123	464	90	144	38	2	25	93	57	0	.310
1984	KC	104	377	42	107	21	3	13	69	38	0	.284
1985	KC	155	550	108	184	38	5	30	112	103	9	.335
1986	KC	124	441	70	128	28	4	16	73	80	1	.290
1987	KC	115	427	71	124	18	2	22	78	72	6	.290
1988	KC	157	589	90	180	42	3	24	103	82	14	.306
1989	KC	124	457	67	129	26	3	12	80	59	14	.282
		2137	8148	1300	2528	514	120	267	1311	908	175	.310

Greg Brock

Birth Date: 6/14/57
Bats: Left
Throws: Right
1989 Club:
Milwaukee Brewers
Contest Code #: 478

Rating: 3

Once considered the next keeper of the Dodgers' first-base flame—the man most likely to follow in the footsteps of Gil Hodges, Wes Parker, and Steve Garvey—Greg Brock has not lived up to his minor-league press notices. Still, he does a sufficiently satisfactory job at first base that his current employers, the Milwaukee Brewers, inked him to a new two-year contract last October.

A good-looking hitter, particularly against right-handed pitching, Brock hit .265 for the Brew Crew in 1989, with a dozen homers and 52 RBI's in only 107 games. (He began the year on the twenty-one-day disabled list with a shoulder injury and didn't return until May 31. He banged a 3-run homer in the delayed-season opener.) Greg's major problems occur on defense. His entire game comes up a bit short, and his range around the bag is simply below average.

Year	Team	G	AB	R	H	2B	3B	HR	RBI	BB	SB	AVG
1982	LA.....	18	17	1	2	1	0	0	1	1	0	.118
1983	LA.....	146	455	64	102	14	2	20	66	83	5	.224
1984	LA.....	88	271	33	61	6	0	14	34	39	8	.225
1985	LA.....	129	438	64	110	19	0	21	66	54	4	.251
1986	LA.....	115	325	33	76	13	0	16	52	37	2	.234
1987	Mil.....	141	532	81	159	29	3	13	85	57	5	.299
1988	Mil.....	115	364	53	77	16	1	6	50	63	6	.212
1989	Mil.....	107	373	40	99	16	0	12	52	43	6	.265
		859	2775	369	686	114	6	102	406	377	36	.247

Bill Buckner

Birth Date: 12/14/49
Bats: Left
Throws: Left
1989 Club:
Kansas City Royals
Contest Code #: 479

Rating: 1

For a promotional program at Shea Stadium last summer, the Mets gave away posters of a memorable Met moment. The photo showed Mookie Wilson's ninth-inning, 2-out grounder eluding Boston first-sacker Bill Buckner, giving the Mets a last-gasp sixth-game 1986 World Series victory. The following night, the Mets won the title.

That memory will always haunt Billy Buck, despite nineteen and a half years as a highly professional big-league hitter. Watching Buckner work out before those World Series games, you knew he was hurting. It was painful to watch him run. It still is. At age forty, it's time for Buckner to give it up.

A lifetime .291 hitter, Buckner struggled to hit .216 in 79 games for the Royals last year. The defense hasn't been there in a while. The power is gone. Buckner can still swing the bat, but virtually every other aspect of his game is shot. Bucks twice led the NL in hitting (.323 and .324 for the Cubs in 1978 and 1980). Watching him slide into mediocrity is difficult.

Year	Team	G	AB	R	H	2B	3B	HR	RBI	BB	SB	AVG
1969	LA.....	1	1	0	0	0	0	0	0	0	0	.000
1970	LA.....	28	68	6	13	3	1	0	4	3	0	.191
1971	LA.....	108	358	37	99	15	1	5	41	11	4	.277
1972	LA.....	105	383	47	122	14	3	5	37	17	10	.319
1973	LA.....	140	575	68	158	20	0	8	46	17	12	.275
1974	LA.....	145	580	83	182	30	3	7	58	30	31	.314
1975	LA.....	92	288	30	70	11	2	6	31	17	8	.243
1976	LA.....	154	642	76	193	28	4	7	60	26	28	.301
1977	ChN....	122	426	40	121	27	0	11	60	21	7	.284
1978	ChN....	117	446	47	144	26	1	5	74	18	7	.323

1979	ChN....	149	591	72	168	34	7	14	66	30	9	.284
1980	ChN....	145	578	69	187	41	3	10	68	30	1	.324
1981	ChN....	106	421	45	131	35	3	10	75	26	5	.311
1982	ChN....	161	657	93	201	34	5	15	105	36	15	.306
1983	ChN....	153	626	79	175	38	6	16	66	25	12	.280
1984	Bos	114	439	51	122	21	2	11	67	24	2	.278
1984	ChN....	21	43	3	9	0	0	0	2	1	0	.209
1985	Bos	162	673	89	201	46	3	16	110	30	18	.299
1986	Bos	153	629	73	168	39	2	18	102	40	6	.267
1987	Cal....	57	183	16	56	12	1	3	32	9	1	.306
1987	Bos	75	286	23	78	6	1	2	42	13	1	.273
1988	Cal....	19	43	1	9	0	0	0	9	4	2	.209
1988	KC.....	89	242	18	62	14	0	3	34	13	3	.256
1989	KC.....	79	176	7	38	4	1	1	16	6	1	.216
		2495	9354	1073	2707	498	49	173	1205	447	183	.289

Jack Daugherty

Birth Date: 6/3/60
Bats: Both
Throws: Left
1989 Club:
Texas Rangers
Contest Code #: 480

Rating: 2

After playing just 11 major-league games with the Montreal Expos in 1987, Jack Daugherty finally got a decent shot at the big time when the Texas Rangers summoned the first baseman to Arlington last July 6. Though the former University of Arizona star may still not be ready for full-time duty, he did make an impression in his three-month visit.

Daugherty made 20 starts for Texas in 1989, 13 at first base, 3 in left, and 4 as the designated hitter. He wound up tying for club leadership in pinch hits with 7 and reached safely 9 times (5 hits, 4 walks) in his last 14 pinch-hitting appearances. Overall, Daugherty hit .302 on 32 hits in 106 at-bats, including 4 doubles, 2 triples, and his first major-league homer. The Rangers would love to see this kind of production for a full year.

Year	Team	G	AB	R	H	2B	3B	HR	RBI	BB	SB	AVG
1987	Mon....	11	10	1	1	1	0	0	1	0	0	.100
1989	Tex	52	106	15	32	4	2	1	10	11	2	.302
		63	116	16	33	5	2	1	11	11	2	.284

Alvin Davis

Birth Date: 9/9/60
Bats: Left
Throws: Right
1989 Club:
Seattle Mariners
Contest Code #: 481

Rating: 5

Has there ever been a time when major-league baseball had so many outstanding first basemen? In other times, the Seattle Mariners' Alvin Davis might be the class of the field. If he were playing in a media center, he would be a household name. As it is, insiders know how good the California native really is.

The 6'1", 190-pounder is a superb first-sacker who makes all the plays. Though his arm is rated average, it's good enough to get it done at first. His speed is, likewise, average. The six-year veteran's biggest asset, however, is his bat. He hits for average and he hits for distance, though he is far more effective against right-handers than against lefties.

The 1984 AL Rookie of the Year, Davis enjoyed his first .300-plus season in 1989 (.305), though he had been in the .280–.290 range in four of his five previous campaigns. And he has been in double figures in homers every season, including 21 (along with 95 RBI's) in 1989.

Year	Team	G	AB	R	H	2B	3B	HR	RBI	BB	SB	AVG
1984	Sea	152	567	80	161	34	3	27	116	97	5	.284
1985	Sea	155	578	78	166	33	1	18	78	90	1	.287

Year	Team	G	AB	R	H	2B	3B	HR	RBI	BB	SB	AVG
1986	Sea	135	479	66	130	18	1	18	72	76	0	.271
1987	Sea	157	580	86	171	37	2	29	100	72	0	.295
1988	Sea	140	478	67	141	24	1	18	69	95	1	.295
1989	Sea	142	498	84	152	30	1	21	95	101	0	.305
		881	3180	461	921	176	9	131	530	531	7	.290

Terry Francona

Birth Date: 4/22/59
Bats: Left
Throws: Left
1989 Club:
Milwaukee Brewers
Contest Code #: 482

Rating: 1

Which pitcher led the Milwaukee Brewers in earned run average last season? It was outfielder-first baseman Terry Francona, whose lone inning against the Oakland A's last May produced no runs and one strikeout. Francona will best be served concentrating on his hitting. At age 31, he has become a situation type or role player. The son of former major-leaguer Tito Francona—who played with nine teams in 15 years, including the Brewers, Terry hit .487 last June when he was filling in full-time at first base for the injured Greg Brock. He struggled the rest of the way, winding up at .232 with 3 homers and 23 RBIs. Still, the Pennsylvania native swings the bat very well, albeit with little or no power. Playing in only 26 games (only 51 at-bats) after the All-Star break doesn't bode well for Terry's future.

Year	Team	G	AB	R	H	2B	3B	HR	RBI	BB	SB	AVG
1981	Mon....	34	95	11	26	0	1	1	8	5	1	.274
1982	Mon....	46	131	14	42	3	0	0	9	8	2	.321
1983	Mon....	120	230	21	59	11	1	3	22	6	0	.257
1984	Mon....	58	214	18	74	19	2	1	18	5	0	.346
1985	Mon....	107	281	19	75	15	1	2	31	12	5	.267
1986	ChN....	86	124	13	31	3	0	2	8	6	0	.250
1987	Cin	102	207	16	47	5	0	3	12	10	2	.227
1988	Cle.....	62	212	24	66	8	0	1	12	5	0	.311
1989	Mil.....	90	233	26	54	10	1	3	23	8	2	.232
		705	1727	162	474	74	6	16	143	65	12	.274

Danny Heep

Birth Date: 7/3/57
Bats: Left
Throws: Left
1989 Club:
Boston Red Sox
Contest Code #: 483

Rating: 2

Danny Heep will probably find a major-league job as long as he can walk. Then he'll become a travel agent. Boston is Heep's fourth big-league stop in ten seasons, and he owns World Series championship rings from his stays in New York and Los Angeles. Let go by the Dodgers after the 1988 season, Heep was a non-roster player with the Sox last spring training, before winning a spot on the big club.

The native Texan is a true professional. He's a fine contact hitter (.300 in 113 games last year) with occasional power (5 homers in 1989 after being shut out the previous two seasons). He does reasonably well in the field, either in the outfield or at first base. His major weakness: speed. Danny's is lower than average. Superstardom is not in Heep's future—or his past. But for a journeyman, he'll always get the job done, no matter where he is.

Year	Team	G	AB	R	H	2B	3B	HR	RBI	BB	SB	AVG
1979	Hou....	14	14	0	2	0	0	0	2	1	0	.143
1980	Hou....	33	87	6	24	8	0	0	6	8	0	.276
1981	Hou....	33	96	6	24	3	0	0	11	10	0	.250
1982	Hou....	85	198	16	47	14	1	4	22	21	0	.237
1983	NYN ...	115	253	30	64	12	0	8	21	29	3	.253
1984	NYN ...	99	199	36	46	9	2	1	12	27	3	.231
1985	NYN ...	95	271	26	76	17	0	7	42	27	2	.280

1986	NYN ...	86	195	24	55	8	2	5	33	30	1	.282
1987	LA	60	98	7	16	4	0	0	9	8	1	.163
1988	LA	95	149	14	36	2	0	0	11	22	2	.242
1989	Bos	113	320	36	96	17	0	5	49	29	0	.300
		828	1880	201	486	94	5	30	218	212	12	.259

Keith Hernandez

Birth Date: 10/20/53
Bats: Left
Throws: Left
1989 Club:
New York Mets
Contest Code #: 484

Rating: 3

Once the National League's finest all-around first baseman, Keith Hernandez now appears near the end of the line. After he had consecutive injury-filled seasons, the Mets' brass decided last October they would not renew Hernandez's $2 million-a-year contract. To add insult to injury, during the off season Bobby Tolan, a manager in the Senior Baseball League, publicly invited Hernandez to join his club and sharpen his skills.

I believe Henandez can still be a productive player. If he were 10 years younger, had been injured for much of two seasons and was in the last year of his contract, the Mets would have re-signed him faster than you can say "Where do I sign?" Yes, most of the injuries have been to his legs, but Hernandez was never a fast runner. I'd still take an injured Hernandez over a healthy, equally slow-footed Dave Magadan. Apparently, the Cleveland Indians agree; they signed Hernandez in the off-season.

Despite the sagging averages the past two seasons, Hernandez remains a professional hitter, whose knowledge is vast enough to compensate for any decline in his abilities.

Year	Team	G	AB	R	H	2B	3B	HR	RBI	BB	SB	AVG
1974	StL	14	34	3	10	1	2	0	2	7	0	.294
1975	StL	64	188	20	47	8	2	3	20	17	0	.250
1976	StL	129	374	54	108	21	5	7	46	49	4	.289
1977	StL	161	560	90	163	41	4	15	91	79	7	.291
1978	StL	159	542	90	138	32	4	11	64	82	13	.255
1979	StL	161	610	116	210	48	11	11	105	80	11	.344
1980	StL	159	595	111	191	39	8	16	99	86	14	.321
1981	StL	103	376	65	115	27	4	8	48	61	12	.306
1982	StL	160	579	79	173	33	6	7	94	100	19	.299
1983	StL	55	218	34	62	15	4	3	26	24	1	.284
1983	NYN ...	95	320	43	98	8	3	9	37	64	8	.306
1984	NYN ...	154	550	83	171	31	0	15	94	97	2	.311
1985	NYN ...	158	593	87	183	34	4	10	91	77	3	.309
1986	NYN ...	149	551	94	171	34	1	13	83	94	2	.310
1987	NYN ...	154	587	87	170	28	2	18	89	81	0	.290
1988	NYN ...	95	348	43	96	16	0	11	55	31	2	.276
1989	NYN ...	75	215	18	50	8	0	4	19	27	0	.233
		2045	7240	1117	2156	424	60	161	1063	1056	98	.298

Kent Hrbek

Birth Date: 5/21/60
Bats: Left
Throws: Right
1989 Club:
Minnesota Twins
Contest Code #: 485

Rating: 4

Everyone in Minnesota keeps waiting for hometown hero Kent Hrbek to have that superstar-type season. They'll just have to keep waiting. Meanwhile, the huge (6'4", 240-pound) Hrbek continues to play some of the best first base in the American League. Herbie doesn't owe anyone anything. For the second straight year, he swatted 25 round-trippers, and raised his RBI total from 76 to 84.

Hrbek's 1987 performance—34 homers and 90 RBI's—may have raised expectations, but that was the year of the suspected rabbit ball. Hrbek, who was born in Minneapolis and played high-school ball in suburban Bloomington, is a solid front-liner, who hits, hits with power, and fields his position well.

His speed is questionable but there are few 6'4", 240-pound speed demons. Some folks wonder whether Hrbek is in the best possible shape, but he is certainly doing the best he can with what he has.

Year	Team	G	AB	R	H	2B	3B	HR	RBI	BB	SB	AVG
1981	Min	24	67	5	16	5	0	1	7	5	0	.239
1982	Min	140	532	82	160	21	4	23	92	54	3	.301
1983	Min	141	515	75	153	41	5	16	84	57	4	.297
1984	Min	149	559	80	174	31	3	27	107	65	1	.311
1985	Min	158	593	78	165	31	2	21	93	67	1	.278
1986	Min	149	550	85	147	27	1	29	91	71	2	.267
1987	Min	143	477	85	136	20	1	34	90	84	5	.285
1988	Min	143	510	75	159	31	0	25	76	67	0	.312
1989	Min	109	375	59	102	17	0	25	84	53	3	.272
		1156	4178	624	1212	224	16	201	724	523	19	.290

Wally Joyner

Birth Date: 6/16/62
Bats: Left
Throws: Left
1989 Club:
California Angels
Contest Code #: 486

Rating: 4

Though the Angels' Wally Joyner seems to have slipped from his first two big-league seasons (he was only the ninth player in history with 100 or more RBI's in each of his first two seasons), he remains one of the finest young players in the AL. The 6'2", 198-pounder, who lost out in the 1986 AL Rookie-of-the-Year balloting to Jose Canseco, is equally talented on offense and defense.

Few first basemen field the position as well as Joyner, who has led the loop in virtually every defensive statistic. Offensively, Joyner can turn on a fastball with the best, though lefties have found that breaking stuff can get him out. He hits for average (.282 in 1989) and power (16 homers last year after a high of 34 in 1987). A three-year star at Brigham Young, Joyner is a great team man who figures to be around well into the next century.

Year	Team	G	AB	R	H	2B	3B	HR	RBI	BB	SB	AVG
1986	Cal.....	154	593	82	172	27	3	22	100	57	5	.290
1987	Cal.....	149	564	100	161	33	1	34	117	72	8	.285
1988	Cal.....	158	597	81	176	31	2	13	85	55	8	.295
1989	Cal.....	159	593	78	167	30	2	16	79	46	3	.282
		620	2347	341	676	121	8	85	381	230	24	.288

Gene Larkin

Birth Date: 10/24/62
Bats: Both
Throws: Right
1989 Club:
Minnesota Twins
Contest Code #: 487

Rating: 2

As an economics graduate of Ivy League Columbia University, Gene Larkin may be the major leaguer most qualified to negotiate his own contract. So long as he keeps up to the standards of his first three seasons with the Twins, he'll have many more contracts to negotiate. Larkin doesn't do anything all that well, but he does everything well enough. A switch-hitter who can fill in well both at first base and in the outfield while DH-ing on the days when he's not needed in the field, Larkin is a valuable addition to his club.

Columbia's first big leaguer since Lou Gehrig, Gene, is nothing if not consistent. In 1987, when he arrived in Minnesota at mid-season, he hit .266. In a full 1988 season, he hit .267. In 1989, it was .267 again. His power dropped a bit (6 homers, 46 RBI's), but he's a reliable player.

Year	Team	G	AB	R	H	2B	3B	HR	RBI	BB	SB	AVG
1987	Min	85	233	23	62	11	2	4	28	25	1	.266
1988	Min	149	505	56	135	30	2	8	70	68	3	.267
1989	Min	136	446	61	119	25	1	6	46	54	5	.267
		370	1184	140	316	66	5	18	144	147	9	.267

Don Mattingly

Birth Date: 4/20/61
Bats: Left
Throws: Left
1989 Club:
New York Yankees
Contest Code #: 488

Rating: 5

Once the unquestioned best first baseman in the game and arguably baseball's best player, Don Mattingly has seemingly slipped a couple of notches the past couple of seasons. Nonetheless, the Indiana native remains one of the game's most awesome threats and likely the most artistic fielder at his position.

From a .352 season in 1986, Don has dropped down to .327, .311, and .303 in the last three campaigns. He increased his power and production in 1989, going from 18 homers and 88 RBI's to 23 round-trippers and 113 ribbies in 1989.

When you think of baseball's best first basemen you now think first of Will Clark and look to the future with Mark Grace. Still, almost anyone would gladly swap first sackers with the Yankees.

Year	Team	G	AB	R	H	2B	3B	HR	RBI	BB	SB	AVG
1982	NYA	7	12	0	2	0	0	0	1	0	0	.167
1983	NYA	91	279	34	79	15	4	4	32	21	0	.283
1984	NYA	153	603	91	207	44	2	23	110	41	1	.343
1985	NYA	159	652	107	211	48	3	35	145	56	2	.324
1986	NYA	162	677	117	238	53	2	31	113	53	0	.352
1987	NYA	141	569	93	186	38	2	30	115	51	1	.327
1988	NYA	144	599	94	186	37	0	18	88	41	1	.311
1989	NYA	158	631	79	191	37	2	23	113	51	3	.303
		1015	4022	615	1300	272	15	164	717	314	8	.323

Fred McGriff

Birth Date: 10/31/63
Bats: Left
Throws: Left
1989 Club:
Toronto Blue Jays
Contest Code #: 489

Rating: 5

Were it not for a powerless and unproductive September, Toronto first baseman Fred McGriff might have been a serious candidate for AL Most Valuable Player honors. Even without a single dinger the last month, the powerful 6'3", 215-pounder led the league with 36 home runs and banged in 92 RBI's. He even drew 119 bases on balls, which says something about the league's respect for the Tampa native.

McGriff kicked around the Yankee and Blue Jay organizations for seven years before he got a 3-game trial with Toronto late in 1986. The following season, he was there to stay. When Willie Upshaw's power went south, McGriff easily beat out his planned platoon-mate, Cecil Fielder, for the starting first-base job. There are few better glove men at first than McGriff, and his arm—while only rated average—is certainly good enough to get it done. McGriff is on the verge of becoming an impact player.

Year	Team	G	AB	R	H	2B	3B	HR	RBI	BB	SB	AVG
1986	Tor.....	3	5	1	1	0	0	0	0	0	0	.200
1987	Tor.....	107	295	58	73	16	0	20	43	60	3	.247
1988	Tor.....	154	536	100	151	35	4	34	82	79	6	.282
1989	Tor.....	161	551	98	148	27	3	36	92	119	7	.269
		425	1387	257	373	78	7	90	217	258	16	.269

Mark McGwire

Birth Date: 10/1/63
Bats: Right
Throws: Right
1989 Club:
Oakland Athletics
Contest Code #: 490

Rating: 5

Mark McGwire isn't likely to approach his rookie year (1987) totals of 49 homers and 118 RBI's, but as the junior partner in the Canseco-McGwire Bash Brothers Act, he's a constant power threat. The former Southern Cal and U.S. Olympic star isn't a good contact hitter and strikes out far too often (94 times last year, down from 131 and 117). But he hits for power and hits with men in scoring position, and that's basically what it's all about.

An imposing 6'5" and 225 pounds, McGwire banged out 33 homers and knocked in 95 runs last season, stop-the-presses numbers on any team without Jose Canseco or in a metropolitan area without Kevin Mitchell. His BA slipped to .231 (from .289 and .260), and he isn't much in the running department. He remains a solid first baseman, albeit with limited range.

Year	Team	G	AB	R	H	2B	3B	HR	RBI	BB	SB	AVG
1986	Oak	18	53	10	10	1	0	3	9	4	0	.189
1987	Oak	151	557	97	161	28	4	49	118	71	1	.289
1988	Oak	155	550	87	143	22	1	32	99	76	0	.260
1989	Oak	143	490	74	113	17	0	33	95	83	1	.231
		467	1650	268	427	68	5	117	321	234	2	.259

Randy Milligan

Birth Date: 11/27/61
Bats: Right
Throws: Right
1989 Club:
Baltimore Orioles
Contest Code #: 492

Rating: 2

A one-time hot Met prospect, Milligan has never really made it. The powerfully built 6'1", 225-pounder has the looks of a hitter who should scare enemy pitchers. That's if the pitchers don't check the stat sheets. Randy excited everyone with his 1987 performance at Tidewater (International). He led the International League with 99 runs scored and 103 RBI's. He also banged out 29 homers. But the Mets still shipped Randy to Pittsburgh, who then dealt him to the O's.

The 1989 numbers were fair—.268 with 12 homers and 45 RBI's in 124 games—but that's all. Our scouts tell us he's still very borderline at the plate, which is better than nothing, and shows occasional power. Surprisingly, he's considered a better-than-average fielder at first base. As the Birds continue to build with youth, the twenty-eight-year-old Milligan could be moved.

Year	Team	G	AB	R	H	2B	3B	HR	RBI	BB	SB	AVG
1987	NYN ...	3	1	0	0	0	0	0	0	1	0	.000
1988	Pit.....	40	82	10	18	5	0	3	8	20	1	.220
1989	Bal	124	365	56	98	23	5	12	45	74	9	.268
		167	448	66	116	28	5	15	53	95	10	.259

Russ Morman

Birth Date: 4/28/62
Bats: Right
Throws: Right
1989 Club:
Chicago White Sox
Contest Code #: 493

Rating: 1

A fter seven years as a professional, Russ Morman has exactly 126 games of major-league experience. Better than many, not good enough for career planning. Morman has always hit on the minor-league level, including .300 and .278 at Vancouver in 1988 and 1989, respectively.

The White Sox's second pick in the June 1983 draft after an All-American career at Wichita State, Morman is basically a first baseman who can play just about anywhere in the outfield. Given his track record, it doesn't look as though the 6'4", 215-pounder, whose power remains suspect, fits into the Chisox's plans for 1990. Comiskey Park will likely not become this Morman's tabernacle.

Year	Team	G	AB	R	H	2B	3B	HR	RBI	BB	SB	AVG
1986	ChA....	49	159	18	40	5	0	4	17	16	1	.252
1988	ChA....	40	75	8	18	2	0	0	3	3	0	.240
1989	ChA....	37	58	5	13	2	0	0	8	6	1	.224
		126	292	31	71	9	0	4	28	25	2	.243

Pete O'Brien

Birth Date: 2/9/58
Bats: Left
Throws: Left
1989 Club:
Cleveland Indians
Contest Code #: 494

Rating: 3

When Pete O'Brien announced that he would file for free-agency after the 1989 season, there were mixed emotions in Cleveland. The California native had played only one season for the Indians after coming to the Tribe from Texas in the Julio Franco deal. He remains one of the consummate artists at first base, but there seems to have been substantial slippage in his offensive game.

In the period between 1985 and 1987, the 6'2", 198-pounder banged out 68 homers and averaged 90 RBI's per season. In 1988 he fell to 16 homers and only 71 RBI's at Texas, and in 1989, with the Indians, the numbers were 12 and 55. Yes, power numbers in baseball have gone down. But Pete's batting numbers have also slipped steadily, from .290, to .286, to .272, and, last year, to .260. The decline was particularly noticeable during the second half of the 1989 season. Nonetheless, the Seattle Mariners saw enough that they liked to sign him during the off season.

Year	Team	G	AB	R	H	2B	3B	HR	RBI	BB	SB	AVG
1982	Tex	20	67	13	16	4	1	4	13	6	1	.239
1983	Tex	154	524	53	124	24	5	8	53	58	5	.237
1984	Tex	142	520	57	149	26	2	18	80	53	3	.287
1985	Tex	159	573	69	153	34	3	22	92	69	5	.267
1986	Tex	156	551	86	160	23	3	23	90	87	4	.290
1987	Tex	159	569	84	163	26	1	23	88	59	0	.286
1988	Tex	156	547	57	149	24	1	16	71	72	1	.272
1989	Cle.....	155	554	75	144	24	1	12	55	83	3	.260
		1101	3905	494	1058	185	17	126	542	487	22	.271

Rafael Palmeiro

Birth Date: 9/24/64
Bats: Left
Throws: Left
1989 Club:
Texas Rangers
Contest Code #: 495

Rating: 3

Everyone keeps waiting for Rafael Palmeiro to have that Hall of Fame year. The Texas Rangers parted with Mitch Williams and others in the massive deal that brought the 6', 180-pound Cuban native to Arlington in 1989. What they got wasn't bad, it just wasn't one of those "drop dead" seasons. Palmeiro, who hit .307 for the Cubs in 1988, dipped to .275 last year, though his runs scored (76) and RBI's (64) set career highs. Palmeiro's season was anything but consistent, which isn't surprising. In fact, he was leading the AL with a .361 batting average on May 28.

Basically, the three-time Mississippi State All-American is a fine contact hitter with occasional power. His career-high 14 homers were hit in the homer-happy year of 1987 and in the friendly confines of Wrigley Field. Defensively, Rafael is adequate whether he's at first base or in the outfield.

Year	Team	G	AB	R	H	2B	3B	HR	RBI	BB	SB	AVG
1986	ChN....	22	73	9	18	4	0	3	12	4	1	.247
1987	ChN....	84	221	32	61	15	1	14	30	20	2	.276
1988	ChN....	152	580	75	178	41	5	8	53	38	12	.307
1989	Tex	156	559	76	154	23	4	8	64	63	4	.275
		414	1433	192	411	83	10	33	159	125	19	.287

Gerald Perry

Birth Date: 10/30/60
Bats: Left
Throws: Right
1989 Club:
Atlanta Braves
Contest Code #: 496

Rating: 2

Yesterday's hero, today's spare part. That was Gerald Perry's fate with the Braves in 1989.

Perry, who can hit for average and power, and can steal bases, had climbed the Braves' minor-league ladder beginning in 1978, and finally made it to the big leagues for good in 1987. That year, Perry batted .270, hit 12 home runs, drove in 74 runs, scored 77 runs, and stole 42 bases. In 1988, Perry earned National League All-Star honors, and wound up batting .300, with 74 RBI's.

Last season, Perry was dogged by shoulder problems that eventually required surgery. During his absence, the Braves tested Tommy Gregg at the position. During the offseason, the Braves signed power-hitting free agent Nick Esasky to take over the starting role in 1990, and traded Perry to the Kansas City Royals.

Year	Team	G	AB	R	H	2B	3B	HR	RBI	BB	SB	AVG
1983	Atl.....	27	39	5	14	2	0	1	6	5	0	.359
1984	Atl.....	122	347	52	92	12	2	7	47	61	15	.265
1985	Atl.....	110	238	22	51	5	0	3	13	23	9	.214
1986	Atl.....	29	70	6	19	2	0	2	11	8	0	.271
1987	Atl.....	142	533	77	144	35	2	12	74	48	42	.270
1988	Atl.....	141	547	61	164	29	1	8	74	36	29	.300
1989	Atl.....	72	266	24	67	11	0	4	21	32	10	.252
		643	2040	247	551	96	5	37	246	213	105	.270

Ken Phelps

Birth Date: 8/6/54
Bats: Left
Throws: Left
1989 Club:
New York Yankees &
Oakland Athletics
Contest Code #: 497

Rating: 2

You figure it out. In all or part of ten major-league seasons, Ken Phelps has 1,734 at-bats and 122 homers. That's one dinger in every 14.2 AB's, classic slugger numbers. Still, no one seems to find a spot in the lineup for the bruiser, who has never batted more than 344 times (Seattle, 1986) in any season.

Now, at age thirty, it isn't likely that Phelps will ever get a regular lineup spot, even as a DH. What Ken does have is a World Series ring. He was languishing around the Yankee bat rack last July when the Bombers did him a favor by dealing him to the high-flying Oakland A's. (Oakland is his fifth major-league whistle-stop, but he owns that big rock now, a decent reward for a hard worker who sits, waits, and delivers.)

Year	Team	G	AB	R	H	2B	3B	HR	RBI	BB	SB	AVG
1980	KC.....	3	4	0	0	0	0	0	0	0	0	.000
1981	KC.....	21	22	1	3	0	1	0	1	1	0	.136
1982	Mon....	10	8	0	2	0	0	0	0	0	0	.250
1983	Sea....	50	127	10	30	4	1	7	16	13	0	.236
1984	Sea....	101	290	52	70	9	0	24	51	61	3	.241
1985	Sea....	61	116	18	24	3	0	9	24	24	2	.207
1986	Sea....	125	344	69	85	16	4	24	64	88	2	.247
1987	Sea....	120	332	68	86	13	1	27	68	80	1	.259
1988	Sea....	72	190	37	54	8	0	14	32	51	1	.284
1988	NYA....	45	107	17	24	5	0	10	22	19	0	.224
1989	NYA....	86	185	26	46	3	0	7	29	27	0	.249
1989	Oak....	11	9	0	1	1	0	0	0	4	0	.111
		705	1734	298	425	62	7	122	307	368	9	.245

Jim Traber

Birth Date: 12/26/61
Bats: Left
Throws: Left
1989 Club:
Baltimore Orioles
Contest Code #: 498

Rating: 2

The scouts look back at a May 1985 knee operation as a turning point (downward) in Jim Traber's career. A decent-to-good minor-league hitter, Traber hit an all-time low (.209) for the Orioles last season. The experts like his aggressiveness and they suggest that he still has home-run power. In fact, 4 of his 49 hits last season were round-trippers.

Still, his batting mark seems to sink every year, and that doesn't bode well. On defense, he's still better at first base than he is in the outfield. The book calls him an adequate first sacker, slightly less so in the outfield. Blessed with a great attitude, Traber is good enough to find work for the time being. But after flirting with the so-called Mendoza Line (.200), the 6', 208-pounder will have to pick up with the bat to stay in the majors.

Year	Team	G	AB	R	H	2B	3B	HR	RBI	BB	SB	AVG
1984	Bal	10	21	3	5	0	0	0	2	2	0	.238
1986	Bal	65	212	28	54	7	0	13	44	18	0	.255
1988	Bal	103	352	25	78	6	0	10	45	19	1	.222
1989	Bal	86	234	14	49	8	0	4	26	19	4	.209
		264	819	70	186	21	0	27	117	58	5	.227

Greg Walker

Birth Date: 10/6/59
Bats: Left
Throws: Right
1989 Club:
Chicago White Sox
Contest Code #: 499

Rating: 3

The brain infection and seizure that ended Greg Walker's 1988 season and nearly ended his life appears to be continuing to plague him. Physical problems have put a severe crimp in his productivity, which leads to questions about his baseball future. His batting average slipped to .210 last season, after hitting .267 in his first six-plus big-league seasons. In only 77 games, he did manage 5 homers and 26 RBI's. But he has never been a good contact man at the plate, and he isn't getting better.

At 6'3" and 210 pounds, he doesn't run well either. His one saving grace is decent ability at first, where both his glove and arm rank as adequate. Everybody roots for Walker, and if prayer produces, Greg will be back.

Year	Team	G	AB	R	H	2B	3B	HR	RBI	BB	SB	AVG
1982	ChA....	11	17	3	7	2	1	2	7	2	0	.412
1983	ChA....	118	307	32	83	16	3	10	55	28	2	.270
1984	ChA....	136	442	62	130	29	2	24	75	35	8	.294
1985	ChA....	163	601	77	155	38	4	24	92	44	5	.258
1986	ChA....	78	282	37	78	10	6	13	51	29	1	.277
1987	ChA....	157	566	85	145	33	2	27	94	75	2	.256
1988	ChA....	99	377	45	93	22	1	8	42	29	0	.247
1989	ChA....	77	233	25	49	14	0	5	26	23	0	.210
		839	2825	366	740	164	19	113	442	265	18	.262

SECOND BASEMEN

Wally Backman

Birth Date: 9/22/59
Bats: Both
Throws: Right
1989 Club:
Minnesota Twins
Contest Code #: 503

Rating: 2

Turns out the trade that sent Wally Backman from the New York Mets to the Minnesota Twins in December 1988 didn't do anyone any good. The Mets lost a sparkplug who helped drive a generally lethargic ball club. And Backman didn't do much of anything in Minnesota, despite being handed a full-time job (something that didn't happen in New York) right out of the blocks.

An energetic 5'9" and 168 pounds, Backman has always been a competent left-handed and so-so (at best) right-handed hitter. A career .283 hitter with the Mets, Wally slumped to .231 in only 87 injury-riddled games last season. Never a power hitter, Backman isn't worth much if he can't get on base, move the runners, and steal the base, none of which he did in 1989. The hope is that a new decade will renew Backman's performance.

Year	Team	G	AB	R	H	2B	3B	HR	RBI	BB	SB	AVG
1980	NYN ...	27	93	12	30	1	1	0	9	11	2	.323
1981	NYN ...	26	36	5	10	2	0	0	0	4	1	.278
1982	NYN ...	96	261	37	71	13	2	3	22	49	8	.272
1983	NYN ...	26	42	6	7	0	1	0	3	2	0	.167
1984	NYN ...	128	436	68	122	19	2	1	26	56	32	.280
1985	NYN ...	145	520	77	142	24	5	1	38	36	30	.273
1986	NYN ...	124	387	67	124	18	2	1	27	36	13	.320
1987	NYN ...	94	300	43	75	6	1	1	23	25	11	.250
1988	NYN ...	99	294	44	89	12	0	0	17	41	9	.303
1989	Min	87	299	33	69	9	2	1	26	32	1	.231
		852	2668	392	739	104	16	8	191	292	107	.277

Marty Barrett

Birth Date: 6/23/58
Bats: Right
Throws: Right
1989 Club:
Boston Red Sox
Contest Code #: 504

Rating: 4

Marty Barrett is just the type of player you love to have on your club. He's steady and sound, a guy who won't hurt you at the plate or in the field. The 5'10", 174-pounder struggled somewhat in 1989, hitting .256 in 86 games, his lowest output in six full seasons with the Red Sox. It's essential, of course, that he return to his pre-1989 form (he played at least 137 games in each of the previous campaigns), but there's little doubt that he can do it. He's a top-flight second baseman, whose instincts on the field match his intelligence at the plate. He can bunt and hit-and-run with the best and, though he doesn't hit with much power, most clubs don't ask their second basemen to drive in a lot of runs.

Year	Team	G	AB	R	H	2B	3B	HR	RBI	BB	SB	AVG
1982	Bos	8	18	0	1	0	0	0	0	0	0	.056
1983	Bos	33	44	7	10	1	1	0	2	3	0	.227
1984	Bos	139	475	56	144	23	3	3	45	42	5	.303
1985	Bos	156	534	59	142	26	0	5	56	56	7	.266
1986	Bos	158	625	94	179	39	4	4	60	65	15	.286
1987	Bos	137	559	72	164	23	0	3	43	51	15	.293
1988	Bos	150	612	83	173	28	1	1	65	40	7	.283
1989	Bos	86	336	31	86	18	0	1	27	32	4	.256
		867	3203	402	899	158	9	17	298	289	53	.281

Lance Blankenship

Birth Date: 12/6/63
Bats: Right
Throws: Right
1989 Club:
Oakland Athletics
Contest Code #: 505

Rating: 2

The only rookie on the world-champion Oakland Athletics' twenty-four-man roster in 1989, Lance Blankenship still seems a couple of years away from becoming an everyday player. Blankenship, the former U. of California star—and the first player ever selected to the All-Pac 10 team for four straight years—doesn't seem to match up to the skill level of his Oakland teammates.

Though he was born in Portland (OR), the 6', 185-pound Blankenship played his high school and college ball within a few miles of the Oakland Coliseum. He can play anywhere around the infield, but the scouts feel he's probably most comfortable at second base. His tools, they say, are below average across the board, and his hitting (.232 in 58 games) remains a question mark.

Year	Team	G	AB	R	H	2B	3B	HR	RBI	BB	SB	AVG
1988	Oak	10	3	1	0	0	0	0	0	0	0	.000
1989	Oak	58	125	22	29	5	1	1	4	8	5	.232
		68	128	23	29	5	1	1	4	8	5	.227

Jerry Browne

Birth Date: 2/13/66
Bats: Both
Throws: Right
1989 Club:
Cleveland Indians
Contest Code #: 506

Rating: 4

The Cleveland Indians can't be too thrilled with the December 1988 trade that sent Julio Franco to the Texas Rangers for three players. First baseman Pete O'Brien declared free agency after the 1989 season and OF Oddibe McDowell was shuffled off to Atlanta. But the Lone (remaining) Ranger has made everything worthwhile. Jerry Browne has done a fine job replacing Franco at second base.

The Virgin Islands native did an outstanding job, offensively and defensively, quickly proving that he has fine range, a good arm, and good baseball sense on the field. At the plate, his ability to make contact makes him a top-notch lead-off hitter. His .299 average in 153 games last season included 31 doubles and a not-shabby 45 RBI's. He has speed to burn and can steal (14 last year, 27 at Texas in 1987). At age twenty-four, Browne's future is outstanding.

Year	Team	G	AB	R	H	2B	3B	HR	RBI	BB	SB	AVG
1986	Tex	12	24	6	10	2	0	0	3	1	0	.417
1987	Tex	132	454	63	123	16	6	1	38	61	27	.271
1988	Tex	73	214	26	49	9	2	1	17	25	7	.229
1989	Cle.....	153	598	83	179	31	4	5	45	68	14	.299
		370	1290	178	361	58	12	7	103	155	48	.280

Julio Franco

Birth Date: 8/23/61
Bats: Right
Throws: Right
1989 Club:
Texas Rangers
Contest Code #: 507

Rating: 5

When the Rangers dealt infielders Jerry Browne and Pete O'Brien and outfielder Oddibe McDowell to Cleveland for Julio Franco in December 1988, they took a major step toward their first AL West pennant. The 6'1", 185-pounder is a first-class hitter. Last year's .316, fifth in the AL, marked his fourth straight in the .300 club.

Another in the long line of outstanding infielders from the Dominican Republic (imagine trying to make a Little League team in San Pedro de Macoris!), Franco rang up the best Ranger average since 1980 and led AL second sackers with 92 RBI's. With a career-high 13 homers, he showed decent if occasional power, and his 21 steals gave him three straight years with 20 or more.

Defense is another question, of course. Franco can scare even the most loyal Ranger fan when the ball is hit his way. Still, he's a key to any team with title aspirations.

Year	Team	G	AB	R	H	2B	3B	HR	RBI	BB	SB	AVG
1982	Phi	16	29	3	8	1	0	0	3	2	0	.276
1983	Cle.	149	560	68	153	24	8	8	80	27	32	.273
1984	Cle.	160	658	82	188	22	5	3	79	43	19	.286
1985	Cle.	160	636	97	183	33	4	6	90	54	13	.288
1986	Cle.	149	599	80	183	30	5	10	74	32	10	.306
1987	Cle.	128	495	86	158	24	3	8	52	57	32	.319
1988	Cle.	152	613	88	186	23	6	10	54	56	25	.303
1989	Tex	150	548	80	173	31	5	13	92	66	21	.316
		1064	4138	584	1232	188	36	58	524	337	152	.298

Jim Gantner

Birth Date: 1/5/54
Bats: Left
Throws: Right
1989 Club:
Milwaukee Brewers
Contest Code #: 508

Rating: 3

Jim Gantner remembers it well. It was June 14, 1987. Tim Stoddard was on the mound for the Yankees and hung a curveball. The Milwaukee second-baseman found the pitch to his liking and deposited into the rightfield seats. Why so memorable? Because the Wisconsin native hasn't done it since—1,027 at-bats in all. Power isn't Gantner's thing. But he has the rest of his game in pretty good working order. An outstanding defensive second-sacker, Jim has loads of game savvy and provides the kind of leadership a manager loves to see on the field. A lifetime .275 hitter, Gantner hit .274 last year before knee surgery and pleased everyone with his 20 stolen bases. He's a good contact man who can get on base, move the runner, steal the base and, in short, get it done for manager Tom Trebelhorn.

Year	Team	G	AB	R	H	2B	3B	HR	RBI	BB	SB	AVG
1976	Mil.....	26	69	6	17	1	0	0	7	6	1	.246
1977	Mil.....	14	47	4	14	1	0	1	2	2	2	.298
1978	Mil.....	43	97	14	21	1	0	1	8	5	2	.216
1979	Mil.....	70	208	29	59	10	3	2	22	16	3	.284
1980	Mil.....	132	415	47	117	21	3	4	40	30	11	.282
1981	Mil.....	107	352	35	94	14	1	2	33	29	3	.267
1982	Mil.....	132	447	48	132	17	2	4	43	26	6	.295
1983	Mil.....	161	603	85	170	23	8	11	74	38	5	.282
1984	Mil.....	153	613	61	173	27	1	3	56	30	6	.282
1985	Mil.....	143	523	63	133	15	4	5	44	33	11	.254
1986	Mil.....	139	497	58	136	25	1	7	38	26	13	.274
1987	Mil.....	81	265	37	72	14	0	4	30	19	6	.272
1988	Mil.....	155	539	67	149	28	2	0	47	34	20	.276
1989	Mil.....	116	409	51	112	18	3	0	34	21	20	.274
		1472	5084	605	1399	215	28	44	478	315	109	.275

Chip Hale

Birth Date: 12/2/64
Bats: Left
Throws: Right
1989 Club:
Minnesota Twins
Contest Code #: 509

Rating: 2

No one was surprised that Chip Hale got a quick shot with the Minnesota Twins in 1989, only a couple of seasons removed from a stellar career at Arizona State. Hale has hit at every level, and manager Tom Kelly believes he'll hit in the big time, too.

The debut was somewhat difficult, as it is for most inexperienced rookies. Hale got into 28 games at Minnesota, hitting only .209, too little to pass judgment. But Hale's track record—defense, power—is sufficient to merit additional time at the Metrodome.

Year	Team	G	AB	R	H	2B	3B	HR	RBI	BB	SB	AVG
1989	Min	28	67	6	14	3	0	0	4	1	0	.209
		28	67	6	14	3	0	0	4	1	0	.209

Tim Hulett

Birth Date: 1/12/60
Bats: Right
Throws: Right
1989 Club:
Baltimore Orioles
Contest Code #: 510

Rating: 2

Tim Hulett has reached that dangerous point in a baseball player's life. After eight years in one organization, the White Sox in Tim's case, he has been tossed around over the past two seasons, playing 33 games for the Baltimore Orioles in 1989 after minor-league duty with the Expos and Birds.

It's something of a strange case. Tim spent all of 1985 and 1986 with the Chisox varsity. His 17 homers in 1986 were second only to slugger Ron Kittle. Then he opened 1987 with the Sox, only to be sent down again at mid-season. He didn't return to the majors until late 1989, when he played in 33 Orioles games. He didn't do badly, either, hitting .278 with 3 homers and 18 RBI's in only 97 at-bats. He isn't a contact hitter but his apparent power offsets that somewhat. Where he goes from here is anyone's guess.

Year	Team	G	AB	R	H	2B	3B	HR	RBI	BB	SB	AVG
1983	ChA....	6	5	0	1	0	0	0	0	0	1	.200
1984	ChA....	8	7	1	0	0	0	0	0	1	1	.000
1985	ChA....	141	395	52	106	19	4	5	37	30	6	.268
1986	ChA....	150	520	53	120	16	5	17	44	21	4	.231
1987	ChA....	68	240	20	52	10	0	7	28	10	0	.217
1989	Bal	33	97	12	27	5	0	3	18	10	0	.278
		406	1264	138	306	50	9	32	127	72	12	.242

Manny Lee

Birth Date: 6/17/65
Bats: Both
Throws: Right
1989 Club:
Toronto Blue Jays
Contest Code #: 511

Rating: 3

Manny Lee has always been a bit on the precocious side. At age twenty-four, he has already played nine seasons of professional baseball. He was only nineteen when he opened the 1985 season in Toronto. At an age when many players are just arriving after college careers, Lee has established himself as a top-flight utility player. Still, only once in his big-league career has Manny played in more than 100 games.

Split seasons and a 1988 disabled-list stay have limited his action. He got into 99 games for the 1989 Jays, at third, short, and second. The latter is probably his best position, mainly because teammate Tony Fernandez promises to be Toronto's shortstop forever. Lee hit .260 in 300 at-bats last year, a fairly major slip from his .291 in 1988. His 3 home runs matched the total of the two previous seasons. He's no power threat. Still another of the Jays' great Dominican players, Lee should battle Nelson Liriano for more playing time at 2B in 1990.

Year	Team	G	AB	R	H	2B	3B	HR	RBI	BB	SB	AVG
1985	Tor.....	64	40	9	8	0	0	0	0	2	1	.200
1986	Tor.....	35	78	8	16	0	1	1	7	4	0	.205
1987	Tor.....	56	121	14	31	2	3	1	11	6	2	.256
1988	Tor.....	116	381	38	111	16	3	2	38	26	3	.291
1989	Tor.....	99	300	27	78	9	2	3	34	20	4	.260
		370	920	96	244	27	9	7	90	58	10	.265

Nelson Liriano

Birth Date: 6/3/64
Bats: Both
Throws: Right
1989 Club:
Toronto Blue Jays
Contest Code #: 512

Rating: 3

Another key member of the Toronto Blue Jays' Dominican connection, Nelson Liriano is coming into his own as a major-league second baseman. That's not good news for Jay rivals. Liriano, who signed with Toronto at age eighteen, arrived in the majors at age twenty-two and is likely to be around a long time. Defensively, he's really learning the position.

His superior speed provides him with excellent range, and he's beginning to learn what to do with the ball once he gets it. His "average" arm can get the job done at second. The 5'10", 172-pounder's offense is beginning to come, too. The switch-hitter's .263 average last season (7 points over his career mark) included 34 extra-base blows (26 doubles, 3 triples, 5 homers) among his 110 hits. He set career highs in each offensive category. Liriano has shown marked improvement in each of the last three seasons. It should continue.

Year	Team	G	AB	R	H	2B	3B	HR	RBI	BB	SB	AVG
1987	Tor.....	37	158	29	38	6	2	2	10	16	13	.241
1988	Tor.....	99	276	36	73	6	2	3	23	11	12	.264
1989	Tor.....	132	418	51	110	26	3	5	53	43	16	.263
		268	852	116	221	38	7	10	86	70	41	.259

Fred Manrique

Birth Date: 11/5/61
Bats: Right
Throws: Right
1989 Club:
Chicago White Sox &
Texas Rangers
Contest Code #: 513

Rating: 3

A July 29, 1989, trade brought Fred Manrique (along with Harold Baines) to the Texas Rangers, his sixth stop in three full and three partial major-league seasons. We can't figure out why he keeps moving along. Manrique, who was born and still lives in Venezuela, is a tough competitor who can play just about anywhere in the infield. Manrique's 47 starts for Texas included 12 at second base, 30 at shortstop, and 5 at third base. That's just about right, though second base appears to be his best position. His arm, which is just adequate at SS, ranks as a plus.

And his bat isn't bad either. The twenty-eight-year-old makes decent contact at the plate. His 111 hits, 25 doubles, and 52 RBI's in 1989 set career highs, and his .388 mark with runners in scoring position was excellent.

Year	Team	G	AB	R	H	2B	3B	HR	RBI	BB	SB	AVG
1981	Tor.....	14	28	1	4	0	0	0	1	0	0	.143
1984	Tor.....	10	9	0	3	0	0	0	1	0	0	.333
1985	Mon....	9	13	5	4	1	1	1	1	1	0	.308
1986	StL	13	17	2	3	0	0	1	1	1	1	.176
1987	ChA....	115	298	30	77	13	3	4	29	19	5	.258
1988	ChA....	140	345	43	81	10	6	5	37	21	6	.235
1989	ChA....	65	187	23	56	13	1	2	30	8	0	.299
1989	Tex	54	191	23	55	12	0	2	22	9	4	.288
		420	1088	127	283	49	11	15	122	59	16	.260

Al Newman

Birth Date: 6/30/60
Bats: Both
Throws: Right
1989 Club:
Minnesota Twins
Contest Code #: 514

Rating: 2

Twins manager Tom Kelly never hesitates to use Al Newman at second, third, or shortstop. He shouldn't. Newman is a first-rate utility infielder who excels at second or third and is adequate at short. You tend to forget about players like Newman until a Gary Gaetti (1988) or Greg Gagne (1989) goes down for an extended period. Newman, a first-round draft choice of the Montreal Expos in 1981 after a career as a second baseman and running back at San Diego State, spent nearly four years in the 'Spos farm system before reaching the big leagues with Montreal in late 1985. Two nonproductive years brought him to Minnesota in time for the 1987 world-championship season.

Last season was Newman's best as a big leaguer. In fact, his batting average has improved every year since he arrived in the majors. His .253 batting average was 38 points over his previous career percentage. Al also set a career-high in stolen bases with 25. It figured. When he stole 63 bases for Memphis in 1982, he broke the club record held by no less talented a runner than Tim Raines.

Year	Team	G	AB	R	H	2B	3B	HR	RBI	BB	SB	AVG
1985	Mon....	25	29	7	5	1	0	0	1	3	2	.172
1986	Mon....	95	185	23	37	3	0	1	8	21	11	.200
1987	Min....	110	307	44	68	15	5	0	29	34	15	.221
1988	Min....	105	260	35	58	7	0	0	19	29	12	.223
1989	Min....	141	446	62	113	18	2	0	38	59	25	.253
		476	1227	171	281	44	7	1	95	146	65	.229

Tony Phillips

Birth Date: 4/15/59
Bats: Both
Throws: Right
1989 Club:
Oakland Athletics
Contest Code #: 515

Rating: 3

Healthy for the first time in five seasons, Tony Phillips reveled in his full-time role for the champion Oakland A's last season. Easily one of the game's most versatile players, Phillips did everything but pitch and catch for the 1988 A's.

Then last year's injury to Walt Weiss forced Mike Gallego to take over at shortstop, leaving the starting role at second to the 5'10", 175-pound Phillips. A .266 marked Tony's best full-year BA in the majors. But he doesn't have to hit any better to maximize his value to a team. Despite possessing just average tools, the Georgia native did a superb job at second and he knows how to play the game.

Though the stats don't show it, he has enough speed to be a base-stealing threat. And most of all, he's the kind of player who can make things happen. Where they happen in 1990 wasn't evident after the last World Series game when Tony filed for free agency.

Year	Team	G	AB	R	H	2B	3B	HR	RBI	BB	SB	AVG
1982	Oak....	40	81	11	17	2	2	0	8	12	2	.210
1983	Oak....	148	412	54	102	12	3	4	35	48	16	.248
1984	Oak....	154	451	62	120	24	3	4	37	42	10	.266
1985	Oak....	42	161	23	45	12	2	4	17	13	3	.280
1986	Oak....	118	441	76	113	14	5	5	52	76	15	.256
1987	Oak....	111	379	48	91	20	0	10	46	57	7	.240
1988	Oak....	79	212	32	43	8	4	2	17	36	0	.203
1989	Oak....	143	451	48	118	15	6	4	47	58	3	.262
		835	2588	354	649	107	25	33	259	342	56	.251

Johnny Ray

Birth Date: 3/1/57
Bats: Both
Throws: Right
1989 Club:
California Angels
Contest Code #: 516

Rating: 4

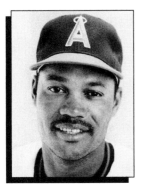

Wake Johnny Ray up in the middle of the night and he'll probably spring into his hitting stance. The man is a hitting machine—from both sides of the plate. Mention defense, and he'll probably go right back to sleep. From his first full big-league season (Pittsburgh, 1982), Ray has been an offensive sensation. Dealt to the Angels during the 1987 pennant chase, Johnny picked up right where he had left off in the NL. He's a constant threat at the stick, as his .289 mark in 1989 shows. He's probably a little better as a lefty than as a righty, particularly when a right-hander grooves a fastball that he can turn on. Defense is another story. Johnny combines limited range with a below-marginal arm and is a liability in the field. But he more than makes up for it as a .291 career hitter who always manages to find a way to get on base.

Year	Team	G	AB	R	H	2B	3B	HR	RBI	BB	SB	AVG
1981	Pit.....	31	102	10	25	11	0	0	6	6	0	.245
1982	Pit.....	162	647	79	182	30	7	7	63	36	16	.281
1983	Pit.....	151	576	68	163	38	7	5	53	35	18	.283
1984	Pit.....	155	555	75	173	38	6	6	67	37	11	.312
1985	Pit.....	154	594	67	163	33	3	7	70	46	13	.274
1986	Pit.....	155	579	67	174	33	0	7	78	58	6	.301
1987	Cal.....	30	127	16	44	11	0	0	15	3	0	.346
1987	Pit.....	123	472	48	129	19	3	5	54	41	4	.273
1988	Cal.....	153	602	75	184	42	7	6	83	36	4	.306
1989	Cal.....	134	530	52	153	16	3	5	62	36	6	.289
		1248	4784	557	1390	271	36	48	551	334	78	.291

Harold Reynolds

Birth Date: 11/26/60
Bats: Both
Throws: Right
1989 Club:
Seattle Mariners
Contest Code #: 517

Rating: 4

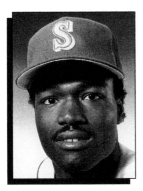

What is there not to like about Harold Reynolds? The best of the ball-playing Reynolds brothers (Don was with the Padres and Mariners, Larry with the Rangers), Seattle's second sacker is the kind of player you can send on the field every day and never worry about his ability to get it done.

After nearly five seasons in the majors, the 5'11", 165-pound Oregon native knows his way around the field. He can make all the plays and rarely makes mistakes (though he did commit 17 errors last year). With a bat in his hand, Harold is becoming increasingly dangerous. His .300 average last season was 17 points better than his previous high and a full 46 points ahead of his career mark. The 1987 AL stolen-base leader (60) pilfered 25 sacks in 1989. Though he failed to homer last season, he did have 9 triples, giving him a two-year total of 20. The report on Reynolds says he's a good man to have on the club. We agree.

Year	Team	G	AB	R	H	2B	3B	HR	RBI	BB	SB	AVG
1983	Sea	20	59	8	12	4	1	0	1	2	0	.203
1984	Sea	10	10	3	3	0	0	0	0	0	1	.300
1985	Sea	67	104	15	15	3	1	0	6	17	3	.144
1986	Sea	126	445	46	99	19	4	1	24	29	30	.222
1987	Sea	160	530	73	146	31	8	1	35	39	60	.275
1988	Sea	158	598	61	169	26	11	4	41	51	35	.283
1989	Sea	153	613	87	184	24	9	0	43	55	25	.300
		694	2359	293	628	107	34	6	150	193	154	.266

Billy Ripken

Birth Date: 12/16/64
Bats: Right
Throws: Right
1989 Club:
Baltimore Orioles
Contest Code #: 518

Rating: 3

Maybe "the other Ripken" has finally found his level. After hitting .308 in 1987, Billy Rip slumped to .207 (the AL's worst for a BA qualifier) in 1988 as the Birds fell through the AL floor. In 1989, for a contending ball club he hit .239, which is probably about right.

A heady player (which doesn't count for much in our League, except to keep your man in the lineup every day), the younger Ripken brother feasts on lefty fastballers and doesn't do much with anything else. Unlike brother Cal, who has had 20 or more homers for the last eight years, Billy has no power whatsoever.

If the Birds come up with a better man (totally conceivable), Billy could wind up on the bench in 1990. If Ripken doesn't get his numbers up, manager Frank Robinson will be looking down the bench when Billy comes up in a late-inning key situation.

Year	Team	G	AB	R	H	2B	3B	HR	RBI	BB	SB	AVG
1987	Bal	58	234	27	72	9	0	2	20	21	4	.308
1988	Bal	150	512	52	106	18	1	2	34	33	8	.207
1989	Bal	115	318	31	76	11	2	2	26	22	1	.239
		323	1064	110	254	38	3	6	80	76	13	.239

Ed Romero

Birth Date: 12/9/57
Bats: Right
Throws: Right
1989 Club:
Atlanta Braves &
Milwaukee Brewers
Contest Code #: 519

Rating: 2

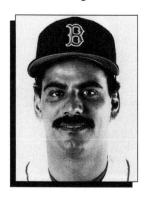

Ed Romero has become a journeyman player in the truest sense of the word. The thirty-two-year-old started 1989 on the Boston Red Sox roster, moved on to the Atlanta Braves and, when Jim Ganter and Billy Bates went down with injuries last August, over to the Milwaukee Brewers, his original big-league club.

The versatile Romero actually came up to the majors (for 10 games) with Milwaukee as a nineteen-year-old in 1977. He was back full-time in 1980, doing utility work all around the infield. Dealt to Boston for the 1986 season, he was hampered by knee surgery in 1988. He had only 19 ABs for the Braves (.263) before arriving in Milwaukee, where he played full-time for about one week. By September he was reduced to part-time action (7 games)and wound up hitting .200.

Year	Team	G	AB	R	H	2B	3B	HR	RBI	BB	SB	AVG
1977	Mil.....	10	25	4	7	1	0	0	2	4	0	.280
1980	Mil.....	42	104	20	27	7	0	1	10	9	2	.260
1981	Mil.....	44	91	6	18	3	0	1	10	4	0	.198
1982	Mil.....	52	144	18	36	8	0	1	7	8	0	.250
1983	Mil.....	59	145	17	46	7	0	1	18	8	1	.317
1984	Mil.....	116	357	36	90	12	0	1	31	29	3	.252
1985	Mil.....	88	251	24	63	11	1	0	21	26	1	.251
1986	Bos	100	233	41	49	11	0	2	23	18	2	.210
1987	Bos	88	235	23	64	5	0	0	14	18	0	.272
1988	Bos	31	75	3	18	3	0	0	5	3	0	.240
1989	Bos	46	113	14	24	4	0	0	6	7	0	.212
1989	Atl	7	19	1	5	1	0	1	1	0	0	.263
1989	Mil.....	15	50	3	10	3	0	0	3	0	0	.200
		698	1842	210	457	76	1	8	151	134	9	.248

Steve Sax

Birth Date: 1/29/60
Bats: Right
Throws: Right
1989 Club:
New York Yankees
Contest Code #: 520

Rating: 5

Long the National League's premier second baseman, Steve Sax moved to the American League and the Yankees last year and took his crown with him. Yankee officials, who outbid the Dodgers by a half-million bucks for Sax's services, were delighted with the play of the 5'11", 179-pounder from California. His work habits and his attitude are without equal.

Steve enjoyed himself, too. His .315 bat mark was his best since a .332 average in 1986 placed him second in the NL standings behind Tim Raines. As usual, Steve played in 158 Yankee games; his 651 at-bats matched his four-year average. Sax is a prototypical lead-off hitter. His on-base percentage was .364 and his 205 hits included 26 doubles and 5 homers. His 63 RBI's set a new career high, major or minor league. And he stole 43 bases, the most since he swiped 56 for the 1983 Dodgers.

Why did the Dodgers slip from a world title to the NL West second division? Steve Sax was in New York.

Year	Team	G	AB	R	H	2B	3B	HR	RBI	BB	SB	AVG
1981	LA.....	31	119	15	33	2	0	2	9	7	5	.277
1982	LA.....	150	638	88	180	23	7	4	47	49	49	.282
1983	LA.....	155	623	94	175	18	5	5	41	58	56	.281
1984	LA.....	145	569	70	138	24	4	1	35	47	34	.243
1985	LA.....	136	488	62	136	8	4	1	42	54	27	.279
1986	LA.....	157	633	91	210	43	4	6	56	59	40	.332
1987	LA.....	157	610	84	171	22	7	6	46	44	37	.280
1988	LA.....	160	632	70	175	19	4	5	57	45	42	.277
1989	NYA....	158	651	88	205	26	3	5	63	52	43	.315
		1249	4963	662	1423	185	38	35	396	415	333	.287

Lou Whitaker

Birth Date: 5/12/57
Bats: Left
Throws: Right
1989 Club:
Detroit Tigers
Contest Code #: 521

Rating: 5

Though the firm of Whitaker & Trammell became a limited partnership thanks to Trammell's back ailment in 1989, veteran Detroit Tiger Lou Whitaker remains one of the better second sackers—and all-around players—in all of baseball. The 1978 AL Rookie of the Year, Whitaker has been doing the job at second base ever since. Except for his speed, which is just average, Sweet Lou (he got the nickname in the Florida State League in 1976) rates among the top offensive and defensive infielders anywhere. He hits (though only .251 last year) and hits with power (28 homers, 17 more than any other Tiger in 1989).

Around the bag, his range remains good, his glove is first-rate, and he turns the double play as well as anyone. He and Trammell have been together since 1978 and figure to stay together a while longer, if both are healthy.

Year	Team	G	AB	R	H	2B	3B	HR	RBI	BB	SB	AVG
1977	Det	11	32	5	8	1	0	0	2	4	2	.250
1978	Det	139	484	71	138	12	7	3	58	61	7	.285
1979	Det	127	423	75	121	14	8	3	42	78	20	.286
1980	Det	145	477	68	111	19	1	1	45	73	8	.233
1981	Det	109	335	48	88	14	4	5	36	40	5	.263
1982	Det	152	560	76	160	22	8	15	65	48	11	.286
1983	Det	161	643	94	206	40	6	12	72	67	17	.320
1984	Det	143	558	90	161	25	1	13	56	62	6	.289
1985	Det	152	609	102	170	29	8	21	73	80	6	.279
1986	Det	144	584	95	157	26	6	20	73	63	13	.269
1987	Det	149	604	110	160	38	6	16	59	71	13	.265
1988	Det	115	403	54	111	18	2	12	55	66	2	.275
1989	Det	148	509	77	128	21	1	28	85	89	6	.251
		1695	6221	965	1719	279	58	149	721	802	116	.276

Frank White

Birth Date: 9/4/50
Bats: Right
Throws: Right
1989 Club:
Kansas City Royals
Contest Code #: 522

Rating: 4

You have to like Frank White. The Mississippi native has given 100 percent every day for more than sixteen seasons, much to the delight of Kansas City teammates, management, and fans. Everyone is waiting for Frank to begin slowing down and, in fact, he has—a little. He'll be forty in September and has rarely taken a day off. But he's out there, working hard, all the time.

Certainly the premier defensive second baseman of the 1980s, White isn't half-bad with at the plate either. He hit .256 last season (the same as Bo Jackson), his best since 1986. But his power has slipped badly (after six straight years of double-digit homers from 1982 to 1987) and so has his production (only 36 RBI's last year). The Royals are diligently preparing for the day when White can't do it anymore. But they could do a lot worse than sticking with Frank for a while longer.

Year	Team	G	AB	R	H	2B	3B	HR	RBI	BB	SB	AVG
1973	KC.....	51	139	20	31	6	1	0	5	8	3	.223
1974	KC.....	99	204	19	45	6	3	1	18	5	3	.221
1975	KC.....	111	304	43	76	10	2	7	36	20	11	.250
1976	KC.....	152	446	39	102	17	6	2	46	19	20	.229
1977	KC.....	152	474	59	116	21	5	5	50	25	23	.245
1978	KC.....	143	461	66	127	24	6	7	50	26	13	.275
1979	KC.....	127	467	73	124	26	4	10	48	25	28	.266
1980	KC.....	154	560	70	148	23	4	7	60	19	19	.264
1981	KC.....	94	364	35	91	17	1	9	38	19	4	.250
1982	KC.....	145	524	71	156	45	6	11	56	16	10	.298
1983	KC.....	146	549	52	143	35	6	11	77	20	13	.260
1984	KC.....	129	479	58	130	22	5	17	56	27	5	.271
1985	KC.....	149	563	62	140	25	1	22	69	28	10	.249
1986	KC.....	151	566	76	154	37	3	22	84	43	4	.272
1987	KC.....	154	563	67	138	32	2	17	78	51	1	.245
1988	KC.....	150	537	48	126	25	1	8	58	21	7	.235
1989	KC.....	135	418	34	107	22	1	2	36	30	3	.256
		2242	7618	892	1954	393	57	158	865	402	177	.256

THIRD BASEMEN

Luis Aguayo

Birth Date: 3/13/59
Bats: Right
Throws: Right
1989 Club:
Cleveland Indians
Contest Code #: 525

Rating: 2

A professional since age 17, Puerto Rico-born Luis Aguayo has begun the journeyman's trek through the concluding days of a major-league career. The 5'9", 188-pound Aguayo spent 12½ pro years with the Phillies' organization before going to the Yankees in mid-1988 when the New Yorkers were dreadfully short of experienced infielders. The Indians were able to pick up the nine-year big-leaguer as a free-agent before the 1989 season. It wasn't a thrilling season for Aguayo who played in only 47 games before heading for the disabled list. His .175 batting average (4 doubles, 8 RBIs) is guaranteed to keep him on the move.

Year	Team	G	AB	R	H	2B	3B	HR	RBI	BB	SB	AVG
1980	Phi	20	47	7	13	1	2	1	8	2	1	.277
1981	Phi	45	84	11	18	4	0	1	7	6	1	.214
1982	Phi	50	56	11	15	1	2	3	7	5	1	.268
1983	Phi	2	4	1	1	0	0	0	0	1	0	.250
1984	Phi	58	72	15	20	4	0	3	11	8	0	.278
1985	Phi	91	165	27	46	7	3	6	21	22	1	.279
1986	Phi	62	133	17	28	6	1	4	13	8	1	.211
1987	Phi	94	209	25	43	9	1	12	21	15	0	.206
1988	NYA....	50	140	12	35	4	0	3	8	7	0	.250
1988	Phi	49	97	9	24	3	0	3	5	13	2	.247
1989	Cle.....	47	97	7	17	4	1	1	8	7	0	.175
		568	1104	142	260	43	10	37	109	94	7	.236

Mike Blowers

Birth Date: 4/24/65
Bats: Right
Throws: Right
1989 Club:
New York Yankees
Contest Code #: 526

Rating: 1

When Mike Blowers got to the Montreal Expos camp last spring, they handed him uniform number 62. He had to know he wasn't long for the place. He wasn't. Picked up by the Yankees organization, Blowers (rhymes with flowers) actually made it to the Bronx in time to play 13 games for the Bombers. He hit .263 (10 hits, all singles, in 38 at-bats), drove in 3 runs, and struckout 13 times. It will be interesting to see what number they give him this year.

Year	Team	G	AB	R	H	2B	3B	HR	RBI	BB	SB	AVG
1989	NYA....	13	38	2	10	0	0	0	3	3	0	.263
		13	38	2	10	0	0	0	3	3	0	.263

Wade Boggs

Birth Date: 6/15/58
Bats: Left
Throws: Right
1989 Club:
Boston Red Sox
Contest Code #: 527

Rating: 5

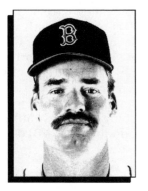

If you like to watch a classic hitter in action, there's no one better than Wade Boggs. At age thirty-one, Bogus just hits and hits and hits. And he's a good third baseman, too. True, his .330 average in 1989 was 26 points below his previous career mark, and ended his streak of four straight AL batting titles (and six overall).

There's no cause for concern, however, because Boggs is also a thinking man's hitter without an obvious weakness—except for occasional lapses against curve balls from left-handed pitchers. He struck out 51 times in 621 at-bats last year, just a smidgen above normal. But he also drew more than 100 walks (107) for the fourth straight year. He doesn't have a lot of speed (14 career stolen bases), but he has an insatiable desire to win and plays hard every day.

Yes, his off-the-field romance dogged him on the field in 1989, though he figures to get his 200 hits for his eighth straight year in 1990.

Year	Team	G	AB	R	H	2B	3B	HR	RBI	BB	SB	AVG
1982	Bos	104	338	51	118	14	1	5	44	35	1	.349
1983	Bos	153	582	100	210	44	7	5	74	92	3	.361
1984	Bos	158	625	109	203	31	4	6	55	89	3	.325
1985	Bos	161	653	107	240	42	3	8	78	96	2	.368
1986	Bos	149	580	107	207	47	2	8	71	105	0	.357
1987	Bos	147	551	108	200	40	6	24	89	105	1	.363
1988	Bos	155	584	128	214	45	6	5	58	125	2	.366
1989	Bos	156	621	113	205	51	7	3	54	107	2	.330
		1183	4534	823	1597	314	36	64	523	754	14	.352

Tom Brookens

Birth Date: 8/10/53
Bats: Right
Throws: Right
1989 Club:
New York Yankees
Contest Code #: 528

Rating: 2

Only a couple of seasons ago, Tom Brookens was the Detroit Tigers' regular third baseman. Now, at age thirty-six, the Pennsylvania native is looking for work. A lifetime .246 career hitter before the 1989 season, Brookens moved onto the Yankees last spring and slumped to .226. Fact is, he played in only 66 games for the Bronx Bombers before moving to the DL for most of the late summer.

The cousin of one-time Tiger pitcher Ike Brookens, the 5'10", 170-pounder put in 9½ seasons in Detroit before moving on. Never an overpowering hitter, he made his way with his glove, providing an excellent accompaniment to the Detroit DP combo of Lou Whitaker and Alan Trammell. It wasn't long ago that the Tigers dealt third baseman Howard Johnson to the Mets, leaving the job to Brookens. Hindsight, as they say, is always 20/20.

Year	Team	G	AB	R	H	2B	3B	HR	RBI	BB	SB	AVG
1979	Det	60	190	23	50	5	2	4	21	11	10	.263
1980	Det	151	509	64	140	25	9	10	66	32	13	.275
1981	Det	71	239	19	58	10	1	4	25	14	5	.243
1982	Det	140	398	40	92	15	3	9	58	27	5	.231
1983	Det	138	332	50	71	13	3	6	32	29	10	.214
1984	Det	113	224	32	55	11	4	5	26	19	6	.246
1985	Det	156	485	54	115	34	6	7	47	27	14	.237
1986	Det	98	281	42	76	11	2	3	25	20	11	.270
1987	Det	143	444	59	107	15	3	13	59	33	7	.241
1988	Det	136	441	62	107	23	5	5	38	44	4	.243
1989	NYA	66	168	14	38	6	0	4	14	11	1	.226
		1272	3711	459	909	168	38	70	411	267	86	.245

Steve Buechele

Birth Date: 9/26/61
Bats: Right
Throws: Right
1989 Club:
Texas Rangers
Contest Code #: 529

Rating: 3

Too bad the American League can't play by National Football League rules. Everytime the Texas Rangers' opponents came to bat, manager Bobby Valentine could send out his defensive unit, led by his designated third baseman, Steve Buechele. Though the 6'2", 190-pounder set career marks for doubles (22) and RBI's (59, though only 6 in his final 37 games) last season and smacked 16 homers, third on the club (and third among AL third basemen), offense simply isn't his strong suit. His .235 batting average was his all-time low-water mark—but not by much.

If the rules makers ever came up with a designated fielder rule, however, Buechele would be an All-Star candidate. Though his speed is basically below average, he owns a vacuum-cleaner glove and throws quickly, hard, and accurately. One scout states flatly, "Buechele is one of the best defensive players in the league."

Year	Team	G	AB	R	H	2B	3B	HR	RBI	BB	SB	AVG
1985	Tex	69	219	22	48	6	3	6	21	14	3	.219
1986	Tex	153	461	54	112	19	2	18	54	35	5	.243
1987	Tex	136	363	45	86	20	0	13	50	28	2	.237
1988	Tex	155	503	68	126	21	4	16	58	65	2	.250
1989	Tex	155	486	60	114	22	2	16	59	36	1	.235
		668	2032	249	486	88	11	69	242	178	13	.239

Gary Gaetti

Birth Date: 8/19/58
Bats: Right
Throws: Right
1989 Club:
Minnesota Twins
Contest Code #: 530

Rating: 4

The American League is loaded with outstanding third basemen. Think offense and you immediately come to Wade Boggs and Carney Lansford. But think all-around third base and Gary Gaetti comes instantly to mind. Though his 1989 production (.251, 19 homers, 75 RBI's) didn't match his All-Star 1988 (.301, 28 homers, 88 RBI's), Gary is the kind of guy any manager would like to have at the hot corner.

He has all the tools: first-rate on defense, good home-run power, excellent hitting skills, a great attitude, and tremendous work habits. He's a throwback to an earlier age, when players come to play every day. Gaetti's toughness is well known throughout the league and has earned him respect from friend and foe alike.

Year	Team	G	AB	R	H	2B	3B	HR	RBI	BB	SB	AVG
1981	Min	9	26	4	5	0	0	2	3	0	0	.192
1982	Min	145	508	59	117	25	4	25	84	37	0	.230
1983	Min	157	584	81	143	30	3	21	78	54	7	.245
1984	Min	162	588	55	154	29	4	5	65	44	11	.262
1985	Min	160	560	71	138	31	0	20	63	37	13	.246
1986	Min	157	596	91	171	34	1	34	108	52	14	.287
1987	Min	154	584	95	150	36	2	31	109	37	10	.257
1988	Min	133	468	66	141	29	2	28	88	36	7	.301
1989	Min	130	498	63	125	11	4	19	75	25	6	.251
		1207	4412	585	1144	225	20	185	673	322	68	.259

Rene Gonzales

Birth Date: 9/3/61
Bats: Right
Throws: Right
1989 Club:
Baltimore Orioles
Contest Code #: 531

Rating: 2

For right now, add the word "utility" to Rene Gonzales' job description. The 6'3", 195-pound Texas native can get it done at third base, shortstop, or second base. But he's no threat to dispossess any of the Oriole starters. The problem is his bat. Gonzales came to Baltimore after a 40-game career (over two seasons) with the Expos. He hit .267 in 37 games for the 1987 O's, but that seems like an aberration. He's basically a .215-or-so hitter (.217 in 1989), and he doesn't have much power. He had 1 homer last year, to go with 3 previous major-league dingers. His glove should keep him on someone's roster, but he'll have to improve at the plate to make any long-range impact in the big time.

Year	Team	G	AB	R	H	2B	3B	HR	RBI	BB	SB	AVG
1984	Mon....	29	30	5	7	1	0	0	2	2	0	.233
1986	Mon....	11	26	1	3	0	0	0	0	2	0	.115
1987	Bal	37	60	14	16	2	1	1	7	3	1	.267
1988	Bal	92	237	13	51	6	0	2	15	13	2	.215
1989	Bal	71	166	16	36	4	0	1	11	12	5	.217
		240	519	49	113	13	1	4	35	32	8	.218

Kelly Gruber

Birth Date: 2/26/62
Bats: Right
Throws: Right
1989 Club:
Toronto Blue Jays
Contest Code #: 532

Rating: 3

The Toronto Blue Jays' Kelly Gruber is the kind of ballplayer who should always carry his American Express card. He has done the job on the field, but a lot of people still don't know who he is. Baseball insiders know. Although the twenty-eight-year-old was Toronto's third baseman during most of 1989 (he started the ALCS at that spot), he also played second, short, and the outfield for the Jays.

In the past couple of seasons, he has also started at least one game in each of the nine slots in the batting order. The one-time Cleveland Indian farmhand was having a super 1988 until a late-season fade left him with a .278 batting average. Off-season conditioning that winter enabled him to last through a grueling 1989 campaign, which he ended at .290 and a career-high 18 homers. A good third baseman with a plus-arm, Gruber is a solid contact hitter with occasional power. Best of all, his overall makeup makes him "a winner."

Year	Team	G	AB	R	H	2B	3B	HR	RBI	BB	SB	AVG
1984	Tor.....	15	16	1	1	0	0	1	2	0	0	.063
1985	Tor.....	5	13	0	3	0	0	0	1	0	0	.231
1986	Tor.....	87	143	20	28	4	1	5	15	5	2	.196
1987	Tor.....	138	341	50	80	14	3	12	36	17	12	.235
1988	Tor.....	158	569	75	158	33	5	16	81	38	23	.278
1989	Tor.....	135	545	83	158	24	4	18	73	30	10	.290
		538	1627	229	428	75	13	52	208	90	47	.263

J.R. Howell

Birth Date: 8/18/61
Bats: Left
Throws: Right
1989 Club:
California Angels
Contest Code #: 533

Rating: 3

The Angels' J. R. Howell is the consummate team player who works at being the best he can be. His best is far short of Hall of Fame, but he does get the most he can out of the tools available to him. Defensively, Howell is a mixed bag. His arm is a big plus, and he's blessed with good hands. In fact, he won awards for his defense during his minor-league career. But insiders contend that his range is limited, and that doesn't help.

J. R. will never hit for a high average, but his power should make up for it. His 20 homers in 1989 give him 59 for his 3 full big-league campaigns. But his RBI contribution fell to 52 from 64 and 63, so that category demands close attention.

Year	Team	G	AB	R	H	2B	3B	HR	RBI	BB	SB	AVG
1985	Cal.....	43	137	19	27	4	0	5	18	16	1	.197
1986	Cal.....	63	151	26	41	14	2	4	21	19	2	.272
1987	Cal.....	138	449	64	110	18	5	23	64	57	4	.245
1988	Cal.....	154	500	59	127	32	2	16	63	46	2	.254
1989	Cal.....	144	474	56	108	19	4	20	52	52	0	.228
		542	1711	224	413	87	13	68	218	190	9	.241

Brook Jacoby

Birth Date: 11/23/59
Bats: Right
Throws: Right
1989 Club:
Cleveland Indians
Contest Code #: 534

Rating: 4

Will the real Brook Jacoby please stand up? The stat sheet on the Cleveland Indians' third sacker is a study in inconsistency. In 1985 and 1986, he knocked in 87 and 80 runs. In 1987, admittedly the year of the home run, he hit .300 and banged out 32 round-trippers but slipped to 69 RBI's. In 1988, his whole game went south after a fast start. He wound up hitting .241 and only had 9 homers.

So where is he now? In 1989, Jacoby finally got the bat back to .273, his career average. He had 13 homers, a little more respectable. And he knocked in 64 runs, a decent-enough improvement. Still, the Jacoby of the mid-1980s is missing. He's a steady defensive player with at least an average arm. The former Atlanta Brave (he arrived in Cleveland via the notorious Len Barker trade) has well-below-average speed. He was successful in only 2 of 7 steal attempts last year. The return of his home-run power is the key to his progression as a major leaguer.

Year	Team	G	AB	R	H	2B	3B	HR	RBI	BB	SB	AVG
1981	Atl.....	11	10	0	2	0	0	0	1	0	0	.200
1983	Atl.....	4	8	0	0	0	0	0	0	0	0	.000
1984	Cle.....	126	439	64	116	19	3	7	40	32	3	.264
1985	Cle.....	161	606	72	166	26	3	20	87	48	2	.274
1986	Cle.....	158	583	83	168	30	4	17	80	56	2	.288
1987	Cle.....	155	540	73	162	26	4	32	69	75	2	.300
1988	Cle.....	152	552	59	133	25	0	9	49	48	2	.241
1989	Cle.....	147	519	49	141	26	5	13	64	62	2	.272
		914	3257	400	888	152	19	98	390	321	13	.273

Carney Lansford

Birth Date: 2/7/57
Bats: Right
Throws: Right
1989 Club:
Oakland Athletics
Contest Code #: 535

Rating: 5

At age thirty-three, Carney Lansford remains one of the wonders of the baseball world. The California native could always hit. He led the American League (for the Boston Red Sox) with a .336 average in 1981. But his career mark was a respectable, if not spectacular, .292 before the 1989 season. Then he hit .336 again, missing his second AL batting title by only 3 points.

Even more remarkable, Lansford stole 37 bases, his career high, after stealing only 23 in four seasons from 1982 to 1985. His speed makes him a better defensive player, too. And though he hit only two homers last year, he was in double figures from 1982 through 1987.

Best of all, Lansford is a solid team player, a key ingredient for a ball club that could tend toward a letdown after two straight AL pennants and a world championship.

Year	Team	G	AB	R	H	2B	3B	HR	RBI	BB	SB	AVG
1978	Cal.....	121	453	63	133	23	2	8	52	31	20	.294
1979	Cal.....	157	654	114	188	30	5	19	79	39	20	.287
1980	Cal.....	151	602	87	157	27	3	15	80	50	14	.261
1981	Bos ...	102	399	61	134	23	3	4	52	34	15	.336
1982	Bos	128	482	65	145	28	4	11	63	46	9	.301
1983	Oak	80	299	43	92	16	2	10	45	22	3	.308
1984	Oak	151	597	70	179	31	5	14	74	40	9	.300
1985	Oak	98	401	51	111	18	2	13	46	18	2	.277
1986	Oak	151	591	80	168	16	4	19	72	39	16	.284
1987	Oak	151	554	89	160	27	4	19	76	60	27	.289
1988	Oak	150	556	80	155	20	2	7	57	35	29	.279
1989	Oak	148	551	81	185	28	2	2	52	51	37	.336
		1588	6139	884	1807	287	38	141	748	465	201	.294

Tom Lawless

Birth Date: 12/19/56
Bats: Right
Throws: Right
1989 Club:
Toronto Blue Jays
Contest Code #: 536

Rating: 2

This may not be Tom Lawless' year. The thirty-three-year-old utility infielder wins a division championship in odd-numbered years. So he doesn't figure in 1990. A former St. Louis Cardinal, he played on the Redbirds' NL East champs team in 1985 and 1987. He came to the Toronto Blue Jays in January 1989 and wound up in another league championship series.

A Pennsylvania native, the 5'11", 170-pounder is the consummate utility man. He can play second, short, or third, though he'll probably never be an everyday starter. What the scouts like most about Lawless is that he does the little things that help his team win. Though Lawless hit only .229 last season, the mark was 22 points over his career average. In fact, in 73 games over the previous two years with St. Louis, he had gone 12-for-90 (.133). However, he suffers from a severe power shortage (two home runs since 1983).

Year	Team	G	AB	R	H	2B	3B	HR	RBI	BB	SB	AVG
1982	Cin	49	165	19	35	6	0	0	4	9	16	.212
1984	Cin	43	80	10	20	2	0	1	2	8	6	.250
1984	Mon....	11	17	1	3	1	0	0	0	0	1	.176
1985	StL	47	58	8	12	3	1	0	8	5	2	.207
1986	StL	46	39	5	11	1	0	0	3	2	8	.282
1987	StL	19	25	5	2	1	0	0	0	3	2	.080
1988	StL	54	65	9	10	2	1	1	3	7	6	.154
1989	Tor.....	59	70	20	16	1	0	0	3	7	12	.229
		328	519	77	109	17	2	2	23	41	53	.210

Steve Lyons

Birth Date: 6/3/60
Bats: Left
Throws: Right
1989 Club:
Chicago White Sox
Contest Code #: 537

Rating: 2

Steve Lyons is the kind of player managers love to keep around. Though the thirty-year-old Lyons will never be a superstar, he does an excellent job at any of five or six positions—which comes in handy in these days of the twenty-four-man roster. Blessed with primarily excellent tools, Lyons is okay in the outfield, but even better at second or third base.

The Washington native came up through the Boston organization and came to the White Sox in a trade that sent future Hall-of-Famer Tom Seaver to Beantown. The former Oregon State star does everything well enough, but rates just above average in speed and arm. At the stick, Lyons hit .264 last year, down a few points from the previous two seasons with the Sox but 3 points over his career mark.

Year	Team	G	AB	R	H	2B	3B	HR	RBI	BB	SB	AVG
1985	Bos	133	371	52	98	14	3	5	30	32	12	.264
1986	Bos	59	124	20	31	7	2	1	14	12	2	.250
1986	ChA	42	123	10	25	2	1	0	6	7	2	.203
1987	ChA	76	193	26	54	11	1	1	19	12	3	.280
1988	ChA	146	472	59	127	28	3	5	45	32	1	.269
1989	ChA	140	443	51	117	21	3	2	50	35	9	.264
		596	1726	218	452	83	13	14	164	130	29	.262

Carlos Martinez

Birth Date: 8/11/65
Bats: Right
Throws: Right
1989 Club:
Chicago White Sox
Contest Code #: 538

Rating: 3

At 6'5" and 175 pounds, Carlos Martinez is an unlikely-looking major leaguer. Tall and gangly, Martinez sees action at both first and third base, and the inside report indicates he can do both well. The native of Venezuela turned pro at age eighteen in the New York Yankee organization and came to the White Sox in a six-player deal in July 1986.

Somebody in Chicago liked what they saw during a late-season trial in 1988, though Carlos hit only .164. In a full shot in 1989, Martinez hit .300 in 109 games. He has some power (22 doubles, 32 RBI's), though his hitting is always somewhat suspect because of his long, looping swing. There are some questions about Martinez's attitude, which can kill a career faster than any on-the-field shortcoming. If he can keep his head on straight, he can contribute to his ball club.

Year	Team	G	AB	R	H	2B	3B	HR	RBI	BB	SB	AVG
1988	ChA	17	55	5	9	1	0	0	0	0	1	.164
1989	ChA	109	350	44	105	22	0	5	32	21	4	.300
		126	405	49	114	23	0	5	32	21	5	.281

Bam-Bam Meulens

Birth Date: 6/23/67
Bats: Right
Throws: Right
1989 Club:
New York Yankees
Contest Code #: 539

Rating: 2

Bam-Bam Meulens is certainly a rare baseball breed. The only major leaguer from Curaçao, in the Netherlands Antilles, he rates right at the top of the list of Yankee prospects. Yankee fans greeted Meulens' promotion to the parent-club roster last August with mixed emotions: They were anxious to see this highly regarded prospect but they realized that he could probably use another year or so at the AAA level.

A strongly built 6'3" and 190 pounds, Muelens has displayed excellent offensive credentials during his minor-league career. At Class-A Prince William in 1987, he led the league with 28 homers and knocked in 103 runs in 116 games. He also hit .300 but struck out 124 times. Those numbers excited Bronx fans who have gone without an American League championship since 1981.

Year	Team	G	AB	R	H	2B	3B	HR	RBI	BB	SB	AVG
1989	NYA....	8	28	2	5	0	0	0	1	2	0	.179
		8	28	2	5	0	0	0	1	2	0	.179

Paul Molitor

Birth Date: 8/22/56
Bats: Right
Throws: Right
1989 Club: Milwaukee Brewers
Contest Code #: 540

Rating: 5

At an age (going on thirty-four) when some players begin to wind down, Milwaukee's Paul Molitor is as good as he's ever been—offensively, defensively, and as a club leader. The one-time U. of Minnesota standout can hurt the opponents in many ways. His nifty .315 average last year was his third straight over .300 and raised his career average to the .300 mark. Molly also had 11 homers, his fourth double-figures year in the last five.

The eyes of America were focused sharply on the 6', 175-pounder in 1987 when he made the AL's best assault on Joe DiMaggio's record of 56 straight games with a hit or more. Molitor's streak stopped at 39 straight. The Brewers' career leader in stolen bases had another 27 last season, though his 11 failed attempts disappointed some. Molitor's work ethic tends to rub off on his teammates. He plays hard all the time and remains a better than decent third sacker. With a plethora of infielders on the Milwaukee roster, Paul is versatile enough to play anywhere Tom Trebelhorn needs him.

Year	Team	G	AB	R	H	2B	3B	HR	RBI	BB	SB	AVG
1978	Mil.....	125	521	73	142	26	4	6	45	19	30	.273
1979	Mil.....	140	584	88	188	27	16	9	62	48	33	.322
1980	Mil.....	111	450	81	137	29	2	9	37	48	34	.304
1981	Mil.....	64	251	45	67	11	0	2	19	25	10	.267
1982	Mil.....	160	666	136	201	26	8	19	71	69	41	.302
1983	Mil.....	152	608	95	164	28	6	15	47	59	41	.270
1984	Mil.....	13	46	3	10	1	0	0	6	2	1	.217
1985	Mil.....	140	576	93	171	28	3	10	48	54	21	.297
1986	Mil.....	105	437	62	123	24	6	9	55	40	20	.281
1987	Mil.....	118	465	114	164	41	5	16	75	69	45	.353
1988	Mil.....	154	609	115	190	34	6	13	60	71	41	.312
1989	Mil.....	155	615	84	194	35	4	11	56	64	27	.315
		1437	5828	989	1751	310	60	119	581	568	344	.300

Rance Mulliniks

Birth Date: 1/15/56
Bats: Left
Throws: Right
1989 Club:
Toronto Blue Jays
Contest Code #: 541

Rating: 3

Rance Mulliniks comes to the Skydome every day ready to play. Where that is, he never knows. At the least, he remains part of a third-base platoon with Kelly Gruber, but since Gruber can play a variety of positions, they often see action together. Mulliniks, who has spent eight seasons with Toronto after three years with the California Angels and two with the Kansas City Royals, does his best defensive work at third but often pops up as Toronto's designated hitter against right-handed pitchers.

Though Rance's batting average slipped to .238 after two straight seasons at .310 and .300, he continued to be a productive hitter. Among his 65 hits, 16 went for extra bases. Throughout his career, more than 30 percent of his hits were extra-base blows.

Year	Team	G	AB	R	H	2B	3B	HR	RBI	BB	SB	AVG
1977	Cal.....	78	271	36	73	13	2	3	21	23	1	.269
1978	Cal.....	50	119	6	22	3	1	1	6	8	2	.185
1979	Cal.....	22	68	7	10	0	0	1	8	4	0	.147
1980	KC.....	36	54	8	14	3	0	0	6	7	0	.259
1981	KC.....	24	44	6	10	3	0	0	5	2	0	.227
1982	Tor.....	112	311	32	76	25	0	4	35	37	3	.244
1983	Tor.....	129	364	54	100	34	3	10	49	57	0	.275
1984	Tor.....	125	343	41	111	21	5	3	42	33	2	.324
1985	Tor.....	129	366	55	108	26	1	10	57	55	2	.295
1986	Tor.....	117	348	50	90	22	0	11	45	43	1	.259
1987	Tor.....	124	332	37	103	28	1	11	44	34	1	.310
1988	Tor.....	119	337	49	101	21	1	12	48	56	1	.300
1989	Tor.....	103	273	25	65	11	2	3	29	34	0	.238
		1168	3230	406	883	210	16	69	395	393	13	.273

Gus Polidor

Birth Date: 10/26/61
Bats: Right
Throws: Right
1989 Club:
Milwaukee Brewers
Contest Code #: 542

Rating: 1

Given a shot to start on opening day by his new employers, the Milwaukee Brewers, Gus Polidor struggled through the entire 1989 season. The former California Angel opened at third base for the Brew Crew, filling in for the injured Paul Molitor. He couldn't do it. The Venezuelan native hit only .156 through the first two months of the season before rallying to hit .400 in June. Then it was back to lack-of-business-as-usual as he slumped to .163 during the second half of the campaign. Overall the 6', 185-pounder hit .194 for the season and was one of only two all-season Brewers to fail to homer. At best, Polidor is a utility player. His bat is weak, and all his tools are below average.

Year	Team	G	AB	R	H	2B	3B	HR	RBI	BB	SB	AVG
1985	Cal.....	2	1	1	1	0	0	0	0	0	0	1.000
1986	Cal.....	6	19	1	5	1	0	0	1	1	0	.263
1987	Cal.....	63	137	12	36	3	0	2	15	2	0	.263
1988	Cal.....	54	81	4	12	3	0	0	4	3	0	.148
1989	Mil.....	79	175	15	34	7	0	0	14	6	3	.194
		204	413	33	88	14	0	2	34	12	3	.213

Jim Presley

Birth Date: 10/23/61
Bats: Right
Throws: Right
1989 Club:
Seattle Mariners
Contest Code #: 543

Rating: 3

At age twenty-eight and after only 5½ years with the Mariners, Jim Presley is one of the team's grand old men. How much longer he stays in Seattle remains a question; almost every big trade discussed in the last two seasons has mentioned Presley's name.

Thanks to a sore back, combined with the super-hard Kingdome playing field, Presley has seemingly lost a step or two at third base. As a result, he has found himself at first base or in the designated-hitter role at times during the past couple of seasons. Unfortunately, he simply hasn't been making good-enough contact of late, as his .236 average, his all-time, full-season low last year, clearly indicates. Still, he maintains enough power to be considered dangerous.

Year	Team	G	AB	R	H	2B	3B	HR	RBI	BB	SB	AVG
1984	Sea	70	251	27	57	12	1	10	36	6	1	.227
1985	Sea	155	570	71	157	33	1	28	84	44	2	.275
1986	Sea	155	616	83	163	33	4	27	107	32	0	.265
1987	Sea	152	575	78	142	23	6	24	88	38	2	.247
1988	Sea	150	544	50	125	26	0	14	62	36	3	.230
1989	Sea	117	390	42	92	20	1	12	41	21	0	.236
		799	2946	351	736	147	13	115	418	177	8	.250

Bobby Rose

Birth Date: 3/15/67
Bats: Right
Throws: Right
1989 Club:
California Angels
Contest Code #: 544

Rating: 2

While an old infielder named Rose was making all the headlines last summer for his off-the-field activities, another, much younger, Rose—the Angels' Bobby Rose—was getting his first taste of major-league action. It was barely a sip (14 games, 38 at-bats), but encouraging nonetheless for a Southern California native with fewer than four minor-league seasons behind him.

The Angels like the way Bobby plays the game, especially with the flashes of power in his arsenal. Though he hit only .211 in his 14 games, 4 of his 8 hits went for extra bases, including a double, 2 triples, and a home run. Rose is still a year or so away from the majors.

Year	Team	G	AB	R	H	2B	3B	HR	RBI	BB	SB	AVG
1989	Cal.....	14	38	4	8	1	2	1	3	2	0	.211
		14	38	4	8	1	2	1	3	2	0	.211

Rick Schu

Birth Date: 1/26/62
Bats: Right
Throws: Right
1989 Club:
Baltimore Orioles &
Detroit Tigers
Contest Code #: 545

Rating: 2

It wasn't long ago that the Philadelphia Phillies moved future Hall-of-Famer Mike Schmidt from his accustomed spot at third base to make room for Rick Schu. The experiment was noble but unsuccessful; the Schu simply didn't fit at third. Now, the Philadelphia native has become an itinerant, after spending the last three seasons with three different clubs.

There's no reason to believe that Schu will be putting down roots anytime soon. His .214 average with the Detroit Tigers last season was easily his major-league low. Schu's glove remains suspect and his power, while occasionally evident, isn't much to write home about. A couple of recent stays on the disabled list don't add to Schu's reputation. A once-bright future appears fairly dim.

Year	Team	G	AB	R	H	2B	3B	HR	RBI	BB	SB	AVG
1984	Phi	17	29	12	8	2	1	2	5	6	0	.276
1985	Phi	112	416	54	105	21	4	7	24	38	8	.252
1986	Phi	92	208	32	57	10	1	8	25	18	2	.274
1987	Phi	92	196	24	46	6	3	7	23	20	0	.235
1988	Bal	89	270	22	69	9	4	4	20	21	6	.256
1989	Bal	1	0	0	0	0	0	0	0	0	0	.000
1989	Det	98	266	25	57	11	0	7	21	24	1	.214
		501	1385	169	342	59	13	35	118	127	17	.247

Kevin Seitzer

Birth Date: 3/26/62
Bats: Right
Throws: Right
1989 Club:
Kansas City Royals
Contest Code #: 546

Rating: 4

There's a little concern in Kansas City that Kevin Seitzer's second and third years in the majors haven't matched his sensational rookie year. It's worth some concern, of course. In 1987, Seitzer hit the big-league scene with a .323 average, 207 hits (tied for the AL lead), 15 homers, and 83 RBI's. In 1988, though, he slipped to .304 with only 5 homers and 60 RBI's. Still he became the first Royal ever to hit .300 or more for his first two years. The downward numbers spiral continued in 1989, however, to .281, 4 homers, and 48 RBI's.

Though the concern is justified, it isn't frightening. Seitzer remains a tough, aggressive hitter and fielder. He makes good contact at the plate and fields well at third base. His attitude makes manager John Wathan proud, and his work habits are beyond reproach. Seitzer knows how to play and will continue to do so. An upward numerical turn is quite conceivable.

Year	Team	G	AB	R	H	2B	3B	HR	RBI	BB	SB	AVG
1986	KC.....	28	96	16	31	4	1	2	11	19	0	.323
1987	KC.....	161	641	105	207	33	8	15	83	80	12	.323
1988	KC.....	149	559	90	170	32	5	5	60	72	10	.304
1989	KC.....	160	597	78	168	17	2	4	48	102	17	.281
		498	1893	289	576	86	16	26	202	273	39	.304

Doug Strange

Birth Date: 4/13/64
Bats: Both
Throws: Right
1989 Club:
Detroit Tigers
Contest Code #: 547

Rating: 1

After all or part of five seasons in the minors, Doug Strange earned a shot at the big time. He didn't hit at the top minor-league levels and kept up the pace in the majors. The one-time N.C. State star didn't rate highly in any of the categories the scouts check. They rated him barely adequate at third base and rated his arm only average. His speed is just borderline.

Similarly, his offensive game left much to be desired. He hit .214 in 64 games with the big club last season, with only 6 extra-base knocks among his 42 hits. His power is way below average, despite 13 homers in a Class AA season in 1987.

Year	Team	G	AB	R	H	2B	3B	HR	RBI	BB	SB	AVG
1989	Det	64	196	16	42	4	1	1	14	17	3	.214
		64	196	16	42	4	1	1	14	17	3	.214

Wayne Tolleson

Birth Date: 9/22/55
Bats: Both
Throws: Right
1989 Club:
New York Yankees
Contest Code #: 548

Rating: 1

His third annual trip to the disabled list marred 1989 for Wayne Tolleson. The former Texas Ranger and Chicago White Sox is a reliable member of the Yankees who has filled in ably while the Yanks have searched for a long-range shortstop. These days, Tolleson is a fringe player at best. The one-time All-American wide receiver at Western Carolina knows how to play the game, but his skills have diminished.

Hitting is the major question mark. He wasn't even within hailing distance of the Mendoza Line (.200) last season, hitting only .164 in 79 games. Power is practically nonexistent. His lone homer last season raised his eight-year major-league total to 9. Tolleson's on-the-field savvy and versatility may enable him to hang on a while longer.

Year	Team	G	AB	R	H	2B	3B	HR	RBI	BB	SB	AVG
1981	Tex	14	24	6	4	0	0	0	1	1	2	.167
1982	Tex	38	70	6	8	1	0	0	2	5	1	.114
1983	Tex	134	470	64	122	13	2	3	20	40	33	.260
1984	Tex	118	338	35	72	9	2	0	9	27	22	.213
1985	Tex	123	323	45	101	9	5	1	18	21	21	.313
1986	ChA	81	260	39	65	7	3	3	29	38	13	.250
1986	NYA	60	215	22	61	9	2	0	14	14	4	.284
1987	NYA	121	349	48	77	4	0	1	22	43	5	.221
1988	NYA	21	59	8	15	2	0	0	5	8	1	.254
1989	NYA	79	140	16	23	5	2	1	9	16	5	.164
		789	2248	289	548	59	16	9	129	213	107	.244

Randy Velarde

Birth Date: 11/24/62
Bats: Right
Throws: Right
1989 Club:
New York Yankees
Contest Code #: 549

Rating: 1

Randy Velarde has to know every bank, every turn, every approach between New York's LaGuardia Airport and the Columbus (OH) airport. Few frequent travelers have made the round-trip as often as the Yankee infielder and, knowing George Steinbrenner, we believe it's likely that Randy will continue to roll up the bonus miles in 1990.

It might be somewhat tougher to send the 6', 185-pound Velarde packing this time, however. In 33 games with the big club in 1989, the Texan pounded out 34 hits in 100 at-bats for an easy-to-figure .340 batting mark. Eight of the 34 hits went for extra bases (4 doubles, 2 triples, 2 homers), producing a .450 slugging percentage. Defense is still Velarde's big weakness. In fact, his 52 errors at Appleton (WI) led the Midwest League in 1986.

Year	Team	G	AB	R	H	2B	3B	HR	RBI	BB	SB	AVG
1987	NYA....	8	22	1	4	0	0	0	1	0	0	.182
1988	NYA....	48	115	18	20	6	0	5	12	8	1	.174
1989	NYA....	33	100	12	34	4	2	2	11	7	0	.340
		89	237	31	58	10	2	7	24	15	1	.245

Craig Worthington

Birth Date: 4/17/65
Bats: Right
Throws: Right
1989 Club:
Baltimore Orioles
Contest Code #: 550

Rating: 3

Craig Worthington is another of the Orioles' fine young prospects. Our reports say that the Tennessee native has a chance to become an outstanding everyday player. Right now, the scouts are looking at his defense. His potential at third base is tremendous. He's blessed with a super arm and a great pair of hands (despite 20 errors a year ago).

That's half the job. The rest isn't bad either. A fair minor-league hitter, Worthington's major-league numbers indicate that he's on his way. He hit .247 in 145 games with the Birds in 1989, including 15 homers and 23 doubles. Scouts focus on the timeliness of his hitting. He's solid with men on base and looks like he can drive in plenty of runs. Worthington's a comer.

Year	Team	G	AB	R	H	2B	3B	HR	RBI	BB	SB	AVG
1988	Bal	26	81	5	15	2	0	2	4	9	1	.185
1989	Bal	145	497	57	123	23	0	15	70	61	1	.247
		171	578	62	138	25	0	17	74	70	2	.239

SHORTSTOPS

Kent Anderson

Birth Date: 8/12/63
Bats: Right
Throws: Right
1989 Club:
California Angels
Contest Code #: 555

Rating: 2

Mike Brumley

Birth Date: 4/9/63
Bats: Both
Throws: Right
1989 Club:
Detroit Tigers
Contest Code #: 556

Rating: 1

Last spring, Kent Anderson wasn't even on California's forty-man roster. After two so-so seasons at AAA Edmonton, it didn't look as though he'd be visiting Disneyland anytime soon. An injury to SS Dick Schofield earned him a ticket to Anaheim, and Anderson gave it his best shot. What he proved is that he belongs on a major-league roster. He's no threat to Schofield or Ozzie Smith or Shawon Dunston at shortstop, though he did a fairly decent job filling in. But he probably is a player.

Managers will love his aggressiveness, both at the plate and in the field. He has tremendous determination. Although he out-hit Schofield by one point (.229–.228), he lacks the starter's power. Anderson can hit and run, however, and he bunts well. The former U. of South Carolina star may be headed for a career as a utility player, but at least it's a career.

Year	Team	G	AB	R	H	2B	3B	HR	RBI	BB	SB	AVG
1989	Cal.....	86	223	27	51	6	1	0	17	17	1	.229
		86	223	27	51	6	1	0	17	17	1	.229

It was kind of a strange year for Mike Brumley. Seemingly set for a shot at the San Diego Padres' roster following a .315 season at Las Vegas in 1988, Brumley was shuffled off to Detroit (in exchange for Luis Salazar, who would wind up in the NLCS with Chicago). Not including a two-week stay in Toledo, Mike wound up starting 58 games in six different positions for the Tigers, and pinch-ran in 17 additional games.

The Oklahoma City native showed absolutely nothing of the offensive firepower he displayed at Vegas. He hit .198, only .181 from the left side. Speed remains a key to his game; he stole 8 bases in 12 attempts. His versatility is notable; he plays mostly at short (36 games) but also at second (16), third (6), and all three outfield spots. At age twenty-six, he should get a full shot one of these years.

Year	Team	G	AB	R	H	2B	3B	HR	RBI	BB	SB	AVG
1987	ChN....	39	104	8	21	2	2	1	9	10	7	.202
1989	Det	92	212	33	42	5	2	1	11	14	8	.198
		131	316	41	63	7	4	2	20	24	15	.199

Mario Diaz

Birth Date: 1/10/62
Bats: Right
Throws: Right
1989 Club:
Seattle Mariners
Contest Code #: 557

Rating: 2

After hitting .304 and .306 in two brief trials (11 and 28 games) with Seattle in 1987 and 1988, Mario Diaz had to figure he was ready for a longer shot. He got it in 1989 and the results weren't pretty. The scouting report on Diaz says that he makes fair contact, but he certainly didn't show it last season; he went 10 for 74 (.135). Diaz has a fine pair of hands and his arm is just short of the "gun" category. Still, with absolutely no power to speak of and a microscopic batting average, he will probably never be anything more than a utility man.

Year	Team	G	AB	R	H	2B	3B	HR	RBI	BB	SB	AVG
1987	Sea	11	23	4	7	0	1	0	3	0	0	.304
1988	Sea	28	72	6	22	5	0	0	9	3	0	.306
1989	Sea	52	74	9	10	0	0	1	7	7	0	.135
		91	169	19	39	5	1	1	19	10	0	.231

Alvaro Espinoza

Birth Date: 2/19/62
Bats: Right
Throws: Right
1989 Club:
New York Yankees
Contest Code #: 558

Rating: 3

Talk about your pleasant surprises. In the spring of 1989, Alvaro Espinoza wasn't even on the Yankees' forty-man roster. A shortstop shortage earned him a trial with the big club, and the Venezuelan made the most of it. It didn't take long for Espo to open some eyes. Espinoza, who played seventy games at second and short over three part-seasons for the Minnesota Twins, took over at short early for the Yankees and never looked back.

Defensively, he did everything he had to, showing good range, a fine arm, and the ability to make the double play. Offensively, he hit .282, better than any year in the majors or minors since a .319 at Visalia in the Class-A California League back in 1983. He doesn't have any power to speak of, but he can bunt and hit and run well and, basically, knows how to play.

Yankee fans are delighted.

Year	Team	G	AB	R	H	2B	3B	HR	RBI	BB	SB	AVG
1985	Min	32	57	5	15	2	0	0	9	1	0	.263
1986	Min	37	42	4	9	1	0	0	1	1	0	.214
1988	NYA....	3	3	0	0	0	0	0	0	0	0	.000
1989	NYA....	146	503	51	142	23	1	0	41	14	3	.282
		218	605	60	166	26	1	0	51	16	3	.274

Felix Fermin

Birth Date: 10/9/63
Bats: Right
Throws: Right
1989 Club:
Cleveland Indians
Contest Code #: 559

Rating: 3

The Indians are pleased with the deal that brought Felix Fermin (Fer-MEEN) to the Tribe from Pittsburgh. Another of the great shortstops from the Dominican Republic, Fermin is probably a better offensive player than last year's .238 average indicates. The book on Fermin says that he's a good contact hitter who seldom strikes out and shows some promise of occasional power. The scouts can't understand why his average isn't better. On defense, he can make all the plays, and his arm is a definite plus. Best of all, the 5'11", 170 pounder has a superb attitude that makes him a good man to have around the ball club while increasing the likelihood that he'll some day fully capitalize on his potential.

Year	Team	G	AB	R	H	2B	3B	HR	RBI	BB	SB	AVG
1987	Pit.....	23	68	6	17	0	0	0	4	4	0	.250
1988	Pit.....	43	87	9	24	0	2	0	2	8	3	.276
1989	Cle.....	156	484	50	115	9	1	0	21	41	6	.238
		222	639	65	156	9	3	0	27	53	9	.244

Tony Fernandez

Birth Date: 6/30/62
Bats: Both
Throws: Right
1989 Club:
Toronto Blue Jays
Contest Code #: 560

Rating: 5

Just another superstar from San Pedro de Macoris in the Dominican Republic. That's Toronto shortstop Tony Fernandez, who's always in the hunt for the AL's All-Star team. For glove work alone, the slick twenty-seven-year-old is easily his league's best. By the time he retires, he'll own enough Gold Gloves to outfit an entire team. He has the range of a 747—and though his arm isn't quite in Shawon Dunston's class, it's better than most. He can throw from anywhere and from any position.

He's getting there as a hitter, too. His 11 homers last season marked a career high. He has averaged nearly 67 RBI's over the last four seasons, including 64 a year ago. And he has been in double figures in steals each of the last five seasons. Originally signed as a seventeen-year-old free agent early in 1979, ever-improving Fernandez should be around for a long time.

Year	Team	G	AB	R	H	2B	3B	HR	RBI	BB	SB	AVG
1983	Tor.....	15	34	5	9	1	1	0	2	2	0	.265
1984	Tor.....	88	233	29	63	5	3	3	19	17	5	.270
1985	Tor.....	161	564	71	163	31	10	2	51	43	13	.289
1986	Tor.....	163	687	91	213	33	9	10	65	27	25	.310
1987	Tor.....	146	578	90	186	29	8	5	67	51	32	.322
1988	Tor.....	154	648	76	186	41	4	5	70	45	15	.287
1989	Tor.....	140	573	64	147	25	9	11	64	29	22	.257
		867	3317	426	967	165	44	36	338	214	112	.292

Scott Fletcher

Birth Date: 7/30/58
Bats: Right
Throws: Right
1989 Club:
Texas Rangers &
Chicago White Sox
Contest Code #: 561

Rating: 4

A key man in the trade that sent Harold Baines from the Chicago White Sox to the Rangers, Fletcher moved right back in at Comiskey Park, where he spent three seasons between 1983 and 1985. A good-enough all-around player, the 5'11", 173-pound infielder will never embarrass himself or his club.

Fletcher is one of those heady players who figure out how to get the job done. The scouts like the way he knows how to use the bat, which means he makes good contact—despite a .253 average, his lowest since 1984. Like most contact hitters, he has little or no power, which isn't a major flaw. Defensively, Scott is versatile, playing shortstop or second base equally well. He has decent range and an average arm.

Back in Chicago, he should show some improvement. The sauna-hot summers in Texas always seemed to exhaust him late in the season. Whether he's worth the $1.2 million he's paid is another question.

Year	Team	G	AB	R	H	2B	3B	HR	RBI	BB	SB	AVG
1981	ChN....	19	46	6	10	4	0	0	1	2	0	.217
1982	ChN....	11	24	4	4	0	0	0	1	4	1	.167
1983	ChA....	114	262	42	62	16	5	3	31	29	5	.237
1984	ChA....	149	456	46	114	13	3	3	35	46	10	.250
1985	ChA....	119	301	38	77	8	1	2	31	35	5	.256
1986	Tex	147	530	82	159	34	5	3	50	47	12	.300
1987	Tex	156	588	82	169	28	4	5	63	61	13	.287
1988	Tex	140	515	59	142	19	4	0	47	62	8	.276
1989	Tex	83	314	47	75	14	1	0	22	38	1	.239
1989	ChA....	59	232	30	63	11	1	1	21	26	1	.272
		997	3268	436	875	147	24	17	302	350	56	.268

Greg Gagne

Birth Date: 11/12/61
Bats: Right
Throws: Right
1989 Club:
Minnesota Twins
Contest Code #: 562

Rating: 4

Thanks to the GG boys, the left side of the Twins' infield is in very competent hands. With Gary Gaetti firmly entrenched at third, Greg Gagne is a perfect partner at short. Gags is a very good shortstop. He has excellent range, a fine arm, and a quick release. He's a heady player who makes the right play virtually every time.

Gagne blossomed in the Twins' run to the world title in 1987, and he has continued to progress ever since. Still, he isn't a major threat on offense. He handles breaking stuff pretty well but usually falls victim to heavy heat. Though he slipped from .265 in 1987 to .236 in 1988, he bounced back with a career-high .272 in 1989, including 9 homers and 48 RBI's. He's a major asset to the club.

Year	Team	G	AB	R	H	2B	3B	HR	RBI	BB	SB	AVG
1983	Min	10	27	2	3	1	0	0	3	0	0	.111
1984	Min	2	1	0	0	0	0	0	0	0	0	.000
1985	Min	114	293	37	66	15	3	2	23	20	10	.225
1986	Min	156	472	63	118	22	6	12	54	30	12	.250
1987	Min	137	437	68	116	28	7	10	40	25	6	.265
1988	Min	149	461	70	109	20	6	14	48	27	15	.236
1989	Min	149	460	69	125	29	7	9	48	17	11	.272
		717	2151	309	537	115	29	47	216	119	54	.250

Mike Gallego

Birth Date: 10/31/60
Bats: Right
Throws: Right
1989 Club:
Oakland Athletics
Contest Code #: 563

Rating: 3

When Walter Weiss went down early last season, the Oakland Athletics didn't miss a beat. There was Mike Gallego, who did well enough that Weiss, the 1988 AL Rookie of the Year, couldn't push him out of the lineup. Though Gallego did an outstanding job at short, scouts still believe that the former UCLA star is probably a better second baseman. Anywhere in the infield, he's a superb fielder, even if he led the A's in errors (19) last year. In 1988, his first full season with Oakland, he made only 2 errors in 277 chances at second base—a rousing .993 fielding percentage.

Questions remain about Gallego's bat, despite his .252 mark last season, a major improvement over his .209 in 1988. He's a pesky hitter who does a better-than-decent job running the bases. Manager Tony LaRussa will find plenty of action for Mike in 1990.

Year	Team	G	AB	R	H	2B	3B	HR	RBI	BB	SB	AVG
1985	Oak	76	77	13	16	5	1	1	9	12	1	.208
1986	Oak	20	37	2	10	2	0	0	4	1	0	.270
1987	Oak	72	124	18	31	6	0	2	14	12	0	.250
1988	Oak	129	277	38	58	8	0	2	20	34	2	.209
1989	Oak	133	357	45	90	14	2	3	30	35	7	.252
		430	872	116	205	35	3	8	77	94	10	.235

Ozzie Guillen

Birth Date: 1/20/64
Bats: Left
Throws: Right
1989 Club:
Chicago White Sox
Contest Code #: 564

Rating: 4

Ozzie Guillen is a top-flight shortstop. Many scouts already rate him with the best in the game. Why not? The Venezuelan has all the tools—excellent range, a great arm, the ability to throw from anywhere.

When Guillen has a bat in his hands, insiders use terms like "Punch and Judy." That's not necessarily a negative, especially on a team with more power than the Chisox. Ozzie hit .253 in 1989, 13 points below his career mark. His single homer was his sixth in five big-league years, but his 54 RBI's set a career high.

Ozzie got his first taste of pro ball at age seventeen in the Padres' chain. He was the key man in a 1984 trade which sent Cy Young-winner LaMarr Hoyt to San Diego. At age twenty-one, he made the big time to stay.

Year	Team	G	AB	R	H	2B	3B	HR	RBI	BB	SB	AVG
1985	ChA....	150	491	71	134	21	9	1	33	12	7	.273
1986	ChA....	159	547	58	137	19	4	2	47	12	8	.250
1987	ChA....	149	560	64	156	22	7	2	51	22	25	.279
1988	ChA....	156	566	58	148	16	7	0	39	25	25	.261
1989	ChA....	155	597	63	151	20	8	1	54	15	36	.253
		769	2761	314	726	98	35	6	224	86	101	.263

Glenn Hoffman

Birth Date: 7/7/58
Bats: Right
Throws: Right
1989 Club:
California Angels
Contest Code #: 565

Rating: 2

Hoffman's best days are a memory. One scout says, "He just can't play anymore." The numbers seem to bear that out. A major leaguer for nearly nine full seasons, Hoffman spent all of 1988 at Boston's Pawtucket farm before joining the Angels as a free agent prior to the 1989 season. His hitting continues to erode, though he has had only one below-Mendoza season (.189 in 64 Red Sox games in 1984). Last year, in 48 games with the Angels, Hoffman hit only .212 with 22 hits, all but 4 singles—not the kind of stuff that moves a general manager to clear dates on his calendar for salary negotiations. At best, Hoffman will find a spot somewhere as a utility player.

Year	Team	G	AB	R	H	2B	3B	HR	RBI	BB	SB	AVG
1980	Bos	114	312	37	89	15	4	4	42	19	2	.285
1981	Bos	78	242	28	56	10	0	1	20	12	0	.231
1982	Bos	150	469	53	98	23	2	7	49	30	0	.209
1983	Bos	143	473	56	123	24	1	4	41	30	1	.260
1984	Bos	64	74	8	14	4	0	0	4	5	0	.189
1985	Bos	96	279	40	77	17	2	6	34	25	2	.276
1986	Bos	12	23	1	5	2	0	0	1	2	0	.217
1987	Bos	21	55	5	11	3	0	0	6	3	0	.200
1987	LA	40	132	10	29	5	0	0	10	7	0	.220
1989	Cal.....	48	104	9	22	3	0	1	3	3	0	.212
		766	2163	247	524	106	9	23	210	136	5	.242

Jeff Kunkel

Birth Date: 3/25/62
Bats: Right
Throws: Right
1989 Club:
Texas Rangers
Contest Code #: 566

Rating: 3

Even after his first full season in the majors (after five split seasons), the jury is still out on Jeff Kunkel. The son of the late major-league pitcher and American League umpire, Bill Kunkel, he started half of Texas' games, mostly at shortstop (53) and center field (21). He also saw action at second base, third base, and left and right fields. Versatility never hurt a big-league career.

The jury's still out because Kunkel seems to be improving. As an infielder, he has both good hands and a good arm. He isn't bad in the outfield, either. Offensively, the bat isn't terrible. His .270 batting average was his career high, along with 79 hits, 21 doubles, 8 homers, 29 RBI's, and 20 bases on balls—all new standards for the 6'2", 190-pounder. Kunkel should be ready for even more service in 1990.

Year	Team	G	AB	R	H	2B	3B	HR	RBI	BB	SB	AVG
1984	Tex	50	142	13	29	2	3	3	7	2	4	.204
1985	Tex	2	4	1	1	0	0	0	0	0	0	.250
1986	Tex	8	13	3	3	0	0	1	2	0	0	.231
1987	Tex	15	32	1	7	0	0	1	2	0	0	.219
1988	Tex	55	154	14	35	9	3	2	15	4	0	.227
1989	Tex	108	293	39	79	21	2	8	29	20	3	.270
		238	638	71	154	32	8	15	55	26	7	.241

Bill Pecota

Birth Date: 2/16/60
Bats: Right
Throws: Right
1989 Club:
Kansas City Royals
Contest Code #: 567

Rating: 2

If they ever created a "designated fielder" position, Bill Pecota could become an All-Star. His line in the Royals' press guide lists him as an infielder. But the California native is likely to pop up anywhere on the field at Royals Stadium—and except for pitcher, he has. The Pecota scouting report is brief. The 6'2", 190-pounder can run. He can field. He can throw. And that's about it.

Offensively, he's a cipher. A lifetime .237 hitter in 168 previous Royals games through 1988, Pecota sank to .205 (17 for 83) in 1989. Interestingly, 3 of his 17 hits were homers, giving him a .410 slugging average. But no one is looking to Pecota for offensive punch. Bill gives it his best shot every time out, but he seems destined to be no more than a major-league fill-in.

Year	Team	G	AB	R	H	2B	3B	HR	RBI	BB	SB	AVG
1986	KC.....	12	29	3	6	2	0	0	2	3	0	.207
1987	KC.....	66	156	22	43	5	1	3	14	15	5	.276
1988	KC.....	90	178	25	37	3	3	1	15	7	7	.208
1989	KC.....	65	83	21	17	4	2	3	5	7	5	.205
		233	446	71	103	14	6	7	36	43	17	.231

Jody Reed

Birth Date: 7/26/62
Bats: Right
Throws: Right
1989 Club:
Boston Red Sox
Contest Code #: 568

Rating: 3

Our scouts are high on Jody Reed. The one-time Florida State star and San Francisco top draft choice gets the job done, no matter what the job is. In two full major-league seasons, he's proven that he can hit .290 consistently. A .300 season in 1990 would surprise absolutely no one. At shortstop, Reed makes all the plays, is sound on the DP, and his arm is solid. But when he's assigned to the outfield or second base, he gets it done there, too. At the plate, he's a fine contact hitter who can hit and run when required. And he can steal the base, though he had only 4 last season. Power is a real deficiency. He had only three homers in 1989 and knocked in only 40 runs. But he drew 73 walks, which helped raise his on-base average to .376, just a shade better than Mike Greenwell's. Just as important, the scouts like Reed's attitude, rating him as a top team player.

Year	Team	G	AB	R	H	2B	3B	HR	RBI	BB	SB	AVG
1987	Bos	9	30	4	9	1	1	0	8	4	1	.300
1988	Bos	109	338	60	99	23	1	1	28	45	1	.293
1989	Bos	146	524	76	151	42	2	3	40	73	4	.288
		264	892	140	259	66	4	4	76	122	6	.290

Cal Ripken, Jr.

Birth Date: 8/24/60
Bats: Right
Throws: Right
1989 Club:
Baltimore Orioles
Contest Code #: 569

Rating: 5

The most reliable guy in baseball? If you're looking for someone who's in the lineup every day, whom else can you pick but Cal Ripken? He has been in there 1,250 consecutive times, since May 30, 1982. Only Everett Scott (1307 straight) and Lou Gehrig (2,130) have played more games without an absence than the Oriole shortstop.

A solid MVP candidate a year ago, Cal's numbers (.257 BA, .317 on-base average, 21 homers, 93 RBI's) weren't quite MVP quality. But he was the key guy (along with manager Frank Robinson) who woke up the Birds and drove them from the bottom to the top. Though Gehrig's consecutive games streak looms ahead (he should get there in June 1995, if he stays healthy), another record could fall next season. Ex-Red Sox Junior Stephens hit 213 homers as an AL shortstop to set the all-time AL mark. Ripken is only 9 behind and he's averaging 25 per season.

Ripken's a superb fastball hitter, though curveballs (particularly against righties) trouble him. He prefers to see sliders from right-handers. He draws lots of walks; but his power (only 21 homers) is beginning to slip a bit.

Year	Team	G	AB	R	H	2B	3B	HR	RBI	BB	SB	AVG
1981	Bal	23	39	1	5	0	0	0	0	1	0	.128
1982	Bal	160	598	90	158	32	5	28	93	46	3	.264
1983	Bal	162	663	121	211	47	2	27	102	58	0	.318
1984	Bal	162	641	103	195	37	7	27	86	71	2	.304
1985	Bal	161	642	116	181	32	5	26	110	67	2	.282
1986	Bal	162	627	98	177	35	1	25	81	70	4	.282
1987	Bal	162	624	97	157	28	3	27	98	81	3	.252
1988	Bal	161	575	87	152	25	1	23	81	102	2	.264
1989	Bal	162	646	80	166	30	0	21	93	57	3	.257
		1315	5055	793	1402	266	24	204	744	553	19	.277

Luis Rivera

Birth Date: 1/3/64
Bats: Right
Throws: Right
1989 Club:
Boston Red Sox
Contest Code #: 570

Rating: 3

One-time Expo Luis Rivera came to the Bosox with right-hander John Dopson for Spike Owen and Dan Gakeler. Looks like Sox GM Lou Gorman came up a winner on that one. Rivera was Montreal's opening day shortstop in 1988. But by the end of the season, the 'Spos were not unhappy to pass him along to Boston. They had to be mildly surprised that Rivera hit .257 in 93 games for the Sox in 1989. Except for a .312 mark in a half-season at AAA Indianapolis in 1987, Rivera had never hit .257 anywhere in his career. Even better for the Sox, Rivera showed good ability in the field. Given time, he could become a front-line major-league shortstop. And he is improving. Rivera even displays occasional power (he smacked 5 homers despite seeing only abbreviated action last season). The 5'10", 170-pounder has real possibilities.

Year	Team	G	AB	R	H	2B	3B	HR	RBI	BB	SB	AVG
1986	Mon....	55	166	20	34	11	1	0	13	17	1	.205
1987	Mon....	18	32	0	5	2	0	0	1	1	0	.156
1988	Mon....	123	371	35	83	17	3	4	30	24	3	.224
1989	Bos	93	323	35	83	17	1	5	29	20	2	.257
		289	892	90	205	47	5	9	73	62	6	.230

Dick Schofield

Birth Date: 11/21/62
Bats: Right
Throws: Right
1989 Club:
California Angels
Contest Code #: 571

Rating: 3

S eems that the sons of major leaguers are among the savviest players themselves. California shortstop Dick Schofield, son of former Cardinal infielder Ducky Schofield, fits the mold perfectly. But unlike the junior versions of Ken Griffey and Cal Ripken, among others, the younger Schofield isn't a tremendous offensive threat. He more than makes up for it with his defense and leadership.

Though injuries limited Schofield to just 91 games last season, he continued to demonstrate that he may well be the Angel shortstop of the present and future. He has good range, fields everything he can get to, and owns a "plus" throwing arm. His speed is suspect, which limits him on defense and on the base paths. But all those years of hanging around with great ballplayers has taught him the finer points of the game, and he uses his knowledge well.

Though his career .231 hit mark (.228 last year) doesn't show it, he's actually improving at the stick. He makes better contact than in the early days of his big-league career and occasionally stings the ball.

Year	Team	G	AB	R	H	2B	3B	HR	RBI	BB	SB	AVG
1983	Cal.....	21	54	4	11	2	0	3	4	6	0	.204
1984	Cal.....	140	400	39	77	10	3	4	21	33	5	.192
1985	Cal.....	147	438	50	96	19	3	8	41	35	11	.219
1986	Cal.....	139	458	67	114	17	6	13	57	48	23	.249
1987	Cal.....	134	479	52	120	17	3	9	46	37	19	.251
1988	Cal.....	155	527	61	126	11	6	6	34	40	20	.239
1989	Cal.....	91	302	42	69	11	2	4	26	28	9	.228
		827	2658	315	613	87	23	47	229	227	87	.231

Gary Sheffield

Birth Date: 11/18/68
Bats: Right
Throws: Right
1989 Club:
Milwaukee Brewers
Contest Code #: 572

Rating: 3

T he 1986 Gatorade National High School Player of the Year out of Tampa's Hillsborough High (the alma mater of Sheffield's uncle, Dwight Gooden), Sheffield has oodles of talent, but his attitude is a potential problem. Sheffield is blessed with excellent speed, an excellent glove and arm, a solid bat, and better-than-decent power. The Class-AA player of the year in 1988, Sheffield also saw action with Denver and the Brewers that season. An injury to Dale Sveum made Sheffield the Brew Crew's opening shortstop in 1989. It was a rocky year (.247, 16 errors) that saw Sheffield demoted, disabled, and crying for a trade. If he can get his act together, he should be super.

Year	Team	G	AB	R	H	2B	3B	HR	RBI	BB	SB	AVG
1988	Mil.....	24	80	12	19	1	0	4	12	7	3	.237
1989	Mil.....	95	368	34	91	18	0	5	32	27	10	.247
		119	448	46	110	19	0	9	44	34	13	.246

Bill Spiers

Birth Date: 6/5/66
Bats: Right
Throws: Right
1989 Club:
Milwaukee Brewers
Contest Code #: 573

Rating: 3

While everyone was looking for Gary Sheffield to be the Brewers' (and the AL's) top rookie a year ago, the surprise out of Milwaukee was the play of shortstop Bill Spiers. The youngster wasn't even on the major-league roster at spring training 1989, but his .400 spring BA and his sparkling defensive play earned him a trip to Wisconsin. He handled it from there.

Spiers excelled defensively, and his bat wasn't half-bad. Though he hit only .255, he showed tremendous offensive potential as well. Within his first two weeks in the bigs, he had his first homer (he wound up with 4), a grand slam off Texas' Brad Arnsberg. Though he was returned to AAA Denver for a couple of weeks (where he hit .362 in 14 games), he returned to the Brewers when Gary Sheffield went down with a broken foot. Scouts love Spiers' aggressiveness—and his future.

Year	Team	G	AB	R	H	2B	3B	HR	RBI	BB	SB	AVG
1989	Mil.....	114	345	44	88	9	3	4	33	21	10	.255
		114	345	44	88	9	3	4	33	21	10	.255

Kurt Stillwell

Birth Date: 6/4/65
Bats: Both
Throws: Right
1989 Club:
Kansas City Royals
Contest Code #: 574

Rating: 3

Former Cincinnati hotshot prospect Kurt Stillwell does a first-rate job as the Kansas City shortstop— which is exactly why the Royals parted with pitcher Danny Jackson and shortstop Angel Salazar for Stillwell and pitcher Ted Power after the 1987 season. The native Californian does everything well enough. He's a good infielder, with good range, good hands, and a good arm. At the plate, he's a contact hitter without much power, but he can occasionally sting the ball.

Anywhere he goes, he's an aggressive player who can get a ball club going. Stillwell made his major-league debut for Cincinnati at age twenty, spending the last half-season filling in for Reds all-timer Dave Concepcion. He filled in for Buddy Bell at third and for Ron Oester at second during his first full season (1987). That was enough for the Royals, who were suffering from a severe case of the shorts at shortstop, to take a shot with Stillwell in 1988. They haven't been disappointed.

Year	Team	G	AB	R	H	2B	3B	HR	RBI	BB	SB	AVG
1986	Cin	104	279	31	64	6	1	0	26	30	6	.229
1987	Cin	131	395	54	102	20	7	4	33	32	4	.258
1988	KC.....	128	459	63	115	28	5	10	53	47	6	.251
1989	KC.....	130	463	52	121	20	7	7	54	42	9	.261
		493	1596	200	402	74	20	21	166	151	25	.252

Alan Trammell

Birth Date: 2/21/58
Bats: Right
Throws: Right
1989 Club:
Detroit Tigers
Contest Code #: 575

Rating: 4

Health is the major question-mark facing Alan Trammell as he prepares for his fourteenth major-league season. A back injury that limited Trammell to 121 games last year threatens to end the Whitaker/Trammell team, which has held together the Tiger infield since 1978. If his back is okay, there's still plenty of baseball in Trammell. Though his game has gone backward somewhat, a healthy Trammell can still make a major contribution to his team. His glove is good, and his arm rates an A-plus from big-league scouts. His speed ranks as average.

Trammell's physical woes contributed mightily to a .243 batting mark in 1989, 47 points below his career mark. The slump followed consecutive seasons of .343 and .311. Likewise, his 5 homers last season were a marked drop from his 1987–88 totals of 28 and 15. Only thirty-two, Trammell should return to his prior numbers if his back is right in 1990.

Year	Team	G	AB	R	H	2B	3B	HR	RBI	BB	SB	AVG
1977	Det	19	43	6	8	0	0	0	0	4	0	.186
1978	Det	139	448	49	120	14	6	2	34	45	3	.268
1979	Det	142	460	68	127	11	4	6	50	43	17	.276
1980	Det	146	560	107	168	21	5	9	65	69	12	.300
1981	Det	105	392	52	101	15	3	2	31	49	10	.258
1982	Det	157	489	66	126	34	3	9	57	52	19	.258
1983	Det	142	505	83	161	31	2	14	66	57	30	.319
1984	Det	139	555	85	174	34	5	14	69	60	19	.314
1985	Det	149	605	79	156	21	7	13	57	50	14	.258
1986	Det	151	574	107	159	33	7	21	75	59	25	.277
1987	Det	151	597	109	205	34	3	28	105	60	21	.343
1988	Det	128	466	73	145	24	1	15	69	46	7	.311
1989	Det	121	449	54	109	20	3	5	43	45	10	.243
		1689	6143	938	1759	292	49	138	721	639	187	.286

Omar Vizquel

Birth Date: 5/15/67
Bats: Right
Throws: Right
1989 Club:
Seattle Mariners
Contest Code #: 576

Rating: 2

If Omar Vizquel wants to remain in the big leagues, he'll either have to crank up his offensive performance or do it as a defensive specialist. He's an excellent infielder, especially for a twenty-two-year-old with one year behind him, blessed with good hands and a plus-arm. Often, when you find a 5'9", 155-pounder, you look for outstanding speed. That's not the case with the native Venezuelan. Call it average (only 1 steal in 5 tries). Vizquel's .220 batting average is probably indicative of his current skill level. He makes fair contact with no home-run power. He will bunt for a base hit and handles the bat well enough to bring it off. Omar was a seventeen-year-old free agent when he was signed by the M's in 1984. He made just about every whistle-stop along Seattle's minor-league trail in five seasons before arriving to play 143 games in the Dome last year.

Year	Team	G	AB	R	H	2B	3B	HR	RBI	BB	SB	AVG
1989	Sea	143	387	45	85	7	3	1	20	28	1	.220
		143	387	45	85	7	3	1	20	28	1	.220

Walt Weiss

Birth Date: 11/28/63
Bats: Both
Throws: Right
1989 Club:
Oakland Athletics
Contest Code #: 577

Rating: 3

When the Oakland Athletics dealt Alfredo Griffin to the L.A. Dodgers before the 1988 season, they handed the job to Walt Weiss, whose total major-league experience encompassed 16 games. The former U. of North Carolina star disappointed no one, banging out 7 hits in his first 15 at-bats, then shoring up his defense by making only one error after July 8. At season's end, he was the shoo-in winner of the AL Rookie-of-the-Year Award.

Though a knee injury knocked Walt out of half of the 1989 season and he lost some of his defensive mobility, he should be back at full speed in 1990. Insiders love Weiss' defensive performance. He's an excellent shortstop, blessed with great range, superb hands, and a good arm. The only reservations revolve around his bat. He hit .250 as a rookie, then came back at .233 in his abbreviated sophomore season, with only 3 homers in each campaign. Still, there's no doubt that Weiss is a solid, everyday player.

Year	Team	G	AB	R	H	2B	3B	HR	RBI	BB	SB	AVG
1987	Oak....	16	26	3	12	4	0	0	1	2	1	.462
1988	Oak....	147	452	44	113	17	3	3	39	35	4	.250
1989	Oak....	84	236	30	55	11	0	3	21	21	6	.233
		247	714	77	180	32	3	6	61	58	11	.252

Paul Zuvella

Birth Date: 10/31/58
Bats: Right
Throws: Right
1989 Club:
Cleveland Indians
Contest Code #: 578

Rating: 2

Indian brass were pleased with the former Stanford star's performance in brief appearances at both shortstop and third base in 1989. Zuvella has fine hands, which make up for his limited range. Even his arm is, at best, borderline.

Zuvella's offense was a plus last season. A lifetime .214 hitter, Paul hit .276 in 24 games in 1989. That's one of Zuvella's problems. Although he has been a major leaguer in all or part of eight seasons, he has never played more than 81 games in any year. What could he do given a full season of action? We may never know.

Year	Team	G	AB	R	H	2B	3B	HR	RBI	BB	SB	AVG
1982	Atl.....	2	1	0	0	0	0	0	0	0	0	.000
1983	Atl.....	3	5	0	0	0	0	0	0	2	0	.000
1984	Atl.....	11	25	2	5	1	0	0	1	2	0	.200
1985	Atl.....	81	190	16	48	8	1	0	4	16	2	.253
1986	NYA....	21	48	2	4	1	0	0	2	5	0	.083
1987	NYA....	14	34	2	6	0	0	0	0	0	0	.176
1988	Cle.....	51	130	9	30	5	1	0	7	8	0	.231
1989	Cle.....	24	58	10	16	2	0	2	6	1	0	.276
		207	491	41	109	17	2	2	20	34	2	.222

CATCHERS

Andy Allanson

Birth Date: 12/22/61
Bats: Right
Throws: Right
1989 Club:
Cleveland Indians
Contest Code #: 583

Rating: 3

The Cleveland Indians' number-one catcher is 6′5″ and weighs 225 pounds—if he wanders into the wrong office at Municipal Stadium, the Browns might think linebacker. But Allanson is too valuable to the Cleveland baseball operation to be considered anything but a catcher. He's a solid backstop whose arm is effective enough. His speed isn't anything to write home about (good-bye, linebacker), and though he's a fair contact hitter, he doesn't have much power—surprising in a player of his size.

No matter. Allanson is a solid citizen behind the plate. After two partial seasons with the Tribe, he became the top catcher in 1988 (.263, 50 RBI's). And with Joel Skinner, he gives Cleveland good depth at the catcher spot. Allanson's batting average slipped to .232 last year, and he knocked in only 17 runs—both causes for concern. But in an age when good catchers who hit .200 are acceptable, Allanson is more than acceptable.

Year	Team	G	AB	R	H	2B	3B	HR	RBI	BB	SB	AVG
1986	Cle.....	101	293	30	66	7	3	1	29	14	10	.225
1987	Cle.....	50	154	17	41	6	0	3	16	9	1	.266
1988	Cle.....	133	434	44	114	11	0	5	50	25	5	.263
1989	Cle.....	111	323	30	75	9	1	3	17	23	4	.232
		395	1204	121	296	33	4	12	112	71	20	.246

Bob Boone

Birth Date: 11/19/47
Bats: Right
Throws: Right
1989 Club:
Kansas City Royals
Contest Code #: 584

Rating: 4

How long can Bob Boone go on catching in the majors? Last time we looked, the new senior league will just have to wait. The son of former major-league infielder Ray Boone—and already the all-time leader in games caught—Bob gives no evidence that he's coming to the end of his career.

He constantly amazes the experts. Though his arm isn't quite what it used to be, he still catches well. Few, if any, backstops handle a staff as well as he does and he calls a fine game. Bret Saberhagen's incredible 23–7 season and the progress of Jeff Montgomery and Flash Gordon can all be attributed, in part at least, to having Boone back of the dish.

Though he's never been a stupendous hitter, his 1989 average (.274) was 21 points better than his career mark. He had only 1 homer, but the last time he hit double figures in round-trippers, Jimmy Carter was in the White House and the shah was still in charge in Iran. Like Ol' Man River, Boonie just keeps rolling along.

Year	Team	G	AB	R	H	2B	3B	HR	RBI	BB	SB	AVG
1972	Phi	16	51	4	14	1	0	1	4	5	1	.275
1973	Phi	145	521	42	136	20	2	10	61	41	3	.261

Year	Team	G	AB	R	H	2B	3B	HR	RBI	BB	SB	AVG
1974	Phi	146	488	41	118	24	3	3	52	35	3	.242
1975	Phi	97	289	28	71	14	2	2	20	32	1	.246
1976	Phi	121	361	40	98	18	2	4	54	45	2	.271
1977	Phi	132	440	55	125	26	4	11	66	42	5	.284
1978	Phi	132	435	48	123	18	4	12	62	46	2	.283
1979	Phi	119	398	38	114	21	3	9	58	49	1	.286
1980	Phi	141	480	34	110	23	1	9	55	48	3	.229
1981	Phi	76	227	19	48	7	0	4	24	22	2	.211
1982	Cal.....	143	472	42	121	17	0	7	58	39	0	.256
1983	Cal.....	142	468	46	120	18	0	9	52	24	4	.256
1984	Cal.....	139	450	33	91	16	1	3	32	25	3	.202
1985	Cal.....	150	460	37	114	17	0	5	55	37	1	.248
1986	Cal.....	144	442	48	98	12	2	7	49	43	1	.222
1987	Cal.....	128	389	42	94	18	0	3	33	35	0	.242
1988	Cal.....	122	352	38	104	17	0	5	39	29	2	.295
1989	KC.....	131	405	33	111	13	2	1	43	49	3	.274
		2224	7128	668	1810	300	26	105	817	646	37	.254

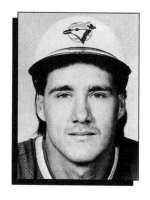

Lance Borders

Birth Date: 5/14/63
Bats: Right
Throws: Right
1989 Club:
Toronto Blue Jays
Contest Code #: 585

Rating: 2

With Ernie Whitt gone, the Blue Jays will look more and more to Pat Borders. Right now, he doesn't look like the guy, but there are enough indications that he could surprise. Borders joined the Toronto organization as a sixth-round draft choice in 1982. He was then a third baseman, too. The Jays loved his bat, but couldn't see him as a major-league third sacker. He had a year at second base, another at first base, and then, in 1986, he became a catcher. Defensively, he is, at best, a platoon-type player. His overall fielding ability is below average, and his arm is strictly borderline. Offensively, the scouts report that Borders' bat "grows on you." He hit .257 in 1989, driving in 29 runs. He even stole a couple of bases, which catchers aren't supposed to do, but former infielders can.

Year	Team	G	AB	R	H	2B	3B	HR	RBI	BB	SB	AVG
1988	Tor.....	56	154	15	42	6	3	5	21	3	0	.273
1989	Tor.....	94	241	22	62	11	1	3	29	11	2	.257
		150	395	37	104	17	4	8	50	14	2	.263

Scott Bradley

Birth Date: 3/22/60
Bats: Left
Throws: Right
1989 Club:
Seattle Mariners
Contest Code #: 586

Rating: 2

After parts of six seasons in the major leagues, Scott Bradley has played himself into the role of a platoon player. Adequate on defense, though not in the class of his teammate Dave Valle, the New Jersey native will see plenty of action against right-handed pitchers—and that's about it. The one-time U. of North Carolina star hit .274 in 103 games in 1989. He makes fairly good contact (in his 376 games with Seattle, he has struck out only 57 times), but he's absolutely no power threat (3 homers in 270 at-bats). He knocked in 37 runs.

In his post-UNC days, Bradley worked his way up through the Yankee organization, finally arriving at Yankee Stadium (only 15 miles from his boyhood home) in 1984. He was dealt to the White Sox in 1986 and played 9 games for the Chisox before being dealt to Seattle, where he has been ever since.

Year	Team	G	AB	R	H	2B	3B	HR	RBI	BB	SB	AVG
1984	NYA....	9	21	3	6	1	0	0	2	1	0	.286
1985	NYA....	19	49	4	8	2	1	0	1	1	0	.163
1986	ChA....	9	21	3	6	0	0	0	0	1	0	.286
1986	Sea....	68	199	17	60	8	3	5	28	12	1	.302

		G	AB	R	H	2B	3B	HR	RBI	BB	SB	AVG
1987	Sea	102	342	34	95	15	1	5	43	15	0	.278
1988	Sea	103	335	45	86	17	1	4	33	17	1	.257
1989	Sea	103	270	21	74	16	0	3	37	21	1	.274
		413	1237	127	335	59	6	17	144	68	3	.271

Rick Cerone

Birth Date: 5/19/54
Bats: Right
Throws: Right
1989 Club:
Boston Red Sox
Contest Code #: 587

Rating: 3

In a league of aging backstops, Rick Cerone is neither the oldest nor the best. But the one-time Seton Hall U. star seems to have a few good years left. The much-traveled thirty-five-year-old has made big-league stops with the Blue Jays, Yankees, Braves, Yankees again, and the Red Sox. He signed with the Yankees yet again during the off-season.

He's still living off a couple of great seasons with the Bronx Bombers. In 1980, for example, he hit .277 with 14 homers and 85 RBI's. On the Cerone career slate, that season sticks out from a basically undistinguished thirteen-years. Still, the chunky 5'11", 195-pounder can hit left-handed pitching pretty well (right-handers kill him) and occasionally takes the ball deep.

Though no more than a platoon player on offense, he still gets it done defensively. His catching mechanics are first-rate; he knows how to call a game, and his arm is still pretty decent. Defense alone should keep him employed through the early 1990s, and if you look at the AL's Boones and Fisks, maybe even longer.

Year	Team	G	AB	R	H	2B	3B	HR	RBI	BB	SB	AVG
1975	Cle.....	7	12	1	3	1	0	0	0	1	0	.250
1976	Cle.....	7	16	1	2	0	0	0	1	0	0	.125
1977	Tor.....	31	100	7	20	4	0	1	10	6	0	.200
1978	Tor.....	88	282	25	63	8	2	3	20	23	0	.223
1979	Tor.....	136	469	47	112	27	4	7	61	37	1	.239
1980	NYA....	147	519	70	144	30	4	14	85	32	1	.277
1981	NYA....	71	234	23	57	13	2	2	21	12	0	.244
1982	NYA....	89	300	29	68	10	0	5	28	19	0	.227
1983	NYA....	80	246	18	54	7	0	2	22	15	0	.220
1984	NYA....	38	120	8	25	3	0	2	13	9	1	.208
1985	Atl.....	96	282	15	61	9	0	3	25	29	0	.216
1986	Mil.....	68	216	22	56	14	0	4	18	15	1	.259
1987	NYA....	113	284	28	69	12	1	4	23	30	0	.243
1988	Bos	84	264	31	71	13	1	3	27	20	0	.269
1989	Bos	102	296	28	72	16	1	4	48	34	0	.243
		1157	3640	353	877	167	15	54	402	282	4	.241

Carlton Fisk

Birth Date: 12/26/47
Bats: Right
Throws: Right
1989 Club:
Chicago White Sox
Contest Code #: 588

Rating: 5

You have to wonder about Carlton Fisk. After two decades in the major leagues, the Chicago White Sox's catcher seems to be getting better and better. How good will he be by the year 2000? If you're betting that Pudge Fisk won't be there, save your money. After a broken hand sidelined the forty-two-year-old backstop for nearly half of the 1988 season, the 6'2", 225-pounder bounced back with another stellar season at the plate, hitting a lofty .293 with 13 homers and 68 RBI's. Not bad for a guy the Red Sox were writing off when they let him go after the 1980 season. (He had been their first draft choice, the fourth player selected nationally, back in 1967.) The Vermont native can still catch, and his arm—

though it has lost some of its strength—still gets it done. His hitting and power are beyond question.

Year	Team	G	AB	R	H	2B	3B	HR	RBI	BB	SB	AVG
1969	Bos	2	5	0	0	0	0	0	0	0	0	.000
1971	Bos	14	48	7	15	2	1	2	6	1	0	.313
1972	Bos	131	457	74	134	28	9	22	61	52	5	.293
1973	Bos	135	508	65	125	21	0	26	71	37	7	.246
1974	Bos	52	187	36	56	12	1	11	26	24	5	.299
1975	Bos	79	263	47	87	14	4	10	52	27	4	.331
1976	Bos	134	487	76	124	17	5	17	58	56	12	.255
1977	Bos	152	536	106	169	26	3	26	102	75	7	.315
1978	Bos	157	571	94	162	39	5	20	88	71	7	.284
1979	Bos	91	320	49	87	23	2	10	42	10	3	.272
1980	Bos	131	478	73	138	25	3	18	62	36	11	.289
1981	ChA	96	338	44	89	12	0	7	45	38	3	.263
1982	ChA	135	476	66	127	17	3	14	65	46	17	.267
1983	ChA	138	488	85	141	26	4	26	86	46	9	.289
1984	ChA	102	359	54	83	20	1	21	43	26	6	.231
1985	ChA	153	543	85	129	23	1	37	107	52	17	.238
1986	ChA	125	457	42	101	11	0	14	63	22	2	.221
1987	ChA	135	454	68	116	22	1	23	71	39	1	.256
1988	ChA	76	253	37	70	8	1	19	50	37	0	.277
1989	ChA	103	375	47	110	25	2	13	68	36	1	.293
		2141	7603	1155	2063	371	46	336	1166	731	117	.271

Rich Gedman

Birth Date: 9/26/59
Bats: Left
Throws: Right
1989 Club:
Boston Red Sox
Contest Code #: 589

Rating: 2

Once the darling of Boston fans, Gedman, at age thirty, has begun to slide backward. Geddy, a native of nearby Worcester, MA, was an instant Fenway favorite when he arrived to stay in 1981 at age twenty-one. When the Sox came within one out of winning the 1986 world title, Gedman was a hero. In fact, during the mid-1980s, he smoked 58 homers and knocked in 217 runs in three seasons.

Since then, however, it hasn't been pretty. The Series loss bugged him, then he tried the free-agent route before returning to Boston, then a thumb injury ruined his 1987 campaign (.205 in 52 games). The bat hasn't come back (.212 in 93 games last season, with only 4 homers and 16 RBI's). And his defensive game was never that good. Fact is, he tends to be lazy behind the plate, and doesn't call a good game. If Geddy regains the offensive touch, he should put his game back together. Now, however, it seems that his days as a front-line player are over.

Year	Team	G	AB	R	H	2B	3B	HR	RBI	BB	SB	AVG
1980	Bos	9	24	2	5	0	0	0	1	0	0	.208
1981	Bos	62	205	22	59	15	0	5	26	9	0	.288
1982	Bos	92	289	30	72	17	2	4	26	10	0	.249
1983	Bos	81	204	21	60	16	1	2	18	15	0	.294
1984	Bos	133	449	54	121	26	4	24	72	29	0	.269
1985	Bos	144	498	66	147	30	5	18	80	50	2	.295
1986	Bos	135	462	49	119	29	0	16	65	37	1	.258
1987	Bos	52	151	11	31	8	0	1	13	10	0	.205
1988	Bos	95	299	33	69	14	0	9	39	18	0	.231
1989	Bos	93	260	24	55	9	0	4	16	23	0	.212
		896	2841	312	738	164	12	83	356	201	3	.260

Bob Geren

Birth Date: 9/22/61
Bats: Right
Throws: Right
1989 Club:
New York Yankees
Contest Code #: 590

Rating: 2

In a season of disappointment for the Yankees, Geren was one of the few pleasant surprises. A ten-year minor leaguer (except for one 10-game-10-at-bat trial with the Yankees in 1988), Geren was a .236 lifetime hitter through stints in the Padres, Cardinals, and New York organizations. What could the Yankees expect from the 6'3", 205-pound catcher? Would you believe a .288 average and 9 home runs? The San Diego native displayed a good-looking swing and the ability to make contact.

The scouts aren't as high on Geren's defensive ability. The book says that he's slow behind the plate and his average arm isn't helped any by his slow release. Whether last year's performance by Geren was an aberration or a portent of good things to come remains to be seen.

Year	Team	G	AB	R	H	2B	3B	HR	RBI	BB	SB	AVG
1988	NYA....	10	10	0	1	0	0	0	0	2	0	.100
1989	NYA....	65	205	26	59	5	1	9	27	12	0	.288
		75	215	26	60	5	1	9	27	14	0	.279

Brian Harper

Birth Date: 10/16/59
Bats: Right
Throws: Right
1989 Club:
Minnesota Twins
Contest Code #: 591

Rating: 5

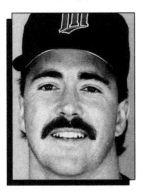

In a day when catchers who hit .210 are acceptable and those who hit .235 are universally hailed, Brian Harper is one of a rare breed. The Los Angeles native has been around, without much prior success. In short stops with the Angels, Pirates, Cardinals, and Tigers, he didn't show much. But a .295 average in a half-season with the Twins in 1988 gave renewed promise. Then the 6'2", 195-pounder followed with a spectacular .325 average, 8 homers, and 57 RBI's in 1989. Everyone took notice.

The news isn't all good. Harper isn't the best receiver in the league. There's no doubt that Harper has improved behind the plate, but he isn't now—nor is he likely to become—a front-line backstop. It's no disaster. Brian can also play at first or third as well as a little bit in the outfield. Anyone who can wield such a big stick will see plenty of action.

Year	Team	G	AB	R	H	2B	3B	HR	RBI	BB	SB	AVG
1979	Cal.....	1	2	0	0	0	0	0	0	0	0	.000
1981	Cal.....	4	11	1	3	0	0	0	1	0	1	.273
1982	Pit.....	20	29	4	8	1	0	2	4	1	0	.276
1983	Pit.....	61	131	16	29	4	1	7	20	2	0	.221
1984	Pit.....	46	112	4	29	4	0	2	11	5	0	.259
1985	StL.....	43	52	5	13	4	0	0	8	2	0	.250
1986	Det	19	36	2	5	1	0	0	3	3	0	.139
1987	Oak	11	17	1	4	1	0	0	3	0	0	.235
1988	Min	60	166	15	49	11	1	3	20	10	0	.295
1989	Min	126	385	43	125	24	0	8	57	13	2	.325
		391	941	91	265	50	2	22	127	36	3	.282

Ron Hassey

Birth Date: 2/27/53
Bats: Left
Throws: Right
1989 Club:
Oakland Athletics
Contest Code #: 592

Rating: 2

After twelve years in the majors, Oakland catcher Ron Hassey continues to be, at best, a platoon catcher. Defensively, he's below average—though his average arm is aided by his quick release. Though the 6'2", 195-pound Hassey still swings a good bat, especially against right-handed pitching, his average swings wildly, including a just-fair .228 mark last year. He has slipped considerably from his career-high .323 with the Yankees and White Sox in 1986.

Since neither Hassey nor his catching mate, Terry Steinbach, is a defensive whiz, some Athletics' pitchers prefer Hassey, merely because of his edge in experience. Originally a Cincinnati Red draft choice after an All-American career at the University of Arizona, Hassey hit the big time with the Indians late in the 1978 season. He also dropped in briefly with the Cubs in 1984 before returning to the American League in 1985.

Year	Team	G	AB	R	H	2B	3B	HR	RBI	BB	SB	AVG
1978	Cle.....	25	74	5	15	0	0	2	9	5	2	.203
1979	Cle.....	75	223	20	64	14	0	4	32	19	1	.287
1980	Cle.....	130	390	43	124	18	4	8	65	49	0	.318
1981	Cle.....	61	190	8	44	4	0	1	25	17	0	.232
1982	Cle.....	113	323	33	81	18	0	5	34	53	3	.251
1983	Cle.....	117	341	48	92	21	0	6	42	38	2	.270
1984	Cle.....	48	149	11	38	5	1	0	19	15	1	.255
1984	ChN....	19	33	5	11	0	0	2	5	4	0	.333
1985	NYA....	92	267	31	79	16	1	13	42	28	0	.296
1986	NYA....	64	191	23	57	14	0	6	29	24	1	.298
1986	ChA....	49	150	22	53	11	1	3	20	22	0	.353
1987	ChA....	49	145	15	31	9	0	3	12	17	0	.214
1988	Oak	107	323	32	83	15	0	7	45	30	2	.257
1989	Oak	97	268	29	61	12	0	5	23	24	1	.228
		1046	3067	325	833	157	7	65	402	345	13	.272

Mike Heath

Birth Date: 2/5/55
Bats: Right
Throws: Right
1989 Club:
Detroit Tigers
Contest Code #: 593

Rating: 3

Maybe they'll rewrite that old song. Doesn't "It's So Nice to Have a Heath Around the House" have a good ring to it? Not only is Mike Heath a top-notch defensive catcher, he can also play—and has played—every other position on the field (okay, he hasn't pitched since a minor-league outing in 1978). And he's a decent contact hitter with occasional power.

A shortstop for the first three years of his pro career, the thirty-five-year-old Floridian splits the Detroit Tigers' catching duties with Matt Nokes, and fills in anywhere Sparky Anderson asks him to. In 1987, for example, that was everywhere except pitcher. Behind the plate, Heath gets the job done physically and also calls a terrific game. At the plate, he's a good contact man (.263 last year) whose 10 home runs was third best among the lowly Tigers. A Yankee second-round draft choice in 1973, Heath remains an aggressive, hard-nosed player.

Year	Team	G	AB	R	H	2B	3B	HR	RBI	BB	SB	AVG
1978	NYA....	33	92	6	21	3	1	0	8	4	0	.228
1979	Oak	74	258	19	66	8	0	3	27	17	1	.256
1980	Oak	92	305	27	74	10	2	1	33	16	3	.243
1981	Oak	84	301	26	71	7	1	8	30	13	3	.236
1982	Oak	101	318	43	77	18	4	3	39	27	8	.242
1983	Oak	96	345	45	97	17	0	6	33	18	3	.281
1984	Oak	140	475	49	118	21	5	13	64	26	7	.248
1985	Oak	138	436	71	109	18	6	13	55	41	7	.250
1986	Det	30	98	11	26	3	0	4	11	4	4	.265

1986	StL	65	190	19	39	8	1	4	25	23	2	.205
1987	Det	93	270	34	76	16	0	8	33	21	1	.281
1988	Det	86	219	24	54	7	2	5	18	18	1	.247
1989	Det	122	396	38	104	16	2	10	43	24	7	.263
		1154	3703	412	932	152	24	78	419	252	47	.252

Ron Karkovice

Birth Date: 8/8/63
Bats: Right
Throws: Right
1989 Club:
Chicago White Sox
Contest Code #: 594

Rating: 3

There's no telling how long he'll have to wait, but it seems evident that Ron Karkovice will eventually succeed Carlton Fisk as the Chicago White Sox's number-one catcher. Given a taste of the major leagues when Fisk went down with a broken hand in 1988, Karko liked what he saw. So did the Sox. Right now, the New Jersey native is one of the top backup catchers in the game.

Someone obviously taught him well. His mechanics are outstanding. His arm ranks just below the gun category, and he gets the ball off well. The major question mark is Karko's bat. He has never hit well, at any level, though he showed some power in the minors. The 6'1", 215-pounder obviously benefited from the teachings of batting instructor Walt Hriniak last season, as he hit .264 in 71 games with a trio of home runs and 24 RBI's. With good catching in relatively short supply, Karko should be around for awhile.

Year	Team	G	AB	R	H	2B	3B	HR	RBI	BB	SB	AVG
1986	ChA....	37	97	13	24	7	0	4	13	9	1	.247
1987	ChA....	39	85	7	6	0	0	2	7	7	3	.071
1988	ChA....	46	115	10	20	4	0	3	9	7	4	.174
1989	ChA....	71	182	21	48	9	2	3	24	10	0	.264
		193	479	51	98	20	2	12	53	33	8	.205

Chad Kreuter

Birth Date: 8/26/64
Bats: Both
Throws: Right
1989 Club:
Texas Rangers
Contest Code #: 595

Rating: 2

Catcher Chad Kreuter's second annual cup of coffee with the Texas Rangers was a decided comedown from his first shot in 1988. In 1988, the 6'2", 190-pounder hit .275 during a 16-game trial with the parent club. But in two stints with Texas in 1989, he was horrid. He opened the season in Arlington, going 0-for-14 before spending a month in the minors. He came back at the end of May to hit .167, providing a final mark of .152.

Kreuter, a switch-hitter who decided to go strictly right-handed after July 25 last year, isn't a gifted catcher. Defensively, he's borderline throughout. Unless the twenty-five-year-old makes some major changes, the scouts don't think he'll ever be more than a backup-type player.

Year	Team	G	AB	R	H	2B	3B	HR	RBI	BB	SB	AVG
1988	Tex	16	51	3	14	2	1	1	5	7	0	.275
1989	Tex	87	158	16	24	3	0	5	9	27	0	.152
		103	209	19	38	5	1	6	14	34	0	.182

Tim Laudner

Birth Date: 6/7/58
Bats: Right
Throws: Right
1989 Club:
Minnesota Twins
Contest Code #: 596

Rating: 3

Every year the Twins come to spring training expecting big things of catcher Tim Laudner. And every year Laudner doesn't quite meet those lofty expectations. Last year was no exception. Off a 1988 All-Star Game appearance, Laudner wound up sharing the catching duties with veteran minor-leaguer Brian Harper. Harper out hit Laudner by 103 points.

Minnesota went nuts when Tim stroked 42 homers and knocked in 104 runs for their Orlando farm club in 1981. He spent parts of 1981 and 1982 with the Twins before settling in full time beginning in 1983. Unfortunately, he hasn't hit better than .255 (as a rookie), slipping to .191 in 1987 and .222 (with 6 homers) last season. A decent defensive catcher, Laudner figures to hang around, for a while, even if only as a backup.

Year	Team	G	AB	R	H	2B	3B	HR	RBI	BB	SB	AVG
1981	Min....	14	43	4	7	2	0	2	5	3	0	.163
1982	Min....	93	306	37	78	19	1	7	33	34	0	.255
1983	Min....	62	168	20	31	9	0	6	18	15	0	.185
1984	Min....	87	262	31	54	16	1	10	35	18	0	.206
1985	Min....	72	164	16	39	5	0	7	19	12	0	.238
1986	Min....	76	193	21	47	10	0	10	29	24	1	.244
1987	Min....	113	288	30	55	7	1	16	43	23	1	.191
1988	Min....	117	375	38	94	18	1	13	54	36	0	.251
1989	Min....	100	239	24	53	11	1	6	27	25	1	.222
		734	2038	221	458	97	5	77	263	190	3	.225

Mike Macfarlane

Birth Date: 4/12/64
Bats: Right
Throws: Right
1989 Club:
Kansas City Royals
Contest Code #: 597

Rating: 2

If Mike Macfarlane is waiting for Bob Boone to give up the starting catcher's position in Kansas City, he may have a long wait. The former U. of Santa Clara star does his job when asked to, but for now, he's simply a backup catcher. The long-range outlook isn't wonderful, either. Macfarlane does a workmanlike job, without a lot of great tools. His arm is decent enough, but his release is extremely slow. At this point, he doesn't call a particularly good game, though one would hope that he's learning from starter Boone.

Scouts rate Macfarlane's bat "way below average." In 69 games last year (157 at-bats), he hit at a .223 clip, not enough for a catcher with defensive deficiencies. Eight of his 35 hits went for extra bases, including a pair of homers. All told, Kaycee simply doesn't have much behind Boone.

Year	Team	G	AB	R	H	2B	3B	HR	RBI	BB	SB	AVG
1987	KC.....	8	19	0	4	1	0	0	3	2	0	.211
1988	KC.....	70	211	25	56	15	0	4	26	21	0	.265
1989	KC.....	69	157	13	35	6	0	2	19	7	0	.223
		147	387	38	95	22	0	6	48	30	0	.245

Bob Melvin

Birth Date: 10/28/61
Bats: Right
Throws: Right
1989 Club:
Baltimore Orioles
Contest Code #: 598

Rating: 3

The Orioles are the third stop of catcher Bob Melvin's major-league odyssey. It may not be the last. An ex-Tiger (briefly) and Giant (three seasons), Melvin's the kind of guy most managers like to have on their rosters. Rate his catching adequate to average. He's a heady guy who gives the club extra leadership on the field. His defensive skills are decent enough and though his arm is just average, his quick release makes him a threat to potential enemy base thieves.

With a bat in his hands, he isn't nearly as dangerous. His .241 average in 1989 marked his major-league high. His best power year was 1987, when he banged out 11 homers for the Giants. He came up 10 short of that personal best in 85 games with the O's last year. Melvin's glove will keep him in the majors.

Year	Team	G	AB	R	H	2B	3B	HR	RBI	BB	SB	AVG
1985	Det	41	82	10	18	4	1	0	4	3	0	.220
1986	SF	89	268	24	60	14	2	5	25	15	3	.224
1987	SF	84	246	31	49	8	0	11	31	17	0	.199
1988	SF	92	273	23	64	13	1	8	27	13	0	.234
1989	Bal	85	278	22	67	10	1	1	32	15	1	.241
		391	1147	110	258	49	5	25	119	63	4	.225

Matt Nokes

Birth Date: 10/31/63
Bats: Left
Throws: Right
1989 Club:
Detroit Tigers
Contest Code #: 599

Rating: 3

Once the Detroit Tigers' "catcher of the future," Matt Nokes simply hasn't completed his defensive game—hence his status as a platoon player. Not that half the teams in the AL wouldn't like the San Diego native as their backstop. His offense is too solid, year in and year out, to give up on. But Nokes simply isn't a good receiver, despite a lot of extra work, and his arm is strictly below average.

The 6'1", 185-pounder was a twentieth-round Giants' selection in the June 1981 draft. He came to the Tigers in a six-man trade in October 1985. When he hit .289 with 32 homers and 87 RBI's in an All-Star rookie year, the Tigers thought they had struck paydirt. But Nokes has slipped to .251 and .250 in the past two years, with only 16 and 9 homers, respectively. The book on Nokes still reports that he can hit and hit with power. But he can't run, and his defensive liabilities limit his future.

Year	Team	G	AB	R	H	2B	3B	HR	RBI	BB	SB	AVG
1985	SF	19	53	3	11	2	0	2	5	1	0	.208
1986	Det	7	24	2	8	1	0	1	2	1	0	.333
1987	Det	135	461	69	133	14	2	32	87	35	2	.289
1988	Det	122	382	53	96	18	0	16	53	34	0	.251
1989	Det	87	268	15	67	10	0	9	39	17	1	.250
		370	1188	142	315	45	2	60	186	88	3	.265

Charles O'Brien

Birth Date: 5/1/61
Bats: Right
Throws: Right
1989 Club:
Milwaukee Brewers
Contest Code #: 600

Rating: 3

The right-handed half of Milwaukee's catching platoon, Charlie O'Brien is also the defensive half. While B.J. Surhoff carries the better bat, O'Brien is the superior backstop. According to the scouts, the Oklahoma native calls a decent game and can catch and throw the baseball.

His weakness is at the plate. After hitting only .220 in his debut in 1988, Obie punched it up to .234 in 1989, with 6 homers among his 44 hits. His 35 RBI's in 62 games were somewhat impressive. It seems evident, however, that until O'Brien picks up his offense, he'll never be an everyday catcher.

Year	Team	G	AB	R	H	2B	3B	HR	RBI	BB	SB	AVG
1985	Oak	16	11	3	3	1	0	0	1	3	0	.273
1987	Mil.....	10	35	2	7	3	1	0	0	4	0	.200
1988	Mil.....	40	118	12	26	6	0	2	9	5	0	.220
1989	Mil.....	62	188	22	44	10	0	6	35	21	0	.234
		128	352	39	80	20	1	8	45	33	0	.227

Lance Parrish

Birth Date: 6/15/56
Bats: Right
Throws: Right
1989 Club:
California Angels
Contest Code #: 601

Rating: 4

It didn't do much for his bat, but Lance Parrish proved he was pleased to return to the American League last year. A six-time AL All-Star Team selection, Parrish flopped in two seasons with Philadelphia (.215 in 1988), where he never learned to deal with NL pitching.

The one-time California high-school football standout (he turned down a grid scholarship offer from UCLA to sign with the Tigers' organization back in 1974) remains a solid defensive catcher who's like a second manager behind the plate. His arm and glove still rate average-plus.

There are questions about his bat. Not that Lance ever hit for a high average, but he always had plenty of pop, with consecutive seasons of 32, 27, 33, 28, and 22 homers for the Tigers between 1982 and 1986. Now his power is only occasional. The 1989 total of 17 round-trippers for the 1989 Angels (with only 50 RBI's) adds to the reservations.

Year	Team	G	AB	R	H	2B	3B	HR	RBI	BB	SB	AVG
1977	Det	12	46	10	9	2	0	3	7	5	0	.196
1978	Det	85	288	37	63	11	3	14	41	11	0	.219
1979	Det	143	493	65	136	26	3	19	65	49	6	.276
1980	Det	144	553	79	158	34	6	24	82	31	6	.286
1981	Det	96	348	39	85	18	2	10	46	34	2	.244
1982	Det	133	486	75	138	19	2	32	87	40	3	.284
1983	Det	155	605	80	163	42	3	27	114	44	1	.269
1984	Det	147	578	75	137	16	2	33	98	41	2	.237
1985	Det	140	549	64	150	27	1	28	98	41	2	.273
1986	Det	91	327	53	84	6	1	22	62	38	0	.257
1987	Phi	130	466	42	114	21	0	17	67	47	0	.245
1988	Phi	123	424	44	91	17	2	15	60	47	0	.215
1989	Cal.....	124	433	48	103	12	1	17	50	42	1	.238
		1523	5596	711	1431	251	26	261	877	470	23	.256

Tony Pena

Birth Date: 6/4/57
Bats: Right
Throws: Right
1989 Club:
St. Louis Cardinals
Contest Code #: 602

Rating: 4

Tony Pena is still among the major leagues' best catchers, but he can't be rated as *the* best because of his inconsistency over the past three seasons. When Pena's in top form, he'll bat in the .280 range, hit 10 home runs, and drive in between 50 and 60 runs. When he's in a slump; he'll take vicious cuts at pitches out of the strike zone and hit weak grounders.

Last season, Pena batted .259, and hit only 4 home runs and drove in just 37 runs. He made good contact—only 33 strikeouts in 424 at-bats—but didn't get results. It's hard to say whether Pena's on the decline, but it's clear he was under pressure in St. Louis, because of the development of Todd Zeile. During the off-season he signed on with the Boston Red Sox, and he could well have value for your team.

Year	Team	G	AB	R	H	2B	3B	HR	RBI	BB	SB	AVG
1980	Pit	8	21	1	9	1	1	0	1	0	0	.429
1981	Pit	66	210	16	63	9	1	2	17	8	1	.300
1982	Pit	138	497	53	147	28	4	11	63	17	2	.296
1983	Pit	151	542	51	163	22	3	15	70	31	6	.301
1984	Pit	147	546	77	156	27	2	15	78	36	12	.286
1985	Pit	147	546	53	136	27	2	10	59	29	12	.249
1986	Pit	144	510	56	147	26	2	10	52	53	9	.288
1987	StL	116	384	40	82	13	4	5	44	36	6	.214
1988	StL	149	505	55	133	23	1	10	51	33	6	.263
1989	StL	141	424	36	110	17	2	4	37	35	5	.259
		1207	4185	438	1146	193	22	82	472	278	59	.274

Geno Petralli

Birth Date: 9/25/59
Bats: Left
Throws: Right
1989 Club:
Texas Rangers
Contest Code #: 603

Rating: 4

The usually sturdy Geno Petralli put in two stints on the disabled list last year. No matter. The Rangers expect the native Californian to return in 1990, with no significant residue from the neck-muscle spasms and partially torn left-knee ligament which shelved him for so much of 1989.

Petralli is a decent major-league catcher. On offense, he's a fine contact hitter. His .304 average last year was second only to Minnesota's Brian Harper among AL backstops. There's little power in Petralli's bat, but catchers who can hit .300 are hard to find these days. Defensively, the former Blue Jay and Indian farmhand is decent. His arm is reasonably strong and accurate.

If he's healthy, Geno should be ready to do a full-time job for the Rangers.

Year	Team	G	AB	R	H	2B	3B	HR	RBI	BB	SB	AVG
1982	Tor	16	44	3	16	2	0	0	1	4	0	.364
1983	Tor	6	4	0	0	0	0	0	0	1	0	.000
1984	Tor	3	3	0	0	0	0	0	0	0	0	.000
1985	Tex	42	100	7	27	2	0	0	11	8	1	.270
1986	Tex	69	137	17	35	9	3	2	18	5	3	.255
1987	Tex	101	202	28	61	11	2	7	31	27	0	.302
1988	Tex	129	351	35	99	14	2	7	36	41	0	.282
1989	Tex	70	184	18	56	7	0	4	23	17	0	.304
		436	1025	108	294	45	7	20	120	103	4	.287

Jamie Quirk

Birth Date: 10/22/54
Bats: Left
Throws: Right
1989 Club:
New York Yankees &
Baltimore Orioles
Contest Code #: 604

Rating: 1

For most of the last few years, Jamie Quirk has been a survivor. A professional since 1972 and a major leaguer for most of the time since late 1975, Quirk has hung on through versatility and sheer tenacity. Quirk turned down a football scholarship to Notre Dame before opting for baseball in 1972. He broke in as the Pioneer League's number-one shortstop, came to the majors as a third baseman, has played virtually every position, and now begins to wind down his career as a backup catcher. His bat, never very potent, is practically gone. He hit .176 in 47 games last year with a single homer and 10 RBI's. Now, at age thirty-five and newly signed with Oakland, even Quirk's versatility and experience (he has been a good pinch-hitter in the past) probably won't be enough.

Year	Team	G	AB	R	H	2B	3B	HR	RBI	BB	SB	AVG
1975	KC.....	14	39	2	10	0	0	1	5	2	0	.256
1976	KC.....	64	114	11	28	6	0	1	15	2	0	.246
1977	Mil.....	93	221	16	48	14	1	3	13	8	0	.217
1978	KC.....	17	29	3	6	2	0	0	2	5	0	.207
1979	KC.....	51	79	8	24	6	1	1	11	5	0	.304
1980	KC.....	62	163	13	45	5	0	5	21	7	3	.276
1981	KC.....	46	100	8	25	7	0	0	10	6	0	.250
1982	KC.....	36	78	8	18	3	0	1	5	3	0	.231
1983	StL	48	86	3	18	2	1	2	11	6	0	.209
1984	ChA	3	2	0	0	0	0	0	1	0	0	.000
1984	Cle....	1	1	1	1	0	0	1	1	0	0	1.000
1985	KC.....	19	57	3	16	3	1	0	4	2	0	.281
1986	KC.....	80	219	24	47	10	0	8	26	17	0	.215
1987	KC.....	109	296	24	70	17	0	5	33	28	1	.236
1988	KC.....	84	196	22	47	7	1	8	25	28	1	.240
1989	NYA	13	24	0	2	0	0	0	0	3	0	.083
1989	Oak	9	10	1	2	0	0	1	1	0	0	.200
1989	Bal	25	51	5	11	2	0	0	9	9	0	.216
		774	1765	152	418	84	5	37	193	131	5	.237

Bill Schroeder

Birth Date: 9/7/58
Bats: Right
Throws: Right
1989 Club: California Angels
Contest Code #: 605

Rating: 2

Here's a player who seems to be living on borrowed time. The former Clemson star has rung up 6½ years in the majors without any single skill that jumps off the scouting report page. The overall evaluation behind the plate is "below average." At best, he's sluggish defensively. His arm is well below average, and his release is extremely slow. The label on his bat is "weak." His 1989 average (.203) was just over the famed Mendoza Line. He struck out nearly once in every three trips to the plate. The Baltimore native did have 6 homers in 138 trips, so there's a little power in his bat. But that's not enough to hang your helmet on. The Angels have to be thinking about someone else to back up Lance Parrish.

Year	Team	G	AB	R	H	2B	3B	HR	RBI	BB	SB	AVG
1983	Mil.....	23	73	7	13	2	1	3	7	3	0	.178
1984	Mil.....	61	210	29	54	6	0	14	25	8	0	.257
1985	Mil.....	53	194	18	47	8	0	8	25	12	0	.242
1986	Mil.....	64	217	32	46	14	0	7	19	9	1	.212
1987	Mil.....	75	250	35	83	12	0	14	42	16	5	.332
1988	Mil.....	41	122	9	19	2	0	5	10	6	0	.156
1989	Cal.....	41	138	16	28	2	0	6	15	3	0	.203
		358	1204	146	290	46	1	57	143	57	6	.241

Joel Skinner

Birth Date: 2/21/61
Bats: Right
Throws: Right
1989 Club:
Cleveland Indians
Contest Code #: 606

Rating: 2

Now with his third major-league club (after previous stays with the White Sox and Yankees), Cleveland's Joel Skinner remains a highly competent catcher whose fortunes would take an enormous leap if he could only hit like his father, Bob Skinner, a former big-league manager and hitting instructor. Joel's .230 mark last year was 11 points better than his career mark, but still wasn't anything to get excited about. He makes fair contact and even demonstrates occasional home run power (though he hit only 1 in 178 at-bats last season). Defensively, he's a savvy receiver whose arm is excellent. He doesn't have much speed. (He's slow.) And although he has spent all or part of seven seasons in the majors, he has never been in more than 88 games (1988 Yankees).

Year	Team	G	AB	R	H	2B	3B	HR	RBI	BB	SB	AVG
1983	ChA....	6	11	2	3	0	0	0	1	0	0	.273
1984	ChA....	43	80	4	17	2	0	0	3	7	1	.213
1985	ChA....	22	44	9	15	4	1	1	5	5	0	.341
1986	ChA....	60	149	17	30	5	1	4	20	9	1	.201
1986	NYA....	54	166	6	43	4	0	1	17	7	0	.259
1987	NYA....	64	139	9	19	4	0	3	14	8	0	.137
1988	NYA....	88	251	23	57	15	0	4	23	14	0	.227
1989	Cle.....	79	178	10	41	10	0	1	13	9	1	.230
		416	1018	80	225	44	2	14	96	59	3	.221

Mike Stanley

Birth Date: 6/25/63
Bats: Right
Throws: Right
1989 Club: Texas Rangers
Contest Code #: 607

Rating: 3

The retirement of Jim Sundberg should produce some extra action for Mike Stanley. The Fort Lauderdale native picked up lots of splinters for the Texas Rangers a year ago, starting only 15 games behind the plate and only 34 games overall. Worse, only 16 starts came before September 4. Stanley is a backup-type catcher. He doesn't call a particularly effective game, and his arm and glove are below average. Compounding the problem, he can't run, either. The 6', 185-pounder does show some offense, however. In his last 35 games last season, he stroked the ball at a .309 pace, raising his average from .167 to .246. The one-time University of Florida star drove in only 3 runs in his first 48 games before banging in 8 in his last 19 games.

Year	Team	G	AB	R	H	2B	3B	HR	RBI	BB	SB	AVG
1986	Tex	15	30	4	10	3	0	1	1	3	1	.333
1987	Tex	78	216	34	59	8	1	6	37	31	3	.273
1988	Tex	94	249	21	57	8	0	3	27	37	0	.229
1989	Tex	67	122	9	30	3	1	1	11	12	1	.246
		254	617	68	156	22	2	11	76	83	5	.253

Terry Steinbach

Birth Date: 3/2/62
Bats: Right
Throws: Right
1989 Club:
Oakland Athletics
Contest Code #: 608

Rating: 5

Terry Steinbach remains one of the American League's top catchers, simply on the strength of his bat. In an era of aging backstops whose hitting skills have deteriorated enormously, Steinbach is still a top-notch offensive threat whose below-average catching work continues to improve—particularly on balls in the dirt. The surprise starter (and even more surprising MVP) of the 1988 All-Star Game, Steinbach hits for average (.273 last year) with a little pop in his bat. He's a perfect addition to an already talented Oakland lineup.

A former U. of Minnesota star (at third base), Steinbach works hard at becoming a complete player behind the plate. He was selected by the Athletics in 1983 and earned a promotion to the parent club after knocking in 132 runs and hitting .325 at Huntsville (Southern) in 1986. If he continues to improve defensively, he could have another ten years of stardom.

Year	Team	G	AB	R	H	2B	3B	HR	RBI	BB	SB	AVG
1986	Oak....	6	15	3	5	0	0	2	4	1	0	.333
1987	Oak....	122	391	66	111	16	3	16	56	32	1	.284
1988	Oak....	104	351	42	93	19	1	9	51	33	3	.265
1989	Oak....	130	454	37	124	13	1	7	42	30	1	.273
		362	1211	148	333	48	5	34	153	96	5	.275

B.J. Surhoff

Birth Date: 8/4/64
Bats: Left
Throws: Right
1989 Club:
Milwaukee Brewers
Contest Code #: 609

Rating: 3

You have to like B. J. Surhoff. An All-American at the U. of North Carolina, he works hard to make the most of what he has. Unfortunately, he doesn't seem to have all that much. At the plate, he hasn't come close to matching his rookie (1987) statistics. The 6'1″, 190-pounder hit .299 and knocked in 68 runs in 115 games in his freshman season. He tumbled to .245 in 1988 and .248 in 1989, so that may well be his level.

His problems continue behind the plate. Though he has worked diligently and has, in fact, improved, he still comes up short as a catcher. Look for Surhoff to continue as a platoon catcher. Possibly his greatest asset is that he's a catcher who hits left-handed. If his defensive improvement continues, he could get more playing time.

Year	Team	G	AB	R	H	2B	3B	HR	RBI	BB	SB	AVG
1987	Mil.....	115	395	50	118	22	3	7	68	36	11	.299
1988	Mil.....	139	493	47	121	21	0	5	38	31	21	.245
1989	Mil.....	126	436	42	108	17	4	5	55	25	14	.248
		380	1324	139	347	60	7	17	161	92	46	.262

Mickey Tettleton

Birth Date: 11/16/60
Bats: Both
Throws: Right
1989 Club:
Baltimore Orioles
Contest Code #: 610

Rating: 4

No one is more surprised about Mickey Tettleton's success in Baltimore than the Oakland A's. The two-time AL champs figured they didn't need Mickey on the second day of the 1988 season and released him. The Birds pounced, picked up the Oklahoma native, and the rest is pleasant history.

Talk about comebacks. Tettleton came back from the baseball dead. His strength—his only strength—is his bat, and that's not bad. He's a catcher with an average arm and one of the slowest releases in the majors—and will probably have to make his living as a DH. But he hits with power, as his team-leading 26 homers in only 117 games before injury clearly prove. The Mick usually has more power from the right side, though he hits for a better average from the left. He's one of only four Bird batters ever with homers from both sides in a single game. If he's healthy, the one-time Oklahoma State Cowboy should find his name in the lineup just about every day.

Year	Team	G	AB	R	H	2B	3B	HR	RBI	BB	SB	AVG
1984	Oak	33	76	10	20	2	1	1	5	11	0	.263
1985	Oak	78	211	23	53	12	0	3	15	28	2	.251
1986	Oak	90	211	26	43	9	0	10	35	39	7	.204
1987	Oak	82	211	19	41	3	0	8	26	30	1	.194
1988	Bal	86	283	31	74	11	1	11	37	28	0	.261
1989	Bal	117	411	72	106	21	2	26	65	73	3	.258
		486	1403	181	337	58	4	59	183	209	13	.240

David Valle

Birth Date: 10/30/60
Bats: Right
Throws: Right
1989 Club:
Seattle Mariners
Contest Code #: 611

Rating: 4

The defensive half of Seattle's catching platoon, Dave Valle is one of the American League's toughest, most aggressive players. His "hard-nosed" label only begins to tell the story. The Bayside, NY, native is terrific behind the plate. He can catch and he can throw.

Baseball insiders call him a workhorse, but he's no thoroughbred. He can't run a lick. At the plate, he makes fairly good contact (.237 last year) with occasional home run power (7 homers in 1989). Fortunately, that's not what the M's pay him for.

A second-round Mariners' draft choice in 1978, the 6'2", 200-pounder spent six full seasons in the minor-league system before arriving for cups of coffee with the M's in 1984, 1985, and 1986. A good AAA hitter, Valle hasn't done it in the big time—but with his defensive ability, he doesn't have to.

Year	Team	G	AB	R	H	2B	3B	HR	RBI	BB	SB	AVG
1984	Sea	13	27	4	8	1	0	1	4	1	0	.296
1985	Sea	31	70	2	11	1	0	0	4	1	0	.157
1986	Sea	22	53	10	18	3	0	5	15	7	0	.340
1987	Sea	95	324	40	83	16	3	12	53	15	2	.256
1988	Sea	92	290	29	67	15	2	10	50	18	0	.231
1989	Sea	94	316	32	75	10	3	7	34	29	0	.237
		347	1080	117	262	46	8	35	160	71	2	.243

OUTFIELDERS

Tony Armas

Birth Date: 7/2/53
Bats: Right
Throws: Right
1989 Club:
California Angels
Contest Code #: 615

Rating: 3

Age has begun to creep up on Tony Armas. The result: a diminution of some of the enormous skills that have made him a crowd favorite through 12½ big-league campaigns. But it isn't over for the Venezuelan native. Even at age thirty-seven (this July), he has too much talent.

The bat may have slowed down, the speed may have deserted him. But he can still play the outfield, and there's enough punch left in the bat to keep him in somebody's lineup. Tony's .257 average in 1989 is right on target with his career mark (.252). And he cranked out 11 homers in only 60 games, giving him a rousing .465 slugging mark. As his bat has slowed, however, more and more pitchers are finding out that they can get Tony with heat. He just can't catch up to some fastballs anymore. His loss of speed hurts him defensively, though most scouts are still impressed with his arm, no mean achievement for someone his age. Tony should be able to hang on a while longer.

Year	Team	G	AB	R	H	2B	3B	HR	RBI	BB	SB	AVG
1976	Pit	4	6	0	2	0	0	0	1	0	0	.333
1977	Oak	118	363	26	87	8	2	13	53	20	1	.240
1978	Oak	91	239	17	51	6	1	2	13	10	1	.213
1979	Oak	80	278	29	69	9	3	11	34	16	1	.248
1980	Oak	158	628	87	175	18	8	35	109	29	5	.279
1981	Oak	109	440	51	115	24	3	22	76	19	5	.261
1982	Oak	138	536	58	125	19	2	28	89	33	2	.233
1983	Bos	145	574	77	125	23	2	36	107	29	0	.218
1984	Bos	157	639	107	171	29	5	43	123	32	1	.268
1985	Bos	103	385	50	102	17	5	23	64	18	0	.265
1986	Bos	121	425	40	112	21	4	11	58	24	0	.264
1987	Cal.....	28	81	8	16	3	1	3	9	1	1	.198
1988	Cal.....	120	368	42	100	20	2	13	49	22	1	.272
1989	Cal.....	60	202	22	52	7	1	11	30	7	0	.257
		1432	5164	614	1302	204	39	251	815	260	18	.252

Harold Baines

Birth Date: 3/15/59
Bats: Left
Throws: Left
1989 Club:
Chicago White Sox &
Texas Rangers
Contest Code #: 616

Rating: 4

When was the last time a ball club retired the uniform number of an active player? That's what the Chicago White Sox did when one of their all-time heroes, Harold Baines, returned to Comiskey Park as a member of the Texas Rangers.

The 6'2", 195-pound Baines, one of baseball's premier hitters over the last decade, went to the Rangers last July 29 in a trade that didn't win the White Sox management too much praise from beleaguered Chisox fans. Though he hit only .285 for Texas in the last 50 games, his season mark of .309 ranked eighth best in the AL. A series of injuries has probably ended Baines' career as an outfielder. But he should be a great DH (he can hit with power, too) for years to come.

Year	Team	G	AB	R	H	2B	3B	HR	RBI	BB	SB	AVG
1980	ChA....	141	491	55	125	23	6	13	49	19	2	.255
1981	ChA....	82	280	42	80	11	7	10	41	12	6	.286
1982	ChA....	161	608	89	165	29	8	25	105	49	10	.271
1983	ChA....	156	596	76	167	33	2	20	99	49	7	.280
1984	ChA....	147	569	72	173	28	10	29	94	54	1	.304
1985	ChA....	160	640	86	198	29	3	22	113	42	1	.309
1986	ChA....	145	570	72	169	29	2	21	88	38	2	.296
1987	ChA....	132	505	59	148	26	4	20	93	46	0	.293
1988	ChA....	158	599	55	166	39	1	13	81	67	0	.277
1989	ChA....	96	333	55	107	20	1	13	56	60	0	.321
1989	Tex	50	172	18	49	9	0	3	16	13	0	.285
		1428	5363	679	1547	276	44	189	835	449	29	.288

Jesse Barfield

Birth Date: 10/29/59
Bats: Right
Throws: Right
1989 Club:
Toronto Blue Jays &
New York Yankees
Contest Code #: 617

Rating: 4

When Dave Winfield went down with a back injury that kept him out for all of 1989, the Yankees called the Toronto Blue Jays and came up with Jesse Barfield. Now, after a decent debut in New York, Barfield looks forward to keeping the position. Barfield's track record (.289, a major-league–leading 40 homers, 108 RBI's in 1986, for example) should earn him a shot.

Defensively, the Illinois native is right up there. He gets to the ball and can make the big throw when he has to. Offensively, despite good power, he has a few problems—as his .234 average shows. Baseball insiders point to "holes" in Barfield's swing. He's a classic bad-ball hitter, often chasing pitches that he can't possibly hit. And although he can smoke most heat (23 homers in 1989), he has a devil of a time with off-speed pitches. (He struck out 150 times last season.) A serious competitor, Barfield should be ready for a better 1990.

Year	Team	G	AB	R	H	2B	3B	HR	RBI	BB	SB	AVG
1981	Tor.....	25	95	7	22	3	2	2	9	4	4	.232
1982	Tor.....	139	394	54	97	13	2	18	58	42	1	.246
1983	Tor.....	128	388	58	98	13	3	27	68	22	2	.253
1984	Tor.....	110	320	51	91	14	1	14	49	35	8	.284
1985	Tor.....	155	539	94	156	34	9	27	84	66	22	.289
1986	Tor.....	158	589	107	170	35	2	40	108	69	8	.289
1987	Tor.....	159	590	89	155	25	3	28	84	58	3	.263
1988	Tor.....	136	468	62	114	21	5	18	56	41	7	.244
1989	Tor.....	21	80	8	16	4	0	5	11	5	0	.200
1989	NYA....	129	441	71	106	19	1	18	56	82	5	.240
		1160	3904	601	1025	181	28	197	583	424	60	.263

George Bell

Birth Date: 10/21/59
Bats: Right
Throws: Right
1989 Club:
Toronto Blue Jays
Contest Code #: 618

Rating: 5

George Bell is one of the most complex men in baseball. On the field, he's at least two people. Bell, the hitter, is one of baseball's most dangerous. Even when he's in a slump, he still commands the respect of every opponent. Bell, the left fielder, is awful. One hopes he'll spend his entire career in the American League where the designated hitter option remains available to him. Off the field, the native of San Pedro de Macoris in the Dominican Republic (yes, another one) is even more complicated. You almost never know where George is coming from. Still, any club in baseball would love to own his bat. There's no doubt about his hitting, including .297 with 41 doubles, 18 homers, and 104 RBI's last year. Only two years ago, in the year of the long ball, Bell

yanked 47 out of sight and knocked in 134 runs to win AL Most-Valuable-Player honors. The one-time Phillie farmhand remains one of the game's most productive hitters.

Year	Team	G	AB	R	H	2B	3B	HR	RBI	BB	SB	AVG
1981	Tor.....	60	163	19	38	2	1	5	12	5	3	.233
1983	Tor.....	39	112	5	30	5	4	2	17	4	1	.268
1984	Tor.....	159	606	85	177	39	4	26	87	24	11	.292
1985	Tor.....	157	607	87	167	28	6	28	95	43	21	.275
1986	Tor.....	159	641	101	198	38	6	31	108	41	7	.309
1987	Tor.....	156	610	111	188	32	4	47	134	39	5	.308
1988	Tor.....	156	614	78	165	27	5	24	97	34	4	.269
1989	Tor.....	153	613	88	182	41	2	18	104	33	4	.297
		1039	3966	574	1145	212	32	181	654	223	56	.289

Joey Belle

Birth Date: 8/25/66
Bats: Right
Throws: Right
1989 Club:
Cleveland Indians
Contest Code #: 619

Rating: 4

Baseball insiders were impressed with Joey Belle's major-league debut last season. Only a couple of years removed from an All-American career at LSU, Belle arrived in time to play 62 games for the Tribe, just enough time to win him a "future star" label.

Belle makes decent contact at the plate, though it's his potential home-run power that excites folks. The 6'2", 200-pounder pounded out 7 homers in only 218 at-bats. Meanwhile, he knocked in 37 runs and hit .225. Like most young power hitters, he struck out about once every 4 at-bats, which matched his minor-league totals. Defensively, he's a better-than-adequate outfielder whose arm falls into the "average" category.

At age twenty-three, Belle has shown that he can get the job done on the major-league level and is still in the early stages of his development.

Year	Team	G	AB	R	H	2B	3B	HR	RBI	BB	SB	AVG
1989	Cle.....	62	218	22	49	8	4	7	37	12	2	.225
		62	218	22	49	8	4	7	37	12	2	.225

Daryl Boston

Birth Date: 1/4/63
Bats: Left
Throws: Left
1989 Club:
Chicago White Sox
Contest Code #: 620

Rating: 2

The strange case of Daryl Boston continues. The Chicago White Sox's outfielder looks like a player, but he doesn't always play like one. He has above-average speed and he's always a threat to hit the ball out of sight. But he doesn't make consistent contact, and his defense borders on the horrible. Worse still, he's a problem child to his coaches; the word "uncoachable" shows up on many scouting reports.

The Cincinnati native has always carried the "potential" label. A first-round draft choice (the seventh player selected) in 1981, Boston passed up a career as a college quarterback to play baseball for Chicago. By 1984 he was in the majors, though he never played a full season in Comiskey Park until 1987. Boston bounced back from a .217 season in 1988 to hit .252 in 1989. But his power slipped from 15 homers in 105 games to only five in 101 games last season.

Year	Team	G	AB	R	H	2B	3B	HR	RBI	BB	SB	AVG
1984	ChA....	35	83	8	14	3	1	0	3	4	6	.169
1985	ChA....	95	232	20	53	13	1	3	15	14	8	.228

1986	ChA....	56	199	29	53	11	3	5	22	21	9	.266
1987	ChA....	103	337	51	87	21	2	10	29	25	12	.258
1988	ChA....	105	281	37	61	12	2	15	31	21	9	.217
1989	ChA....	101	218	34	55	3	4	5	23	24	7	.252
		495	1350	179	323	63	13	38	123	109	51	.239

Phil Bradley

Birth Date: 3/11/59
Bats: Right
Throws: Right
1989 Club:
Baltimore Orioles
Contest Code #: 621

Rating: 4

Returning to the American League (the former Mariner spent one season with the Phillies before the O's got him back for Ken Howell) is the best thing that ever happened to Phil Bradley. Never mind that the Phillies were a last-place team while the Birds nearly zoomed to the top of the AL East. Phil seems a lot more comfortable in the junior circuit.

A three-time .300 hitter with Seattle, Bradley is likely to do it again. The reports call him an outstanding "top of the lineup" hitter who knows how to play situation baseball: bunt, hit-and-run, etc. He's excellent on the bases (his 20 steals in 1989 were a typical Bradley figure) and he's a fine defensive outfielder. At the plate, he's a decent contact man who will occasionally hit the long ball. Phil is an asset to any ball club.

Year	Team	G	AB	R	H	2B	3B	HR	RBI	BB	SB	AVG
1983	Sea....	23	67	8	18	2	0	0	5	8	3	.269
1984	Sea....	124	322	49	97	12	4	0	24	34	21	.301
1985	Sea....	159	641	100	192	33	8	26	88	55	22	.300
1986	Sea....	143	526	88	163	27	4	12	50	77	21	.310
1987	Sea....	158	603	101	179	38	10	14	67	84	40	.297
1988	Phi....	154	569	77	150	30	5	11	56	54	11	.264
1989	Bal....	144	545	83	151	23	10	11	55	70	20	.277
		905	3273	506	950	165	41	74	345	382	138	.290

Glenn Braggs

Birth Date: 10/17/62
Bats: Right
Throws: Right
1989 Club:
Milwaukee Brewers
Contest Code #: 622

Rating: 2

The Milwaukee Brewers continue to wait on Glenn Braggs. The powerfully built 6'3", 210-pounder possesses the power the ball club really needs, though there are shortcomings in the rest of his game. When the power fails, so does Braggs.

The native Californian, who missed a major chunk of the 1988 season, bounced back physically in 1989. By mid-season, he looked as though he was on his way, hitting .270 with 11 homers and 42 RBI's. But after the All-Star break, it was almost all downhill (.210, only 4 homers, and 24 RBI's). Still he set career highs in homers (15), stolen bases (17), and games played (144).

A free swinger with excellent power potential, Glenn must simply begin to make more consistent contact at the plate. Defensively, the outfield is a real adventure at times, and Braggs' arm rates below average. The wait for Braggs continues.

Year	Team	G	AB	R	H	2B	3B	HR	RBI	BB	SB	AVG
1986	Mil.....	58	215	19	51	8	2	4	18	11	1	.237
1987	Mil.....	132	505	67	136	28	7	13	77	47	12	.269
1988	Mil.....	72	272	30	71	14	0	10	42	14	6	.261
1989	Mil.....	144	514	77	127	12	3	15	66	42	17	.247
		406	1506	193	385	62	12	42	203	114	36	.256

Greg Briley

Birth Date: 5/24/65
Bats: Left
Throws: Right
1989 Club:
Seattle Mariners
Contest Code #: 623

Rating: 2

A one-time all-Atlantic Coast Conference star at North Carolina State, Greg Briley spent his third full season in pro baseball in Seattle. A combination second baseman and outfielder, Briley can make a major contribution to his team with his bat.

The book on the 5'9", 170-pounder likes his offensive potential. He's a good contact hitter who hit .266 last season. What's more important is his power, which is in the average-to-above-average range. He hit 13 dingers in his major-league debut and also banged out 22 doubles and 4 triples among his 105 hits. His .442 slugging percentage impressed the scouts.

Defensively, the label is "adequate." His speed, which enabled him to steal 11 bases last year, helps him get to any balls hit into his neighborhood. He is probably better off in the outfield than at second, though his arm from the outfield is just about borderline.

Year	Team	G	AB	R	H	2B	3B	HR	RBI	BB	SB	AVG
1988	Sea	13	36	6	9	2	0	1	4	5	0	.250
1989	Sea	115	394	52	105	22	4	13	52	39	11	.266
		128	430	58	114	24	4	14	56	44	11	.265

Jay Buhner

Birth Date: 8/13/64
Bats: Right
Throws: Right
1989 Club:
Seattle Mariners
Contest Code #: 624

Rating: 2

Baseball people keep waiting for Jay Buhner to move into the big-time slugger class. The wait continues. The Texas strongman—he's 6'3" and 205—has hit some balls into orbit during his career. Trouble is, he doesn't do it often enough.

The Yankees gave up on Buhner during the 1988 season when they thought they needed 1B-DH Ken Phelps. Buhner has hit at every level, including .275 last year, when he hit 9 homers in 58 games.

He isn't bad defensively either, blessed with a better-than-decent arm. Originally a second-round draft pick by the Pittsburgh Pirates, Buhner moved to the Yankees after one season in the Bucs' system. For a couple of seasons, he was on the Yankees' Bronx/Columbus shuttle before the deal that sent him to the Mariners.

Year	Team	G	AB	R	H	2B	3B	HR	RBI	BB	SB	AVG
1987	NYA....	7	22	0	5	2	0	0	1	1	0	.227
1988	NYA....	25	69	8	13	0	0	3	13	3	0	.188
1988	Sea	60	192	28	43	13	1	10	25	25	1	.224
1989	Sea	58	204	27	56	15	1	9	33	19	1	.275
		150	487	63	117	30	2	22	72	48	2	.240

Ellis Burks

Birth Date: 9/11/64
Bats: Right
Throws: Right
1989 Club:
Boston Red Sox
Contest Code #: 625

Rating: 5

Every time Boston GM Lou Gorman answers a phone call from a rival GM, it seems that Ellis Burks is a prime topic of conversation. Why not? The 6'2", 195-pound Mississippi native has all the tools—and knows how to use them.

The only question mark about Burks is his health. He missed the start of the 1988 season after having bone chips removed from his right ankle. And he put in a couple of tours on the DL in 1989, which limited him to 97 games and 399 at-bats.

That question aside, Burks' future is brilliant. The scouts report that Burks is an excellent outfielder, blessed with good speed and good judgment. At the plate, he makes good contact (.303 last season) with decent power (12 homers, 61 RBI's). He's a genuine pain for most left-handed pitchers, and righties who rely on breaking stuff have trouble dealing with him. His speed produced 21 stolen bases, tops on the ball club, in his abbreviated season. The bottom line is that Burks is a potential impact player who can turn a ball club around. Gorman and every other big-league GM love that kind of guy.

Year	Team	G	AB	R	H	2B	3B	HR	RBI	BB	SB	AVG
1987	Bos	133	558	94	152	30	2	20	59	41	27	.272
1988	Bos	144	540	93	159	37	5	18	92	62	25	.294
1989	Bos	97	399	73	121	19	6	12	61	36	21	.303
		374	1497	260	432	86	13	50	212	139	73	.289

Randy Bush

Birth Date: 10/5/58
Bats: Left
Throws: Left
1989 Club:
Minnesota Twins
Contest Code #: 626

Rating: 3

After 7 ½ seasons with the Twins, Randy Bush should be a bigger cog in the Tom Kelly machine. When Minnesota dealt Tom Brunansky to the Cardinals in 1988, they fully expected that Bush would fill his large shoes. He really hasn't.

Of course, there are a lot of clubs that would love to have a consistent player like the 6'1", 186-pounder who was a college All-American at the U. of New Orleans. For the past four seasons, Randy has hit within a 16-point range. His 14 home runs in 1989 tied his major-league high, his 54 RBI's marked his highest total in the last six years, and his .263 batting average was a respectable 11 points higher than his career average. He's also a reliable pinch-hitter, and his outfield skills are reasonably good.

The disappointment is that Randy has never enjoyed the kind of blow-'em-out season that the Twins have been seeking since he stroked 22 homers and knocked in 94 runs for their Orlando farm club in 1981.

Year	Team	G	AB	R	H	2B	3B	HR	RBI	BB	SB	AVG
1982	Min	55	119	13	29	6	1	4	13	8	0	.244
1983	Min	124	373	43	93	24	3	11	56	34	0	.249
1984	Min	113	311	46	69	17	1	11	43	31	1	.222
1985	Min	97	234	26	56	13	3	10	35	24	3	.239
1986	Min	130	357	50	96	19	7	7	45	39	5	.269
1987	Min	122	293	46	74	10	2	11	46	43	10	.253
1988	Min	136	394	51	103	20	3	14	51	58	8	.261
1989	Min	141	391	60	103	17	4	14	54	48	5	.263
		918	2472	335	623	126	24	82	343	285	32	.252

Ivan Calderon

Birth Date: 3/19/62
Bats: Right
Throws: Right
1989 Club:
Chicago White Sox
Contest Code #: 627

Rating: 3

If you can keep Ivan Calderon out of trouble defensively, you have one productive baseball player. The White Sox outfielder enjoyed his best major-league season at the plate last year, and at age twenty-eight this year, figures to continue to produce. The native Puerto Rican hit the ball at a .286 clip in 1989, bouncing back from a horrendous 1988 (.212) which was marred by surgery on his left shoulder.

The 6'1", 205-pounder is a professional hitter who was Seattle's hot candidate for Rookie-of-the-Year honors in 1985, before a hand injury ended his season in early August. Calderon came to the White Sox in exchange for catcher Scott Bradley in mid-1986, and has continued to produce offensively. His 14 homers and 87 RBI's last season offered a perfect complement to his first-rate average.

Year	Team	G	AB	R	H	2B	3B	HR	RBI	BB	SB	AVG
1984	Sea	11	24	2	5	1	0	1	1	2	1	.208
1985	Sea	67	210	37	60	16	4	8	28	19	4	.286
1986	Sea	37	131	13	31	5	0	2	13	6	3	.237
1986	ChA	13	33	3	10	2	1	0	2	3	0	.303
1987	ChA	144	542	93	159	38	2	28	83	60	10	.293
1988	ChA	73	264	40	56	14	0	14	35	34	4	.212
1989	ChA	157	622	83	178	34	9	14	87	43	7	.286
		502	1826	271	499	110	16	67	249	167	29	.273

Jose Canseco

Birth Date: 7/2/64
Bats: Right
Throws: Right
1989 Club:
Oakland Athletics
Contest Code #: 628

Rating: 5

The most dominant player in baseball? Could it be anyone other than Oakland's Jose Canseco? About the only person who could prevent the Cuban-born, Miami-educated outfielder from becoming an all-timer is Jose himself. He seems to gravitate to trouble, but if he keeps his nose clean, his talent can take him to incredible heights. At 6'3" and 230, the A's right-fielder is presumably without a weakness.

Offensively, his power is without question (17 homers in 65 post-injury games in 1989, after 33, 31, and 42 in his first three seasons). Some of his long balls are the stuff that legends are made of, and they seem to get out of the park before the pitcher completes his follow-through. It's awesome. But that's only part of it.

Jose is an outstanding fielder, though he tends to be lazy in the outfield at times. His arm is close to "gun" quality. And, as the only member of baseball's 40-40 club (homers/steals), he can certainly run. There is absolutely no limit on Jose's potential, though his self-destructive tendencies frighten loyal Oakland rooters.

Year	Team	G	AB	R	H	2B	3B	HR	RBI	BB	SB	AVG
1985	Oak	29	96	16	29	3	0	5	13	4	1	.302
1986	Oak	157	600	85	144	29	1	33	117	65	15	.240
1987	Oak	159	630	81	162	35	3	31	113	50	15	.257
1988	Oak	158	610	120	187	34	0	42	124	78	40	.307
1989	Oak	65	227	40	61	9	1	17	57	23	6	.269
		568	2163	342	583	110	5	128	424	220	77	.270

Carmen Castillo

Birth Date: 6/8/58
Bats: Right
Throws: Right
1989 Club:
Minnesota Twins
Contest Code #: 629

Rating: 2

After 11 seasons in the Cleveland Indians' organization, the last seven with the parent club, Carmen Castillo packed his bags for Minnesota in 1989. Long just an average player, Castillo remains an average player. A lifetime .256 hitter, he hit .257 last year. His 8 home runs in 94 games was just about right.

Another of those quick, talented Dominican Republic natives, Castillo originally signed with the Philadelphia Phillies at age twenty and moved to the Cleveland organization after that initial (1978) season. He reached the big leagues in 1982 with the Indians, though he never played more than 89 games in any season with the Tribe. His 94 games in 1989 set an all-time career high.

Year	Team	G	AB	R	H	2B	3B	HR	RBI	BB	SB	AVG
1982	Cle.....	47	120	11	25	4	0	2	11	6	0	.208
1983	Cle.....	23	36	9	10	2	1	1	3	4	1	.278
1984	Cle.....	87	211	36	55	9	2	10	36	21	1	.261
1985	Cle.....	67	184	27	45	5	1	11	25	11	3	.245
1986	Cle.....	85	205	34	57	9	0	8	32	9	2	.278
1987	Cle.....	89	220	27	55	17	0	11	31	16	1	.250
1988	Cle.....	66	176	12	48	8	0	4	14	5	6	.273
1989	Min	94	218	23	56	13	3	8	33	15	1	.257
		558	1370	179	351	67	7	55	185	87	15	.256

Dave Clark

Birth Date: 9/3/62
Bats: Left
Throws: Right
1989 Club:
Cleveland Indians
Contest Code #: 630

Rating: 3

After parts of three seasons with Cleveland, it looked as though 1989 would be Dave Clark's year. The twenty-seven-year-old outfielder was the Tribe's first-round draft choice in 1983 after starring at Jackson State. But Clark hit only .237, most of it as a designated hitter and pinch hitter.

His defensive performance may relegate him to those roles throughout his career. Even though his arm is a definite plus, the rest of his defensive game is shabby. Offensively, he's a fairly good contact guy, with occasional home-run power. He has hit the long ball in the minors (30 round-trippers in 108 games with Buffalo in 1987, when he also hit .340).

A guy like Clark will have to improve both his power and average to have a shot at longevity. And in 1990, he'll have to go after it in Wrigley Field. The Cubs traded Mitch Webster to the Tribe for Clark.

Year	Team	G	AB	R	H	2B	3B	HR	RBI	BB	SB	AVG
1986	Cle.....	18	58	10	16	1	0	3	9	7	1	.276
1987	Cle.....	29	87	11	18	5	0	3	12	2	1	.207
1988	Cle.....	63	156	11	41	4	1	3	18	17	0	.263
1989	Cle.....	102	253	21	60	12	0	8	29	30	0	.237
		212	554	53	135	22	1	17	68	56	2	.244

Darnell Coles

Birth Date: 6/2/62
Bats: Right
Throws: Right
1989 Club:
Seattle Mariners
Contest Code #: 631

Rating: 2

Darnell Coles' first full season back with his original club, the Seattle Mariners, produced mixed results. The California native was the M's first-round selection (the sixth player picked) in the 1980 draft and made his Seattle debut late in the 1983 season. After brief stints with Detroit and Pittsburgh, he returned to the Kingdome in late 1988 (for outfielder Glenn Wilson).

Coles is the type of player who frustrates managers. When he's hot, he's beautiful. When he's not, forget it. A premier utility man, he's at home in the infield or the outfield, though the scouting report advises keeping him in the outer gardens. In general, he's not a terrific defensive player. Offensively, the 6'2", 185-pounder shows occasional power (10 homers last season and 20 for the 1986 Tigers).

Year	Team	G	AB	R	H	2B	3B	HR	RBI	BB	SB	AVG
1983	Sea	27	92	9	26	7	0	1	6	7	0	.283
1984	Sea	48	143	15	23	3	1	0	6	17	2	.161
1985	Sea	27	59	8	14	4	0	1	5	9	0	.237
1986	Det	142	521	67	142	30	2	20	86	45	6	.273
1987	Det	53	149	14	27	5	1	4	15	15	0	.181
1987	Pit	40	119	20	27	8	0	6	24	19	1	.227
1988	Sea	55	195	32	57	10	1	10	34	17	3	.292
1988	Pit	68	211	20	49	13	1	5	36	20	1	.232
1989	Sea	146	535	54	135	21	3	10	59	27	5	.252
		606	2024	239	500	101	9	57	271	176	18	.247

Henry Cotto

Birth Date: 1/5/61
Bats: Right
Throws: Right
1989 Club:
Seattle Mariners
Contest Code #: 632

Rating: 2

Two years after the trade that brought Henry Cotto and Steve Trout from the Yankees to Seattle for Lee Guetterman, Clay Parker, and Wade Taylor, the Mariners aren't complaining. The 6'2", 178-pound Cotto, a native of the Bronx who lives in Puerto Rico, has become a first-rate player, offensively and defensively.

Speed is Cotto's greatest asset. It makes him a better outfielder and a bigger threat at the plate and on the bases. Despite an arm that can only be rated average, Cotto gets to as many balls as anyone. At the plate, Henry makes good, consistent contact and displays some power. Cotto's .264 average last year included 9 homers. A one-time Chicago Cub, Cotto spent four seasons shuffling between the minors and majors before arriving full-time with the Mariners in the 1988 season.

Year	Team	G	AB	R	H	2B	3B	HR	RBI	BB	SB	AVG
1984	ChN....	105	146	24	40	5	0	0	8	10	9	.274
1985	NYA....	34	56	4	17	1	0	1	6	3	1	.304
1986	NYA....	35	80	11	17	3	0	1	6	2	3	.213
1987	NYA....	68	149	21	35	10	0	5	20	6	4	.235
1988	Sea	133	386	50	100	18	1	8	33	23	27	.259
1989	Sea	100	295	44	78	11	2	9	33	12	10	.264
		475	1112	154	287	48	3	24	106	56	54	.258

Chili Davis

Birth Date: 1/17/60
Bats: Both
Throws: Right
1989 Club:
California Angels
Contest Code #: 633

Rating: 4

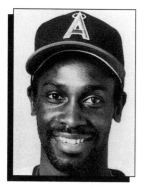

There are two Chili Davises. With a glove on his left hand, he can scare his manager to death. He makes mistakes—breaks the wrong way, throws to the wrong base. He has a tendency to butcher ground balls. You know the type.

With a bat in his hands, however, he scares the opponents. Even after nine big-league campaigns, he retains all of his offensive tools. The long-time San Francisco Giant who arrived in California via the free-agent route before the 1988 season can fall victim to heavy smoke, but he handles breaking stuff well. In fact, he seems to be handling the bat better with the Angels than he did with the Giants. He enjoyed his second straight 90-RBI year while hitting .271. His 22 homers marked his third straight season with 21 or more. The added power has put him in triple digits in strikeouts (109 last year), but it's a small price to pay for a hitter who can break up any game.

Year	Team	G	AB	R	H	2B	3B	HR	RBI	BB	SB	AVG
1981	SF	8	15	1	2	0	0	0	0	1	2	.133
1982	SF	154	641	86	167	27	6	19	76	45	24	.261
1983	SF	137	486	54	113	21	2	11	59	55	10	.233
1984	SF	137	499	87	157	21	6	21	81	42	12	.315
1985	SF	136	481	53	130	25	2	13	56	62	15	.270
1986	SF	153	526	71	146	28	3	13	70	84	16	.278
1987	SF	149	500	80	125	22	1	24	76	72	16	.250
1988	Cal.....	158	600	81	161	29	3	21	93	56	9	.268
1989	Cal.....	154	560	81	152	24	1	22	90	61	3	.271
		1186	4308	594	1153	197	24	144	601	478	107	.268

Rob Deer

Birth Date: 9/29/60
Bats: Right
Throws: Right
1989 Club:
Milwaukee Brewers
Contest Code #: 634

Rating: 2

Rob Deer struck out 158 times last season. No news, you say. Right. One of the most aggressive, free-swinging hitters in baseball, Deer remains one of the premier strikeout artists, though he hits the ball into adjacent counties often enough to make fans and managers forget.

A part-time member of the San Francisco Giants for a couple of seasons (1984–85), Deer came to the Brewers and became a full-time player in 1986. He has averaged 27½ homers per season with Milwaukee, though his strikeout totals for the last three years read 186 (the AL record), 153, and 158. In addition, his batting average spun out wildly last season, down to .210 from .252 in 1988.

Scouts who like Deer rate him as an adequate outfielder; those who don't say he isn't quite that good. A further reduction in strikeouts and improved outfield play are essential to Rob's future.

Year	Team	G	AB	R	H	2B	3B	HR	RBI	BB	SB	AVG
1984	SF	13	24	5	4	0	0	3	3	7	1	.167
1985	SF	78	162	22	30	5	1	8	20	23	0	.185
1986	Mil.....	134	466	75	108	17	3	33	86	72	5	.232
1987	Mil.....	134	474	71	113	15	2	28	80	86	12	.238
1988	Mil.....	135	492	71	124	24	0	23	85	51	9	.252
1989	Mil.....	130	466	72	98	18	2	26	65	60	4	.210
		624	2084	316	477	79	8	121	339	299	31	.229

Mike Devereaux

Birth Date: 4/10/63
Bats: Right
Throws: Right
1989 Club:
Baltimore Orioles
Contest Code #: 635

Rating: 4

A one-time Dodger hot prospect, Mike Devereaux arrived in Baltimore last spring in time to make a major impression, offensively and defensively, and play a major role in Baltimore's 1989 near-miracle. A first-rate defensive player in centerfield, Devereaux is also an outstanding low-ball hitter who should improve on his .266 BA in 1989. The book on Devereaux also indicates the presence of good power, though his 8 homers in 122 games last season didn't offer clearcut proof. Devereaux also possesses good speed, which is a major factor on defense, and his 22 stolen bases was tops on the Orioles last year. The bottom line on Devereaux is that he's a tough out who doesn't get his team in trouble in any facet of the game.

Year	Team	G	AB	R	H	2B	3B	HR	RBI	BB	SB	AVG
1987	LA	19	54	7	12	3	0	0	4	3	3	.222
1988	LA	30	43	4	5	1	0	0	2	2	0	.116
1989	Bal	122	391	55	104	14	3	8	46	36	22	.266
		171	488	66	121	18	3	8	52	41	25	.248

Brian Downing

Birth Date: 10/9/50
Bats: Right
Throws: Right
1989 Club:
California Angels
Contest Code #: 636

Rating: 4

So Brian Downing can't play defense anymore. So what? Approaching his fortieth birthday, he makes a tremendous contribution on offense and, in this age of the designated hitter, that makes him a valuable commodity. In fact, the 5'10", 200-pounder's .283 bat mark was his best since 1980, when he hit .290. Not bad for a player who took plenty of lumps as a catcher before switching to the outfield in the early 1980s.

Downing, who played his high school ball in the shadow of Anaheim Stadium, is a constant threat at the plate. A 100-percent team player, Brian's aggressiveness gives him a major leadership role on the ball club. His selfless attitude helped produce a .354 on-base percentage last year. It was the second straight year he led the Angels in that department. Downing looks as though he can go on hitting for several more years.

Year	Team	G	AB	R	H	2B	3B	HR	RBI	BB	SB	AVG
1973	ChA	34	73	5	13	1	0	2	4	10	0	.178
1974	ChA	108	293	41	66	12	1	10	39	51	0	.225
1975	ChA	138	420	58	101	12	1	7	41	76	13	.240
1976	ChA	104	317	38	81	14	0	3	30	40	7	.256
1977	ChA	69	169	28	48	4	2	4	25	34	1	.284
1978	Cal.	133	412	42	105	15	0	7	46	52	3	.255
1979	Cal.	148	509	87	166	27	3	12	75	77	3	.326
1980	Cal.	30	93	5	27	6	0	2	25	12	0	.290
1981	Cal.	93	317	47	79	14	0	9	41	46	1	.249
1982	Cal.	158	623	109	175	37	2	28	84	86	2	.281
1983	Cal.	113	403	68	99	15	1	19	53	62	1	.246
1984	Cal.	156	539	65	148	28	2	23	91	70	0	.275
1985	Cal.	150	520	80	137	23	1	20	85	78	5	.263
1986	Cal.	152	513	90	137	27	4	20	95	90	4	.267
1987	Cal.	155	567	110	154	29	3	29	77	106	5	.272
1988	Cal.	135	484	80	117	18	2	25	64	81	3	.242
1989	Cal.	142	544	59	154	25	2	14	59	56	0	.283
		2018	6796	1012	1807	307	24	234	934	1027	48	.266

Jim Eisenreich

Birth Date: 4/18/59
Bats: Left
Throws: Left
1989 Club:
Kansas City Royals
Contest Code #: 637

Rating: 3

One day they'll make a movie out of the Jim Eisenreich story. Don't miss it. After an outstanding and brief minor-league career, Jim came up to the Minnesota Twins for the 1982 season. After a marvelous spring training, he got off to an equally marvelous start, hitting .303 in his first 34 games.

Then disaster struck Jim down. A mysterious nervous disorder, later identified as Tourette Syndrome, knocked Eisenreich out of the game. He tried it again for 2 games in 1983 and 12 in 1984 before packing it in. No one expected to see Eisenreich in the majors again. After two years of amateur ball in St. Cloud, MN, the Royals gave him a final shot. This time it worked. It took awhile but Eisenreich finally played a full season last year, hitting .293 to lead Kaycee. His 33 doubles helped him to a lofty .448 slugging percentage. Jim has the tools: speed, defense, and, only slightly less so, offense.

An all-out player every time out, he's great to have on your club.

Year	Team	G	AB	R	H	2B	3B	HR	RBI	BB	SB	AVG
1982	Min	34	99	10	30	6	0	2	9	11	0	.303
1983	Min	2	7	1	2	1	0	0	0	1	0	.286
1984	Min	12	32	1	7	1	0	0	3	2	2	.219
1987	KC	44	105	10	25	8	2	4	21	7	1	.238
1988	KC	82	202	26	44	8	1	1	19	6	9	.218
1989	KC	134	475	64	139	33	7	9	59	37	27	.293
		308	920	112	247	57	10	16	111	64	39	.268

Cecil Espy

Birth Date: 1/20/63
Bats: Both
Throws: Right
1989 Club:
Texas Rangers
Contest Code #: 638

Rating: 3

If Cecil Espy continues his 1989 improvement, the Texas Rangers have the makings of an outstanding lead-off hitter. The San Diego native has all it takes; it's up to him how good he gets. Speed is the stock in trade of a first-rate number-one hitter, and Espy has it to burn. Cecil stole 45 bases last year, second only to another fair lead-off man (Rickey Henderson, 77). In Texas history, only Bump Wills and Dave Nelson have exceeded Espy's total.

Espy's hitting numbers reflect his position in the lineup. He hit .257, 9 points better than in 1988. He doesn't have much power, with only 22 extra-base blows among his 122 hits. Defensively, Espy continues to improve in the outfield, which combined with his speed, should earn him an everyday spot for years to come.

Year	Team	G	AB	R	H	2B	3B	HR	RBI	BB	SB	AVG
1983	LA	20	11	4	3	1	0	0	1	1	0	.273
1987	Tex	14	8	1	0	0	0	0	0	1	2	.000
1988	Tex	123	347	46	86	17	6	2	39	20	33	.248
1989	Tex	142	475	65	122	12	7	3	31	38	45	.257
		299	841	116	211	30	13	5	71	60	80	.251

Dwight Evans

Birth Date: 11/3/51
Bats: Right
Throws: Right
1989 Club:
Boston Red Sox
Contest Code #: 639

Rating: 4

So Ol' Dewey Evans is washed up? Forget it. Forget that the California native is thirty-eight. Forget that he has survived shifts from right field to first base and back to right. It may seem amazing, but Evans remains one of the game's most productive players.

Signed by the Sox in June 1969, he joined the ball club in 1972 and hasn't budged. Why would he? The man practically owns Fenway Park. He's a dead fastball hitter, which makes the Green Monster even more inviting. Though righties can get him with the curveball, he handles lefty curveballs well. Evans is a model of consistency. He has never hit more than .305 (1987) or less than .247 (1978). Last year's figures of 20 homers and 100 RBI's are also fairly typical, though some of his power seems to be eroding.

Just as pleasant for Boston management, Evans remains a very fine outfielder with a strong, accurate arm. And when the game is on the line, there's no one better in Boston than Evans to send the fans home. How long can he keep it up? Who knows?

Year	Team	G	AB	R	H	2B	3B	HR	RBI	BB	SB	AVG
1972	Bos	18	57	2	15	3	1	1	6	7	0	.263
1973	Bos	119	282	46	63	13	1	10	32	40	5	.223
1974	Bos	133	463	60	130	19	8	10	70	38	4	.281
1975	Bos	128	412	61	113	24	6	13	56	47	3	.274
1976	Bos	146	501	61	121	34	5	17	62	57	6	.242
1977	Bos	73	230	39	66	9	2	14	36	28	4	.287
1978	Bos	147	497	75	123	24	2	24	63	65	8	.247
1979	Bos	152	489	69	134	24	1	21	58	69	6	.274
1980	Bos	148	463	72	123	37	5	18	60	64	3	.266
1981	Bos	108	412	84	122	19	4	22	71	85	3	.296
1982	Bos	162	609	122	178	37	7	32	98	112	3	.292
1983	Bos	126	470	74	112	19	4	22	58	70	3	.238
1984	Bos	162	630	121	186	37	8	32	104	96	3	.295
1985	Bos	159	617	110	162	29	1	29	78	114	7	.263
1986	Bos	152	529	86	137	33	2	26	97	97	3	.259
1987	Bos	154	541	109	165	37	2	34	123	106	4	.305
1988	Bos	149	559	96	164	31	7	21	111	76	5	.293
1989	Bos	146	520	82	148	27	3	20	100	99	3	.285
		2382	8281	1369	2262	456	69	366	1283	1270	73	.273

Mike Felder

Birth Date: 11/18/62
Bats: Both
Throws: Right
1989 Club:
Milwaukee Brewers
Contest Code #: 640

Rating: 2

Blessed with a world of speed, Mike Felder has decent major-league potential. Yet his questionable bat and his occasionally questionable on-field attitude create reasonable doubt about his future. Speed? You bet. Felder stole 26 bases in 1989, one behind club leader Paul Molitor, who played 38 additional games. Felder cracked an inside-the-park homer against Baltimore last September. He can move.

What he can't do—or hasn't up until now—is hit. Despite hitting .305 last July, Felder finished at only .241 for the season, with 3 homers and 23 RBI's. Though he can fly in the outfield, his judgment is occasionally questionable and he tends to be lazy on defense. There's no doubt that Felder has some talent, but he must make better use of it.

Year	Team	G	AB	R	H	2B	3B	HR	RBI	BB	SB	AVG
1985	Mil.....	15	56	8	11	1	0	0	0	5	4	.196
1986	Mil.....	44	155	24	37	2	4	1	13	13	16	.239
1987	Mil.....	108	289	48	77	5	7	2	31	28	34	.266

1988	Mil.....	50	81	14	14	1	0	0	5	0	8	.173
1989	Mil.....	117	315	50	76	11	3	3	23	23	26	.241
		334	896	144	215	20	14	6	72	69	88	.240

Junior Felix

Birth Date: 10/3/67
Bats: Both
Throws: Right
1989 Club:
Toronto Blue Jays
Contest Code #: 641

Rating: 2

The Toronto Blue Jays' Dominican connection has come up with another winner. Junior Felix is the latest addition to the Jay roster of stars from the Dominican Republic, which now includes pitcher Jose Nunez, outfielder George Bell, shortstop Tony Fernandez, second baseman Nelson Liriano, and infielder Manny Lee. Bell and Fernandez are already All-Stars; Felix could be next.

Despite an occasional lapse, Felix is a defensive whiz. He has amazing speed and utilizes it in the outfield as well as on the bases. His arm rates above average.

A potential lead-off hitter supreme, the twenty-two-year-old will have to learn to maneuver his bat better. But the speed that serves him so well on defense also makes him a major threat on offense. Though he was caught on 12 of 30 stealing attempts last season, that figure should improve too. Junior even had an inside-the-park grand-slam homer last June. That's the ultimate salute to speed.

Year	Team	G	AB	R	H	2B	3B	HR	RBI	BB	SB	AVG
1989	Tor.....	110	415	62	107	14	8	9	46	33	18	.258
		110	415	62	107	14	8	9	46	33	18	.258

Dave Gallagher

Birth Date: 9/20/60
Bats: Right
Throws: Right
1989 Club:
Chicago White Sox
Contest Code #: 642

Rating: 1

Dave Gallagher doesn't do anything extraordinarily well, but he does everything he does well enough to be a solid major leaguer. The only White Sox to play in every one of the club's 161 games last year, Dave saw his batting average slip to .266 from his spectacular .303 in 1988.

Nonetheless, the life-long resident of Trenton, NJ, remains a steady, winning player who does what it takes to help his club. A former Cleveland Indian (for 15 games in 1987), Gallagher came to the Sox as a free-agent in January 1988, and spent 34 games at AAA Vancouver before arriving to stay at Comiskey Park. He's a fine number-two hitter who makes good contact, can bunt, and can steal, and he can play the outfield. Gallagher is a steady, winning player.

Year	Team	G	AB	R	H	2B	3B	HR	RBI	BB	SB	AVG
1987	Cle.....	15	36	2	4	1	1	0	1	2	2	.111
1988	ChA....	101	347	59	105	15	3	5	31	29	5	.303
1989	ChA....	161	601	74	160	22	2	1	46	46	5	.266
		277	984	135	269	38	6	6	78	77	12	.273

Dan Gladden

Birth Date: 7/7/57
Bats: Right
Throws: Right
1989 Club:
Minnesota Twins
Contest Code #: 643

Rating: 3

At age thirty-two, Dan Gladden of the Minnesota Twins remains one of baseball's solid citizens. The long-time San Francisco Giant was dealt to the Twins in 1987, just in time to help lead the club to the 1987 world title. A lifetime .272 hitter going into the 1989 campaign, Gladden enjoyed a full-season career-high .295 last year. A competent outfielder, the former Fresno State ace has enjoyed productive seasons in the Humphreydome, with 62 RBI's in 1988 and 46 in 1989, his two top run-producing years.

Speed has never been a question, both in the outfield and on the bases. Gladden had 23 stolen bases last year, his sixth straight season with 20 or more. Defensively, he combines with center fielder Kirby Puckett to get everything gettable in the homer-happy Minneapolis launching pad.

Year	Team	G	AB	R	H	2B	3B	HR	RBI	BB	SB	AVG
1983	SF	18	63	6	14	2	0	1	9	5	4	.222
1984	SF	86	342	71	120	17	2	4	31	33	31	.351
1985	SF	142	502	64	122	15	8	7	41	40	32	.243
1986	SF	102	351	55	97	16	1	4	29	39	27	.276
1987	Min	121	438	69	109	21	2	8	38	38	25	.249
1988	Min	141	576	91	155	32	6	11	62	46	28	.269
1989	Min	121	461	69	136	23	3	8	46	23	23	.295
		731	2733	425	753	126	22	43	256	224	170	.276

Mike Greenwell

Birth Date: 7/18/63
Bats: Left
Throws: Right
1989 Club:
Boston Red Sox
Contest Code #: 644

Rating: 4

With a stick in his hands, Mike Greenwell scares the daylights out of Red Sox opponents. With a glove on his hand, Greenwell scares the daylights out of the Red Sox. But the damage he can wreak on offense far outweighs his defensive deficiencies. Simply put, Greenwell is one of the best hitters in the game. Mike hit .308 in 1989, just about his career average. He slipped somewhat from his 1987 and 1988 marks of .328 and .325, but there's no cause for concern. He banged out 14 homers and 36 doubles among his 178 hits in 145 games. Not bad. Despite being blessed with only average speed, he managed 13 stolen bases. Only Ellis Burks (21) had more for the Sox.

After only three major-league seasons, one thing is clear: When Greenwell gets hot (which is fairly frequently), he is very capable of carrying the ball club. Over the past fifty years, the Sox have employed only four left fielders—Ted Williams, Carl Yastrzemski, Jim Rice, and Greenwell. They needn't worry about the spot until about 2004.

Year	Team	G	AB	R	H	2B	3B	HR	RBI	BB	SB	AVG
1985	Bos	17	31	7	10	1	0	4	8	3	1	.323
1986	Bos	31	35	4	11	2	0	0	4	5	0	.314
1987	Bos	125	412	71	135	31	6	19	89	35	5	.328
1988	Bos	158	590	86	192	39	8	22	119	87	16	.325
1989	Bos	145	578	87	178	36	0	14	95	56	13	.308
		476	1646	255	526	109	14	59	315	186	35	.320

Ken Griffey, Jr.

Birth Date: 11/21/69
Bats: Left
Throws: Left
1989 Club:
Seattle Mariners
Contest Code #: 645

Rating: 4

Ken Griffey, Sr., has had a remarkable baseball career. At age forty, he's still going strong. But his greatest contribution to the national pastime may be still to come. The veteran's son, Ken, Jr., is on the verge of superstardom. He has everything going for him. The former Cincinnati high school sensation is big at 6'3" and 195 pounds and strong, and he can fly. Although he stole only 16 bases last season, he was able to get to balls in the outfield that mere speedsters couldn't touch. At age twenty, he has impressed scouts with his awesome defensive ability. His possibilities on offense aren't bad either. He looks terrific at the plate, where he hit .264 in his rookie year. He popped 16 homers and knocked in 61 runs in 127 games. Young Mr. Griffey has some improving to do, but he has "great" written all over him.

Year	Team	G	AB	R	H	2B	3B	HR	RBI	BB	SB	AVG
1989	Sea	127	455	61	120	23	0	16	61	44	16	.264
		127	455	61	120	23	0	16	61	44	16	.264

Mel Hall

Birth Date: 9/16/60
Bats: Left
Throws: Left
1989 Club:
New York Yankees
Contest Code #: 646

Rating: 4

When Cleveland got Mel Hall, Joe Carter, and two other players from the Cubs in a 1984 trade, Hall looked like the key guy. These days, Carter is a borderline superstar and Hall is on a treadmill. Mel makes contact at the plate. Though his average slipped to .260 last year, he's probably a better hitter than that. He'd never hit less than .280 the four previous years and seems destined to be in that range again. But he doesn't possess much power, despite 17 homers in 1989. Oddly, he only had 9 doubles.

The rap on Hall is that he isn't a very good outfielder—and that's being generous. His arm is fair, but he takes far too long to get his throws off. Insiders point to Hall's poor work habits as the reason for his failure to meet previous expectations.

Year	Team	G	AB	R	H	2B	3B	HR	RBI	BB	SB	AVG
1981	ChN....	10	11	1	1	0	0	1	2	1	0	.091
1982	ChN....	24	80	6	21	3	2	0	4	5	0	.262
1983	ChN....	112	410	60	116	23	5	17	56	42	6	.283
1984	Cle.....	83	257	43	66	13	1	7	30	35	1	.257
1984	ChN....	48	150	25	42	11	3	4	22	12	2	.280
1985	Cle.....	23	66	7	21	6	0	0	12	8	0	.318
1986	Cle.....	140	442	68	131	29	2	18	77	33	6	.296
1987	Cle.....	142	485	57	136	21	1	18	76	20	5	.280
1988	Cle.....	150	515	69	144	32	4	6	71	28	7	.280
1989	NYA....	113	361	54	94	9	0	17	58	21	0	.260
		845	2777	390	772	147	18	88	408	205	27	.278

Dave Henderson

Birth Date: 7/21/58
Bats: Right
Throws: Right
1989 Club:
Oakland Athletics
Contest Code #: 647

Rating: 3

Forget Dave Henderson's career year in 1988. His .304 batting average with 24 homers and 94 RBI's was a major surprise, and the Oakland Athletics loved it. Henderson is not a .304 hitter, and he doesn't have that much power. But don't forget what Dave Henderson can do for you in an ordinary year. He hits a little better than his .250 average last year. He hits around 15 homers, as he did last year. He knocks in runs, though probably not the 80 he did last year.

One of the heroes of the Boston Red Sox's 1986 ALCS title, Henderson came to the A's (from San Francisco) as a free agent in late 1987, and has proven a valuable pickup. He's solid on defense, getting to everything in center field, occasionally making the spectacular play, and throwing quickly, accurately, and usually to the right base. Although his offense has returned to more normal figures, he's tough with runners in scoring position and even tougher when the chips are down.

Year	Team	G	AB	R	H	2B	3B	HR	RBI	BB	SB	AVG
1981	Sea	59	126	17	21	3	0	6	13	16	2	.167
1982	Sea	104	324	47	82	17	1	14	48	36	2	.253
1983	Sea	137	484	50	130	24	5	17	55	28	9	.269
1984	Sea	112	350	42	98	23	0	14	43	19	5	.280
1985	Sea	139	502	70	121	28	2	14	68	48	6	.241
1986	Sea	103	337	51	93	19	4	14	44	37	1	.276
1986	Bos	36	51	8	10	3	0	1	3	2	1	.196
1987	Bos	75	184	30	43	10	0	8	25	22	1	.234
1987	SF	15	21	2	5	2	0	0	1	8	2	.238
1988	Oak	146	507	100	154	38	1	24	94	47	2	.304
1989	Oak	152	579	77	145	24	3	15	80	54	8	.250
		1078	3465	494	902	191	16	127	474	317	39	.260

Rickey Henderson

Birth Date: 12/25/58
Bats: Right
Throws: Right
1989 Club:
New York Yankees &
Oakland Athletics
Contest Code #: 648

Rating: 5

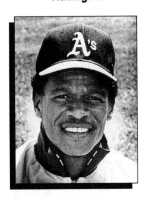

Rickey Henderson is one of baseball's $3-million-per-year-men. Evidently, Oakland was willing to risk those once-unthinkable numbers on an outfielder who sometimes sulks, sometimes screws up, and sometimes—often key times—can ignite his ball club. Henderson is a fearsome force on the field. The 5'10", 185-pound speedball can do more things better than almost anyone in the game. An outstanding lead-off hitter (.411 on-base average last year) who can also hit the long ball (12 homers in 1989), he should become baseball's all-time stolen-base leader (he needs 65) this season. Though he hit only .274 in 1989, he should hit 20 points better in 1990. Though his moodiness occasionally affects his outfield play, he is better than adequate in the outfield. When you reflect upon his ALCS MVP performance, and his .474 World Series average, with a double, 2 triples, and a homer, plus 3 stolen bases (a 4-game Series record), you get an idea of the damage Rickey can do.

Year	Team	G	AB	R	H	2B	3B	HR	RBI	BB	SB	AVG
1979	Oak	89	351	49	96	13	3	1	26	34	33	.274
1980	Oak	158	591	111	179	22	4	9	53	117	100	.303
1981	Oak	108	423	89	135	18	7	6	35	64	56	.319
1982	Oak	149	536	119	143	24	4	10	51	116	130	.267
1983	Oak	145	513	105	150	25	7	9	48	103	108	.292
1984	Oak	142	502	113	147	27	4	16	58	86	66	.293
1985	NYA	143	547	146	172	28	5	24	72	99	80	.314

Year	Team	G	AB	R	H	2B	3B	HR	RBI	BB	SB	AVG
1986	NYA....	153	608	130	160	31	5	28	74	89	87	.263
1987	NYA....	95	358	78	104	17	3	17	37	80	41	.291
1988	NYA....	140	554	118	169	30	2	6	50	82	93	.305
1989	NYA....	65	235	41	58	13	1	3	22	56	25	.247
1989	Oak....	85	306	72	90	13	2	9	35	70	52	.294
		1472	5524	1171	1603	261	47	138	561	996	871	.290

Pete Incaviglia

Birth Date: 4/2/64
Bats: Right
Throws: Right
1989 Club:
Texas Rangers
Contest Code #: 649

Rating: 4

How does the other half live? Don't ask Pete Incaviglia. The Ranger outfielder and DH is one of the few big leaguers (Bob Horner and Dave Winfield are the other current club members) who never spent a minute in the minors. An original Montreal Expos' first-round draftee out of Oklahoma State, the 6'1", 220-pounder refused to sign with the Canadian club, then was traded to the Rangers in November 1985. The following spring he opened in right field in Arlington.

Pete has always carried the "big swinger" label, and he isn't likely to lose it. He tied for or led the AL in strikeouts in two of his first three seasons, averaging 169 K's per year. He cut that to only 136 in 1989, but his power dipped, too (an all-time low 21 homers), which is some cause for concern. Still, he became the first Ranger to top the 20-homer mark for four straight seasons. Defensively, he has very limited range in the outfield and his arm is only average. Still, if you're willing to make peace with the 150 strikeouts, Pete can be a constant threat offensively

Year	Team	G	AB	R	H	2B	3B	HR	RBI	BB	SB	AVG
1986	Tex	153	540	82	135	21	2	30	88	55	3	.250
1987	Tex	139	509	85	138	26	4	27	80	48	9	.271
1988	Tex	116	418	59	104	19	3	22	54	39	6	.249
1989	Tex	133	453	48	107	27	4	21	81	32	5	.236
		541	1920	274	484	93	13	100	303	174	23	.252

Bo Jackson

Birth Date: 11/30/62
Bats: Right
Throws: Right
1989 Club:
Kansas City Royals
Contest Code #: 650

Rating: 5

Bo Jackson is (a) the best running back in the American League, (b) the best hitter in the National Football League, (c) the best all-around athlete in America, (d) all of the above.

C'mon, that's a gimme. If SAT questions were that easy, no athlete would fail to meet the Proposition 48 standards. Bo is a wonder. The MVP of the 1989 All-Star game with 2 prodigious home runs, he took his annual ten-day vacation before taking over at tailback for the L.A. Raiders. That sets Royals management into a fit of prayer, hoping that their budding baseball superstar doesn't mangle any extremity that would negatively affect his baseball prowess.

The former Auburn football All-American and Heisman Trophy winner has all the tools to be a baseball immortal. He's improving at the plate, making better contact than ever. He hit .256, his major-league high last season, but his 172 strikeouts are still too many. He also possesses superstar power (32 homers, 105 RBI's, despite missing 27 games), superstar speed (26 steals, with the sky the limit), and a superstar throwing arm. Bo, who often refers to himself in the third person, can be about as good as Bo wants to be.

Year	Team	G	AB	R	H	2B	3B	HR	RBI	BB	SB	AVG
1986	KC.....	25	82	9	17	2	1	2	9	7	3	.207
1987	KC.....	116	396	46	93	17	2	22	53	30	10	.235
1988	KC.....	124	439	63	108	16	4	25	68	25	27	.246
1989	KC.....	135	515	86	132	15	6	32	105	39	26	.256
		409	1432	204	350	50	13	81	235	101	66	.244

Chris James

Birth Date: 10/4/62
Bats: Right
Throws: Right
1989 Clubs:
Philadelphia Phillies &
San Diego Padres
Contest Code #: 651

Rating: 3

Once upon a time, the Phillies were grooming Chris James to be one of the team cornerstones. James, whose brother, Craig, is a running back for the NFL's New England Patriots, was signed as a free agent by the Phillies in 1981. James put up great numbers in his first three minor-league seasons: a league-leading 19 doubles at Class-A Bend in 1982; a league-leading 121 RBI's at Class-A Spartanburg in 1983; a league-leading 12 home runs at Double-A Reading; and a .316 batting average at Triple-A Portland.

In his three-plus seasons in Philadelphia, James, playing in the outfield, hit for power. Former Phillies general manager Paul Owens envisioned James as Mike Schmidt's heir apparent at third base. But the Phillies removed Owens after the 1988 season, and new general manager Lee Thomas had other plans for James. Last summer he sent James to the Padres for John Kruk and Randy Ready. James joined the Cleveland Indians during the off-season; James should rebound from his sub-par 1989 season.

Year	Team	G	AB	R	H	2B	3B	HR	RBI	BB	SB	AVG
1986	Phi	16	46	5	13	3	0	1	5	1	0	.283
1987	Phi	115	358	48	105	20	6	17	54	27	3	.293
1988	Phi	150	566	57	137	24	1	19	66	31	7	.242
1989	Phi	45	179	14	37	4	0	2	19	4	3	.207
1989	SD.....	87	303	41	80	13	2	11	46	22	2	.264
		413	1452	165	372	64	9	50	190	85	15	.256

Dion James

Birth Date: 11/9/62
Bats: Left
Throws: Left
1989 Club:
Atlanta Braves &
Cleveland Indians
Contest Code #: 652

Rating: 3

Dion James, whose defense in Atlanta left so much to be desired, seemed to find himself when he arrived in Cleveland late last summer. James' offensive capability is well documented, so if he can put his game back together at age twenty-seven, he could enjoy his stay in Ohio.

The James number book is a little inconsistent. The NL's number-five hitter in 1987 (.312), he slipped to .256 in 1988. He seemed to get it back together when he came to Cleveland. In his 71 games in an Indian costume, he hit .306 (shades of 1987) and knocked in 29 runs. The scouting report calls James a good contact hitter with occasional home-run power. Surprisingly, his speed has been downgraded to borderline. (He failed on 4 out of 5 base-stealing attempts with Cleveland.) Still, he can go and get the ball in the outfield, and his arm is rated as adequate. The ball is strictly in Dion's court.

Year	Team	G	AB	R	H	2B	3B	HR	RBI	BB	SB	AVG
1983	Mil.....	11	20	1	2	0	0	0	1	2	1	.100
1984	Mil.....	128	387	52	114	19	5	1	30	32	10	.295
1985	Mil.....	18	49	5	11	1	0	0	3	6	0	.224
1987	Atl.....	134	494	80	154	37	6	10	61	70	10	.312
1988	Atl.....	132	386	46	99	17	5	3	30	58	9	.256
1989	Atl.....	63	170	15	44	7	0	1	11	25	1	.259
1989	Cle.....	71	245	26	75	11	0	4	29	24	1	.306
		557	1751	225	499	92	16	19	165	217	32	.285

Stan Javier

Birth Date: 9/1/65
Bats: Both
Throws: Right
1989 Club:
Oakland Athletics
Contest Code #: 653

Rating: 2

Stan Javier is not the kind of player you build your team around. But his ability to make contact at the plate, run well on the bases and in the field, and play in both left and right fields means he earns his spot on the roster. The son of one-time St. Louis Cardinal infielder Julian Javier, Stan kicked around the Card and Yankee organizations before finally arriving in Oakland in 1986.

As befits the offspring of a major leaguer, Javier is quite comfortable batting in the number-two spot in the lineup. He can bunt, hit-and-run, move the runner, and do all the right things in that key lineup spot. In 112 games for the world champs last year, the Dominican Republic native hit .248, 18 points better than his previous career mark.

Year	Team	G	AB	R	H	2B	3B	HR	RBI	BB	SB	AVG
1984	NYA....	7	7	1	1	0	0	0	0	0	0	.143
1986	Oak....	59	114	13	23	8	0	0	8	16	8	.202
1987	Oak....	81	151	22	28	3	1	2	9	19	3	.185
1988	Oak....	125	397	49	102	13	3	2	35	32	20	.257
1989	Oak....	112	310	42	77	12	3	1	28	31	12	.248
		384	979	127	231	36	7	5	80	98	43	.236

Stanley Jefferson

Birth Date: 12/4/62
Bats: Both
Throws: Left
1989 Club:
Baltimore Orioles
Contest Code #: 654

Rating: 2

Here's another one of those one-time Met farm-system hotshots who simply hasn't made it—and may not. His legs are his strongest asset now. It seems that Stanley Jefferson's major claim to fame is his participation in some of baseball's biggest trades. When the Mets acquired Kevin McReynolds from San Diego, Stan (and Kevin Mitchell) went to the Padres. When the Yankees picked up Jefferson from the Padres, slugger Jack Clark went the other way. Though the Bronx native's 1989 season was his most statistically impressive (.246), it still didn't excite anyone. Time is beginning to run out on the former phenom.

Year	Team	G	AB	R	H	2B	3B	HR	RBI	BB	SB	AVG
1986	NYN ...	14	24	6	5	1	0	1	3	2	0	.208
1987	SD.....	116	422	59	97	8	7	8	29	39	34	.230
1988	SD.....	49	111	16	16	1	2	1	4	9	5	.144
1989	NYA....	10	12	1	1	0	0	0	1	0	1	.083
1989	Bal	35	127	19	33	7	0	4	20	4	9	.260
		224	696	101	152	17	9	14	57	54	49	.218

Lance Johnson

Birth Date: 7/7/63
Bats: Left
Throws: Left
1989 Club:
Chicago White Sox
Contest Code #: 655

Rating: 2

What a difference a year makes! When Lance Johnson was handed the Chicago White Sox's starting center-fielder spot for the 1988 season, he flopped. He hit .190 and lasted just 22 games before being demoted to Vancouver. Recalled in September, he managed to drop a few more points to .185. Given another shot in 1989, a different Johnson showed up. In 50 big-league contests, Johnson banged the ball at a .300 clip, with 10 extra-base blows among his 54 hits. Speed is probably his greatest asset. He swiped 16 bases in 19 attempts, producing a major-league total of 28 for 34. He's a burner.

A whippet-like 5'11", 155-pounder, Johnson will never be a power threat, but if he can turn a single into a triple, à la Rickey Henderson, his value will increase incrementally. The Cincinnati native, who played at Triton Junior College in Illinois with Kirby Puckett, came to the Sox from St. Louis in the Jose DeLeon trade in February 1988.

Year	Team	G	AB	R	H	2B	3B	HR	RBI	BB	SB	AVG
1987	StL	33	59	4	13	2	1	0	7	4	6	.220
1988	ChA....	33	124	11	23	4	1	0	6	6	6	.185
1989	ChA....	50	180	28	54	8	2	0	16	17	16	.300
		116	363	43	90	14	4	0	29	27	28	.248

Roberto Kelly

Birth Date: 10/1/64
Bats: Right
Throws: Right
1989 Club:
New York Yankees
Contest Code #: 656

Rating: 4

They went nuts for Roberto Kelly at Yankee Stadium last year. They knew he could run. They knew he could play defense. But when he hit .302, he became one of the bright spots in an otherwise dismal Yankee season. The Panamanian played like a Panamaniac right from the start of the season. In fact, he was the glue in a Yankee outfield that saw Dave Winfield go down with back surgery, Jesse Barfield and Mel Hall and Luis Polonia arrive, and Rickey Henderson leave for Oakland.

Kelly had mixed success in two previous stints with the Yanks, although injuries led to his limited play in 1988. Among his 133 hits were 18 doubles and 9 homers, along with 48 RBI's. With Henderson gone, the 6'4", 185-pound Kelly joined Steve Sax as a Yankee base-stealing threat. Roberto pilfered 35 sacks in 47 tries.

Year	Team	G	AB	R	H	2B	3B	HR	RBI	BB	SB	AVG
1987	NYA....	23	52	12	14	3	0	1	7	5	9	.269
1988	NYA....	38	77	9	19	4	1	1	7	3	5	.247
1989	NYA....	137	441	65	133	18	3	9	48	41	35	.302
		198	570	86	166	25	4	11	62	49	49	.291

Ron Kittle

Birth Date: 1/5/58
Bats: Right
Throws: Right
1989 Club:
Chicago White Sox
Contest Code #: 657

Rating: 3

When is Ron Kittle going to be healthy enough to play a full major-league season? The thirty-two-year-old, who moved from Cleveland to Chicago for the 1989 season, got into only 51 games for the Chisox. When he was there, he was a constant threat at the plate, hitting .302 with 11 homers in only 169 at-bats, again one of the best homers-per-at-bat mark in the game. Trouble is, the games-played column for Kittle the last three years reads 59, 75, and 51. At least the Indiana native doesn't get hurt playing defense. He's a major liability in the outfield. A healthy Kittle can be an offensive powerhouse.

Year	Team	G	AB	R	H	2B	3B	HR	RBI	BB	SB	AVG
1982	ChA....	20	29	3	7	2	0	1	7	3	0	.241
1983	ChA....	145	520	75	132	19	3	35	100	39	8	.254
1984	ChA....	139	466	67	100	15	0	32	74	49	3	.215
1985	ChA....	116	379	51	87	12	0	26	58	31	1	.230
1986	ChA....	86	296	34	63	11	0	17	48	28	2	.213
1986	NYA....	30	80	8	19	2	0	4	12	7	2	.237
1987	NYA....	59	159	21	44	5	0	12	28	10	0	.277
1988	Cle.....	75	225	31	58	8	0	18	43	16	0	.258
1989	ChA....	51	169	26	51	10	0	11	37	22	0	.302
		721	2323	316	561	84	3	156	407	205	16	.241

Brad Komminsk

Birth Date: 4/4/61
Bats: Right
Throws: Right
1989 Club:
Cleveland Indians
Contest Code #: 658

Rating: 2

Brad Komminsk has never measured up to his pre-career press clippings. Could be that the Cleveland Indians are providing him with his last chance at big-league stardom. It's hard to believe that Komminsk's .237 1989 batting average was a full 20 points better than his career mark. He made better contact than he had in a while, upgrading his contact mark to "fair."

There is, and always has been, occasional home-run power in the Ohio native's bat. He hit 8 homers in 71 games (198 at-bats), after hitting only 12 in 227 previous big-league contests over five previous full or partial seasons. The 6'2", 205-pounder is an excellent defensive center fielder, parlaying an average arm and better than average speed.

Year	Team	G	AB	R	H	2B	3B	HR	RBI	BB	SB	AVG
1983	Atl.....	19	36	2	8	2	0	0	4	5	0	.222
1984	Atl.....	90	301	37	61	10	0	8	36	29	18	.203
1985	Atl.....	106	300	52	68	12	3	4	21	38	10	.227
1986	Atl.....	5	5	1	2	0	0	0	1	0	0	.400
1987	Mil.....	7	15	0	1	0	0	0	0	1	1	.067
1989	Cle.....	71	198	27	47	8	2	8	33	24	8	.237
		298	855	119	187	32	5	20	95	97	37	.219

Rick Leach

Birth Date: 5/4/57
Bats: Left
Throws: Left
1989 Club:
Texas Rangers
Contest Code #: 659

Rating: 1

Insiders report that Rick Leach is a fine guy to have around the clubhouse. Why not? He knows how to deal with pressure. You get the hang of it by starting three straight Rose Bowls as the University of Michigan quarterback. Though he was a fifth-round NFL draft choice (Denver Broncos), Leach, who set most of Michigan's baseball records, has been a baseball man ever since, first with Detroit, later with Toronto, before coming to the Rangers for the 1989 season.

Whether he's at first base (only once last year) or in the outfield, Leach is a competent defensive player. For a thirty-two-year-old, he still runs pretty well and still has the rest of the tools. He's a good left-handed bat to bring off the bench. He hit .272 last season (including 32 games as the Ranger DH), though he really slumped after hitting .351 in the first 30 games. Rick loves playing indoors. At Minnesota and Seattle, he's hitting .403.

Year	Team	G	AB	R	H	2B	3B	HR	RBI	BB	SB	AVG
1981	Det	54	83	9	16	3	1	1	11	16	0	.193
1982	Det	82	218	23	52	7	2	3	12	21	4	.239
1983	Det	99	242	22	60	17	0	3	26	19	2	.248
1984	Tor.....	65	88	11	23	6	2	0	7	8	0	.261
1985	Tor.....	16	35	2	7	0	1	0	1	3	0	.200
1986	Tor.....	110	246	35	76	14	1	5	39	13	0	.309
1987	Tor.....	98	195	26	55	13	1	3	25	25	0	.282
1988	Tor.....	87	199	21	55	13	1	0	23	18	0	.276
1989	Tex	110	239	32	65	14	1	1	23	32	2	.272
		721	1545	181	409	87	10	16	167	155	8	.265

Chet Lemon

Birth Date: 2/12/55
Bats: Right
Throws: Right
1989 Club:
Detroit Tigers
Contest Code #: 660

Rating: 3

Chet Lemon starts his sixteenth straight major-league season with most of his skills fully intact. Throughout the history of sports, almost every athlete named Chet has been nicknamed "The Jet." Lemon is no longer in the supersonic category (if he ever was), though his speed remains sufficient to get the job done in the Tiger Stadium outfield. Once a premier center fielder, he moved to right in 1988 with no loss of effectiveness. His arm remains a weapon.

The 6', 190-pounder has slipped a bit at the plate. He simply doesn't make enough contact, as his .237 average in 1989 indicates. It was his least productive season ever, though he hasn't exactly been killing the ball over the past five years. Chet's power remains below average, though his 7 homers last season marked his first year under double-figures since 1981.

Year	Team	G	AB	R	H	2B	3B	HR	RBI	BB	SB	AVG
1975	ChA....	9	35	2	9	2	0	0	1	2	1	.257
1976	ChA....	132	451	46	111	15	5	4	38	28	13	.246
1977	ChA....	150	553	99	151	38	4	19	67	52	8	.273
1978	ChA....	105	357	51	107	24	6	13	55	39	5	.300
1979	ChA....	148	556	79	177	44	2	17	86	56	7	.318
1980	ChA....	147	514	76	150	32	6	11	51	71	6	.292
1981	ChA....	94	328	50	99	23	6	9	50	33	5	.302
1982	Det	125	436	75	116	20	1	19	52	56	1	.266
1983	Det	145	491	78	125	21	5	24	69	54	0	.255
1984	Det	141	509	77	146	34	6	20	76	51	5	.287
1985	Det	145	517	69	137	28	4	18	68	45	0	.265
1986	Det	126	403	45	101	21	3	12	53	39	2	.251
1987	Det	146	470	75	130	30	3	20	75	70	0	.277
1988	Det	144	512	67	135	29	4	17	64	59	1	.264
1989	Det	127	414	45	98	19	2	7	47	46	1	.237
		1884	6546	934	1792	380	57	210	852	701	55	.274

Jeffrey Leonard

Birth Date: 9/22/55
Bats: Right
Throws: Right
1989 Club:
Seattle Mariners
Contest Code #: 661

Rating: 2

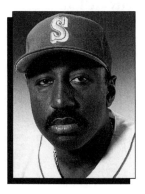

Jeffrey Leonard has this nasty habit of wearing out his welcome very quickly. Yes, he spent six full and two partial seasons with the San Francisco Giants, but it was one season and out with Milwaukee. Who knows how long it will last in Seattle? Old number 00 never hesitates to open his mouth. He offends people who've never even met him. Everyone seems to be his enemy. The Philadelphia native is a classic baseball head case, a problem child who tends to be a disruptive influence in any locker room where he hangs his doubleknits.

Perhaps the only reason he's still around is his bat. He can really swing and makes fairly good contact. He can sting the ball and sometimes hits it a long way. In 150 games last year, he had 24 homers (tops in Seattle) and knocked in 93 runs. Not bad. Though a good change-up can drive him nuts, he's still a valuable bat in the lineup. Defense? Forget it. The Mouth Man is a horrible outfielder.

Year	Team	G	AB	R	H	2B	3B	HR	RBI	BB	SB	AVG
1977	LA	11	10	1	3	0	1	0	2	1	0	.300
1978	Hou	8	26	2	10	2	0	0	4	1	0	.385
1979	Hou	134	411	47	119	15	5	0	47	46	23	.290
1980	Hou	88	216	29	46	7	5	3	20	19	4	.213
1981	Hou	7	18	1	3	1	1	0	3	0	1	.167
1981	SF	37	127	20	39	11	3	4	26	12	4	.307
1982	SF	80	278	32	72	16	1	9	49	19	18	.259
1983	SF	139	516	74	144	17	7	21	87	35	26	.279
1984	SF	136	514	76	155	27	2	21	86	47	17	.302
1985	SF	133	507	49	122	20	3	17	62	21	11	.241
1986	SF	89	341	48	95	11	3	6	42	20	16	.279
1987	SF	131	503	70	141	29	4	19	63	21	16	.280
1988	Mil	94	374	45	88	19	0	8	44	16	10	.235
1988	SF	44	160	12	41	8	1	2	20	9	7	.256
1989	Sea	150	566	69	144	20	1	24	93	38	6	.254
		1281	4567	575	1222	203	37	134	648	305	159	.268

Fred Lynn

Birth Date: 2/3/52
Bats: Left
Throws: Left
1989 Club:
Detroit Tigers
Contest Code #: 662

Rating: 2

The off-season line on Fred Lynn reads as it has in so many previous years: "recuperating from injuries." Long one of basball's premier offensive and defensive outfielders, Lynn has seen his game sink precipitously; the Chicago-area native must know that his major-league days are numbered. The 6'1", 190-pounder's decline can best be measured on defense. He doesn't run as well as in the past, his throwing arm has deteriorated, and he doesn't make the plays he once did—though he's still savvy enough to get to some balls you wouldn't expect him to get to.

Once an outstanding contact hitter, Lynn's batting average slipped to .241 last season—far below his .287 career mark. These days he's a streaky hitter, though he occasionally can hit the long ball (11 homers last year, second on the club to Lou Whitaker).

Year	Team	G	AB	R	H	2B	3B	HR	RBI	BB	SB	AVG
1974	Bos	15	43	5	18	2	2	2	10	6	0	.419
1975	Bos	145	528	103	175	47	7	21	105	62	10	.331
1976	Bos	132	507	76	159	32	8	10	65	48	14	.314
1977	Bos	129	497	81	129	29	5	18	76	51	2	.260
1978	Bos	150	541	75	161	33	3	22	82	75	3	.298
1979	Bos	147	531	116	177	42	1	39	122	82	2	.333
1980	Bos	110	415	67	125	32	3	12	61	58	12	.301
1981	Cal	76	256	28	56	8	1	5	31	38	1	.219

Year	Team	G	AB	R	H	2B	3B	HR	RBI	BB	SB	AVG
1982	Cal.....	138	472	89	141	38	1	21	86	58	7	.299
1983	Cal.....	117	437	56	119	20	3	22	74	55	2	.272
1984	Cal.....	142	517	84	140	28	4	23	79	77	2	.271
1985	Bal	124	448	59	118	12	1	23	68	53	7	.263
1986	Bal	112	397	67	114	13	1	23	67	53	2	.287
1987	Bal	111	396	49	100	24	0	23	60	39	3	.253
1988	Bal	87	301	37	76	13	1	18	37	28	2	.252
1988	Det	27	90	9	20	1	0	7	19	5	0	.222
1989	Det	117	353	44	85	11	1	11	46	47	1	.241
		1879	6729	1045	1913	385	42	300	1088	835	70	.284

Lee Mazzilli

Birth Date: 3/25/55
Bats: Both
Throws: Right
1989 Club:
New York Mets &
Toronto Blue Jays
Contest Code #: 663

Rating: 2

Anybody need a premier pinch hitter? The last word out of Toronto was that Lee Mazzilli was available. The swarthy Brooklyn native was the darling of fans of the hapless Mets of the late 1970s. Dealt to Texas for Ron Darling, Mazz has spent his declining years as a premier pinch hitter for the Mets and, beginning last July, the pennant-chasing Blue Jays.

Mazzilli can still play a little first base and outfield and probably has a couple of more years left in his game. Mazz hit .227 (including 4 homers) in 28 games for the Jays in his brief Canadian stay last year. His value doesn't lie strictly in numbers like that. Managers like his confidence, leadership, and versatility. (In high school, he was even a switch-thrower.)

Year	Team	G	AB	R	H	2B	3B	HR	RBI	BB	SB	AVG
1976	NYN ...	24	77	9	15	2	0	2	7	14	5	.195
1977	NYN ...	159	537	66	134	24	3	6	46	72	22	.250
1978	NYN ...	148	542	78	148	28	5	16	61	69	20	.273
1979	NYN ...	158	597	78	181	34	4	15	79	93	34	.303
1980	NYN ...	152	578	82	162	31	4	16	76	82	41	.280
1981	NYN ...	95	324	36	74	14	5	6	34	46	17	.228
1982	Tex	58	195	23	47	8	0	4	17	28	11	.241
1982	NYA....	37	128	20	34	2	0	6	17	15	2	.266
1983	Pit.....	109	246	37	59	9	0	5	24	49	15	.240
1984	Pit.....	111	266	37	63	11	1	4	21	40	8	.237
1985	Pit.....	92	117	20	33	8	0	1	9	29	4	.282
1986	Pit.....	61	93	18	21	2	1	1	8	26	3	.226
1986	NYN ...	39	58	10	16	3	0	2	7	12	1	.276
1987	NYN ...	88	124	26	38	8	1	3	24	21	5	.306
1988	NYN ...	68	116	9	17	2	0	0	12	12	4	.147
1989	NYN ...	48	60	10	11	2	0	2	7	17	3	.183
1989	Tor.....	28	66	12	15	3	0	4	11	17	2	.227
		1475	4124	571	1068	191	24	93	460	642	197	.259

Keith Moreland

Birth Date: 5/2/64
Bats: Right
Throws: Right
1989 Club:
Detroit Tigers &
Baltimore Orioles
Contest Code #: 664

Rating: 1

Once a premier major-league hitter, Keith Moreland will probably be best advised to check out the senior league in Florida. His best big-league days seem to be behind him. The Texas native's career has had its memorable moments. As a collegian, he was an All-American third baseman as he led the Texas Longhorns to an NCAA College World Series title.

A slugger of note, the 6'0", 200-pounder was always a run producer, reaching the 106 RBI mark (while hitting .307) for the 1985 Chicago Cubs. Defense has never been

his strong suit, but his bat always found him a spot in the lineup. His versatility also contributed to his success, as a catcher, first and third baseman, and an outfielder. Moreland hit .278 in 123 games with Detroit and Baltimore last year, but with only 6 homers and 45 RBI's.

Year	Team	G	AB	R	H	2B	3B	HR	RBI	BB	SB	AVG
1978	Phi	1	2	0	0	0	0	0	0	0	0	.000
1979	Phi	14	48	3	18	3	2	0	8	3	0	.375
1980	Phi	62	159	13	50	8	0	4	29	8	3	.314
1981	Phi	61	196	16	50	7	0	6	37	15	1	.255
1982	ChN....	138	476	50	124	17	2	15	68	46	0	.261
1983	ChN....	154	533	76	161	30	3	16	70	68	0	.302
1984	ChN....	140	495	59	138	17	3	16	80	34	1	.279
1985	ChN....	161	587	74	180	30	3	14	106	68	12	.307
1986	ChN....	156	586	72	159	30	0	12	79	53	3	.271
1987	ChN....	153	563	63	150	29	1	27	88	39	3	.266
1988	SD	143	511	40	131	23	0	5	64	40	2	.256
1989	Det	90	318	34	95	16	0	5	35	27	3	.299
1989	Bal	33	107	11	23	4	0	1	10	4	0	.215
		1306	4581	511	1279	214	14	121	674	405	28	.279

Lloyd Moseby

Birth Date: 11/5/59
Bats: Left
Throws: Right
1989 Club:
Toronto Blue Jays
Contest Code #: 665

Rating: 4

The Toronto Blue Jays' career leader in just about every offensive category except home runs, Lloyd Moseby seems to be on an irreversible slide. His .221 batting average last season marked one more downward step since he hit .315 in 1983 and was 40 points under his career mark. Left-handed pitching is especially bothersome to the thirty-year-old, who first came to Toronto early in the 1980 season.

These days, even his defense is suspect. Though his arm remains strong, he occasionally doesn't know where the ball is going. On the plus side, Moseby retains occasional home-run power at the plate and his speed is good enough to enable him to steal 24 bases last season, his ninth straight year in double figures. Detroit, which signed him during the off-season, evidently hopes Moseby still has some production left in him.

Year	Team	G	AB	R	H	2B	3B	HR	RBI	BB	SB	AVG
1980	Tor.....	114	389	44	89	24	1	9	46	25	4	.229
1981	Tor.....	100	378	36	88	16	2	9	43	24	11	.233
1982	Tor.....	147	487	51	115	20	9	9	52	33	11	.236
1983	Tor.....	151	539	104	170	31	7	18	81	51	27	.315
1984	Tor.....	158	592	97	166	28	15	18	92	78	39	.280
1985	Tor.....	152	584	92	151	30	7	18	70	76	37	.259
1986	Tor.....	152	589	89	149	24	5	21	86	64	32	.253
1987	Tor.....	155	592	106	167	27	4	26	96	70	39	.282
1988	Tor.....	128	472	77	113	17	7	10	42	70	31	.239
1989	Tor.....	135	502	72	111	25	3	11	43	56	24	.221
		1392	5124	768	1319	242	60	149	651	547	255	.257

John Moses

Birth Date: 8/9/57
Bats: Both
Throws: Left
1989 Club:
Minnesota Twins
Contest Code #: 666

Rating: 3

Quietly, John Moses has cut out a role for himself in the Minnesota Twins' outfield. Moses' outlook wasn't brilliant when the Seattle Mariners released him following the 1987 season. Signed by Cleveland in January 1988, he didn't make it through spring training. The Twins then decided to give him a shot (his last?) and after 17 games at AAA Portland, they brought him to Minnesota. Success, at last.

After hitting .316 in 105 Minny games in 1988, Moses came back with an equally impressive .281 combined with excellent defensive work. It's unlikely that Moses will ever be an everyday starter, but as a role player, he can contribute. Moses' versatility is a key to his future plans. He can play any outfield spot and can fill in admirably at first base. His fundamentals are sound; he can run, he can bunt. Best of all, he's a good man to have around the club.

Year	Team	G	AB	R	H	2B	3B	HR	RBI	BB	SB	AVG
1982	Sea	22	44	7	14	5	1	1	3	4	5	.318
1983	Sea	93	130	19	27	4	1	0	6	12	11	.208
1984	Sea	19	35	3	12	1	1	0	2	2	1	.343
1985	Sea	33	62	4	12	0	0	0	3	2	5	.194
1986	Sea	103	399	56	102	16	3	3	34	34	25	.256
1987	Sea	116	390	58	96	16	4	3	38	29	23	.246
1988	Min	105	206	33	65	10	3	2	12	15	11	.316
1989	Min	129	242	33	68	12	3	1	31	19	14	.281
		620	1508	213	396	64	16	10	129	117	95	.263

Joe Orsulak

Birth Date: 5/31/62
Bats: Left
Throws: Left
1989 Club:
Baltimore Orioles
Contest Code #: 667

Rating: 3

In the two seasons since ex-Pirate Joe Orsulak arrived in Baltimore, he has proven what everyone already knew: The man can hit. He's no threat to Kirby Puckett or Wade Boggs. But when he's healthy, he always seems to flirt with .300 (.285 last season). No, he doesn't hit with a lot of power (though he has shown more than he did in Pittsburgh) and he isn't the world's prettiest outfielder. But he makes contact—and that's what the weak-hitting Orioles need.

He hasn't been particularly productive throughout his career, hitting far better with the bases empty than with runners in scoring position. Still, he set a career-high with 34 extra-base hits (22 doubles, 5 triples, 7 homers) in 1989. He has lost a step or so after stealing 24 bases each in 1985 and 1986. But he'll get the job done with his bat.

Year	Team	G	AB	R	H	2B	3B	HR	RBI	BB	SB	AVG
1983	Pit	7	11	0	2	0	0	0	1	0	0	.182
1984	Pit	32	67	12	17	1	2	0	3	1	3	.254
1985	Pit	121	397	54	119	14	6	0	21	26	24	.300
1986	Pit	138	401	60	100	19	6	2	19	28	24	.249
1988	Bal	125	379	48	109	21	3	8	27	23	9	.288
1989	Bal	123	390	59	111	22	5	7	55	41	5	.285
		546	1645	233	458	77	22	17	126	119	65	.278

Dave Parker

Birth Date: 6/9/51
Bats: Left
Throws: Right
1989 Club:
Oakland Athletics
Contest Code #: 668

Rating: 3

The Cobra can still strike. That's the word on Dave Parker, who remains a long-ball terror at the plate even at age thirty-nine in June.

The 16½-year veteran who rocked National League pitching for Pittsburgh and Cincinnati until 1988 and who signed with Milwaukee during the off-season has been a premier hitter for as long as anyone can remember. He doesn't hit for a high average anymore (.295 career before last year's .264), but he looks so imposing at the plate that he scares enemy pitchers. At 6'5" and 230 pounds, Parker owes his current existence to the AL's designated-hitter rule. He simply can't play defense anymore. But when he strides to the plate swinging a bat that looks like a toy next to his huge body, he adds quite a punch to a team's lineup. His 22 homers last season marked a superb comeback from the 12 he hit in his AL debut.

Year	Team	G	AB	R	H	2B	3B	HR	RBI	BB	SB	AVG
1973	Pit.....	54	139	17	40	9	1	4	14	2	1	.288
1974	Pit.....	73	220	27	62	10	3	4	29	10	3	.282
1975	Pit.....	148	558	75	172	35	10	25	101	38	8	.308
1976	Pit.....	138	537	82	168	28	10	13	90	30	19	.313
1977	Pit.....	159	637	107	215	44	8	21	88	58	17	.338
1978	Pit.....	148	581	102	194	32	12	30	117	57	20	.334
1979	Pit.....	158	622	109	193	45	7	25	94	67	20	.310
1980	Pit.....	139	518	71	153	31	1	17	79	25	10	.295
1981	Pit.....	67	240	29	62	14	3	9	48	9	6	.258
1982	Pit.....	73	244	41	66	19	3	6	29	22	7	.270
1983	Pit.....	144	552	68	154	29	4	12	69	28	12	.279
1984	Cin	156	607	73	173	28	0	16	94	41	11	.285
1985	Cin	160	635	88	198	42	4	34	125	52	5	.312
1986	Cin	162	637	89	174	31	3	31	116	56	1	.273
1987	Cin	153	589	77	149	28	0	26	97	44	7	.253
1988	Oak	101	377	43	97	18	1	12	55	32	0	.257
1989	Oak	144	553	56	146	27	0	22	97	38	0	.264
		2177	8246	1154	2416	470	70	307	1342	609	147	.293

Gary Pettis

Birth Date: 4/3/58
Bats: Both
Throws: Right
1989 Club:
Detroit Tigers
Contest Code #: 669

Rating: 3

Thanks to a superb glove and quick legs, Gary Pettis remains one of the most exciting players in baseball. A perennial Gold Glove winner, Pettis gets to everything hit anywhere in his neighborhood. Even at age thirty-one, he hasn't lost a step, which also makes him a major threat on the base paths, where he stole 43 bases in 1989.

Unfortunately, Pettis is a weak hitter. Too often, he fails to make contact—a major shortcoming for a speed-type player. His .257 average was 19 points better than his career mark. But in his best full season (1986), he only hit .258. Combined with a total lack of power (17 homers in eight seasons), Pettis' value on offense is limited to his ability to get on base and steal.

A number-six draft selection by the California Angels in 1979, Pettis hit the big time full-time with the Angels in 1984. He came to Detroit for pitcher Dan Petry in December 1987, and will play for Texas in 1990.

Year	Team	G	AB	R	H	2B	3B	HR	RBI	BB	SB	AVG
1982	Cal.....	10	5	5	1	0	0	1	1	0	0	.200
1983	Cal.....	22	85	19	25	2	3	3	6	7	8	.294
1984	Cal.....	140	397	63	90	11	6	2	29	60	48	.227
1985	Cal.....	125	443	67	114	10	8	1	32	62	56	.257

Year	Team	G	AB	R	H	2B	3B	HR	RBI	BB	SB	AVG
1986	Cal.....	154	539	93	139	23	4	5	58	69	50	.258
1987	Cal.....	133	394	49	82	13	2	1	17	52	24	.208
1988	Det	129	458	65	96	14	4	3	36	47	44	.210
1989	Det	119	444	77	114	8	6	1	18	84	43	.257
		832	2765	438	661	81	33	17	197	381	273	.239

Luis Polonia

Birth Date: 10/12/64
Bats: Left
Throws: Left
1989 Club:
Oakland Athletics &
New York Yankees
Contest Code #: 670

Rating: 2

How far can you fall? For Luis Polonia, all the way. He started last season with the eventual world champion Oakland Athletics. He finished it with the mediocre New York Yankees. Then he spent part of his off-season in a Wisconsin jail, where the stripes are a little thicker than pinstripes.

Courtroom activities aside, Polonia isn't a bad offensive player. His skills are perfectly suited to a lead-off role. He makes good contact and runs well. The Dominican native has always hit, and last season was no exception. His combined Oakland–New York totals included a .300 average with 130 hits (17 doubles, 6 triples, 3 homers). Defense is another story. Rumor was that he was improving. Don't believe all the rumors you hear. If the little guy (5'8", 155 pounds) can get his act—and his defense—together, he can make a contribution to any team.

Year	Team	G	AB	R	H	2B	3B	HR	RBI	BB	SB	AVG
1987	Oak	125	435	78	125	16	10	4	49	32	29	.287
1988	Oak	84	288	51	84	11	4	2	27	21	24	.292
1989	Oak	59	206	31	59	6	4	1	17	9	13	.286
1989	NYA....	66	227	39	71	11	2	2	29	16	9	.313
		334	1156	199	339	44	20	9	122	78	75	.293

Kirby Puckett

Birth Date: 3/14/61
Bats: Right
Throws: Right
1989 Club:
Minnesota Twins
Contest Code #: 671

Rating: 5

Is there anything that Kirby Puckett can't do? If there is, no one in the American League has figured it out yet. The Minnesota Twins' fireplug—and baseball's first $3-million-per-year-man—hasn't got a weakness, offensively or defensively. Would that the Twins had a supporting cast to go with Puckett. He deserves it.

Though Kirby's BA slipped from .356 to .339 last season, it was good enough to win his first AL batting title, the first won by a right-handed hitter since 1981. He's in there, working hard, every day. The 5'8", 210-pounder has averaged more than 657 at-bats for each of the last five years. Though his RBI total fell from 121 to 85 in 1989, much of the blame goes to his teammates, who simply weren't aboard when Kirby came to the plate.

He's just as good on defense. How he propels his chunky body high enough to bring enemy homers back from over the fence defies all laws of physics. His glove takes away a variety of shorter base hits as well. The little guy hits, hits with power, runs, fields, and throws well. As they say in the cartoons, "That's all, folks!"

Year	Team	G	AB	R	H	2B	3B	HR	RBI	BB	SB	AVG
1984	Min	128	557	63	165	12	5	0	31	16	14	.296
1985	Min	161	691	80	199	29	13	4	74	41	21	.288

Year	Team	G	AB	R	H	2B	3B	HR	RBI	BB	SB	AVG
1986	Min	161	680	119	223	37	6	31	96	34	20	.328
1987	Min	157	624	96	207	32	5	28	99	32	12	.332
1988	Min	158	657	109	234	42	5	24	121	23	6	.356
1989	Min	159	635	75	215	45	4	9	85	41	11	.339
		924	3844	542	1243	197	38	96	506	187	84	.323

Carlos Quintana

Birth Date: 8/26/65
Bats: Right
Throws: Right
1989 Club:
Boston Red Sox
Contest Code #: 672

Rating: 3

Talk about auspicious debuts. In Carlos Quintana's first major-league plate appearance, he pinch-hit for Boston all-timer Jim Rice and walked with the bases loaded to drive in a run against the Yankees. The native Venezuelan had a close encounter with the famous Mendoza Line in his second shot at the big leagues in 1989. In 34 games (77 at-bats), the 6'2", 195-pounder hit only .208 (with 5 doubles among his 16 hits).

Boston is optimistic that the twenty-four-year-old will be able to hit in the majors as he did in the minors (.325 at Greensboro in 1986, .311 at New Britain in 1987, and .285 at Pawtucket in 1988). Unfortunately, he has struck out a little more than once in every 6 at-bats in his brief Boston visits.

Year	Team	G	AB	R	H	2B	3B	HR	RBI	BB	SB	AVG
1988	Bos	5	6	1	2	0	0	0	2	2	0	.333
1989	Bos	34	77	6	16	5	0	0	6	7	0	.208
		39	83	7	18	5	0	0	8	9	0	.217

Kevin Andrew Romine

Birth Date: 5/23/61
Bats: Right
Throws: Right
1989 Club:
Boston Red Sox
Contest Code #: 673

Rating: 3

Though Kevin Romine hit .274 in 1989, 50 points better than his previous career mark, the jury is still out on his bat. It's a positive sign that Ro got into 92 games in Boston last season. Four previous trials resulted in only 125 games and 165 at-bats. The problem is that Romine will turn twenty-nine this May, and it's getting to be a question of now or never.

The scouts have mixed reviews. They like his speed and report that his arm is decent. That's a plus. To establish a big-league career, however, he'll need to add power to the mix. And with only 2 homers and 21 doubles in 217 major-league games, it doesn't seem to be there. Right now, the best that Romine can hope for is a spot as a number-four or -five outfielder on a big-league club and wait for a long-range chance.

Year	Team	G	AB	R	H	2B	3B	HR	RBI	BB	SB	AVG
1985	Bos	24	28	3	6	2	0	0	1	1	1	.214
1986	Bos	35	35	6	9	2	0	0	2	3	2	.257
1987	Bos	9	24	5	7	2	0	0	2	2	0	.292
1988	Bos	57	78	17	15	2	1	1	6	7	2	.192
1989	Bos	92	274	30	75	13	0	1	23	21	1	.274
		217	439	61	112	21	1	2	34	34	6	.255

Larry Sheets

Birth Date: 12/6/59
Bats: Left
Throws: Right
1989 Club:
Baltimore Orioles
Contest Code #: 674

Rating: 3

Here's a career that's beginning to fade. After five full seasons with Baltimore, including an All-Star-like year in 1988, Larry Sheets looks as if he's going backward. His play in the outfield is shoddy, which means that he probably won't be an everyday player very often. More likely, he's headed for a designated-hitter slot. But the Birds have better candidates. The strong 6'3", 215-pounder can still pound the ball. But he had only 7 homers and drove in 33 runs in 304 at-bats last season and that's not good enough.

It's hard to believe that only a couple of seasons earlier Larry stroked 31 homers and knocked in 94 runs. He has trouble with left-handed pitching, and that won't help win him a spot in the lineup. Chances are manager Frank Robinson will look to Sheets as his power pinch hitter against righties.

Year	Team	G	AB	R	H	2B	3B	HR	RBI	BB	SB	AVG
1984	Bal	8	16	3	7	1	0	1	2	1	0	.438
1985	Bal	113	328	43	86	8	0	17	50	28	0	.262
1986	Bal	112	338	42	92	17	1	18	60	21	2	.272
1987	Bal	135	469	74	148	23	0	31	94	31	1	.316
1988	Bal	136	452	38	104	19	1	10	47	42	1	.230
1989	Bal	102	304	33	74	12	1	7	33	26	1	.243
		606	1907	233	511	80	3	84	286	149	5	.268

Ruben Sierra

Birth Date: 10/6/65
Bats: Both
Throws: Right
1989 Club:
Texas Rangers
Contest Code #: 675

Rating: 5

If you could bottle a season for future use, Ruben Sierra would put a vacuum cap on his 1989. It wasn't just that the lifetime .260 hitter hit .306, though that in itself was an achievement. The Puerto Rico–born outfielder led the majors in triples (14) and topped the AL with 119 RBI's, 344 total bases, a .543 slugging percentage, and 78 extra-base hits. His other stats, including 101 runs scored, 194 hits, 29 homers, 53 multi-hit games, and 162 games played put him right up among the league leaders. The kind of season you want to save? You bet.

At least one organization named Sierra the AL's Most Valuable Player. The book on Sierra calls him one of the top front-line players in the game. The 6'1", 175-pounder has it all—good hitter, good power, good speed, good arm. At age twenty-four, he's still just an average outfielder, but he's improving there, too.

Year	Team	G	AB	R	H	2B	3B	HR	RBI	BB	SB	AVG
1986	Tex	113	382	50	101	13	10	16	55	22	7	.264
1987	Tex	158	643	97	169	35	4	30	109	39	16	.263
1988	Tex	156	615	77	156	32	2	23	91	44	18	.254
1989	Tex	162	634	101	194	35	14	29	119	43	8	.306
		589	2274	325	620	115	30	98	374	148	49	.273

Cory Snyder

Birth Date: 11/11/62
Bats: Right
Throws: Right
1989 Club:
Cleveland Indians
Contest Code #: 676

Rating: 4

Just when it looked as though former U.S. Olympic baseball ace Cory Snyder was about to blossom into a bona fide major-league superstar, he slipped back in 1989, resurrecting old doubts. It was a tremendous disappointment. There's no doubt about Cory's power. Although he hit only 18 homers last year, his previous totals of 24, 33, and 26 give evidence of his ability to jerk the ball out of the park. But after hitting .272 in 1988, there were big hopes for 1989. They never materialized. He hit only .215, easily the worst year of his career, and he struck out 134 times, again well over his average. His ability to make contact with the ball was poor.

Defense is another story. The 6'3", 185-pounder has a gun attached to his right shoulder—perhaps the best outfield throwing arm in baseball. Just as important, he gets the ball off quickly and almost always hits the target. The Tribe seems willing to wait for him.

Year	Team	G	AB	R	H	2B	3B	HR	RBI	BB	SB	AVG
1986	Cle.....	103	416	58	113	21	1	24	69	16	2	.272
1987	Cle.....	157	577	74	136	24	2	33	82	31	5	.236
1988	Cle.....	142	511	71	139	24	3	26	75	42	5	.272
1989	Cle.....	132	489	49	105	17	0	18	59	23	6	.215
		534	1993	252	493	86	6	101	285	112	18	.247

Sammy Sosa

Birth Date: 11/10/68
Bats: Right
Throws: Right
1989 Club:
Texas Rangers &
Chicago White Sox
Contest Code #: 677

Rating: 1

Sammy Sosa must have developed his super speed racing for meals at home. The native of that baseball hotbed, San Pedro de Macoris in the Dominican Republic, grew up as one of eleven Sosa children. That's plenty of motivation. Like so many Dominicans, the 6', 165-pound Sosa signed his first pro contract at age seventeen and got to the big leagues at age twenty, making the jump from Class A.

His 12 triples at Port Charlotte in 1988 placed him second in all of organized baseball and caught the scouts' eyes. So did his 42 stolen bases, though he was also caught stealing 24 times. A model of consistency, Sosa hit .258 in three minor-league seasons, then hit .257 in his first 58 major-league contests (and nary a triple in the lot!). Dealt from the Rangers to the White Sox in mid-summer, Sammy poked 4 homers, but remained inconsistent on the bases, stealing 7 sacks but being caught 5 times. Sosa is a project, but some of the key ingredients are there.

Year	Team	G	AB	R	H	2B	3B	HR	RBI	BB	SB	AVG
1989	Tex	25	84	8	20	3	0	1	3	0	0	.238
1989	ChA....	33	99	19	27	5	0	3	10	11	7	.273
		58	183	27	47	8	0	4	13	11	7	.257

Pat Tabler

Birth Date: 2/2/58
Bats: Right
Throws: Right
1989 Club:
Kansas City Royals
Contest Code #: 678

Rating: 2

As long as Pat Tabler can hit, he'll find a spot on a major-league roster. A lifetime .291 hitter, Tabler slipped to .259 in 1989, his worst full season in the bigs. Still, his bat remains his number-one asset. Defensively, he just can't do it on a regular basis anymore. He'll be limited to spot fill-in duty at first base or in the outfield.

Tabler has earned a healthy respect from AL rivals with his clutch hitting over the years. With men on base, he has few equals. From 1982 to 1988, his average with the bases loaded was a lofty .579. Nobody does it better. The Cincinnati native was a top three-sport high-school athlete before signing with the Yankees in 1976. He eventually arrived in the majors in two brief stints with the Cubs. His first full-time assignment came with the 1985 Indians, where he enjoyed two .300-plus seasons (.326 in 1986 and .307 in 1987) before the trade to Kaycee in 1988.

Year	Team	G	AB	R	H	2B	3B	HR	RBI	BB	SB	AVG
1981	ChN....	35	101	11	19	3	1	1	5	13	0	.188
1982	ChN....	25	85	9	20	4	2	1	7	6	0	.235
1983	Cle.....	124	430	56	125	23	5	6	65	56	2	.291
1984	Cle.....	144	473	66	137	21	3	10	68	47	3	.290
1985	Cle.....	117	404	47	111	18	3	5	59	27	0	.275
1986	Cle.....	130	473	61	154	29	2	6	48	29	3	.326
1987	Cle.....	151	553	66	170	34	3	11	86	51	5	.307
1988	Cle.....	41	143	16	32	5	1	1	17	23	1	.224
1988	KC....	89	301	37	93	17	2	1	49	23	2	.309
1989	KC.....	123	390	36	101	11	1	2	42	37	0	.259
		979	3353	405	962	165	23	44	446	312	16	.287

Danny Tartabull

Birth Date: 10/30/62
Bats: Right
Throws: Right
1989 Club:
Kansas City Royals
Contest Code #: 679

Rating: 4

Like father, like son? Well, not exactly. In nine major-league seasons, Jose Tartabull swatted exactly two home runs. His "little" boy, the 6'1", 205-pound Danny has stroked 106 in a shade more than four years. The differences don't end there. Jose was practically a model citizen throughout his career. Danny, on the other hand, is carrying an "attitude problem" label which he brought from Seattle to Kansas City three seasons ago.

About the only tool missing from Tartabull's arsenal is speed. The lack thereof probably prevents him from becoming an outstanding defensive player. Other than that, he can do it all. He hits (.268 in 1989, with a .309 season in 1987), hits with power, and throws very well. Though he slipped to 62 RBI's last season, he knocked in 101 and 102 runs for Kaycee in 1987 and 1988. Danny has what it takes to have a superior career—if he has his head on straight.

Year	Team	G	AB	R	H	2B	3B	HR	RBI	BB	SB	AVG
1984	Sea	10	20	3	6	1	0	2	7	2	0	.300
1985	Sea	19	61	8	20	7	1	1	7	8	1	.328
1986	Sea	137	511	76	138	25	6	25	96	61	4	.270
1987	KC.....	158	582	95	180	27	3	34	101	79	9	.309
1988	KC.....	146	507	80	139	38	3	26	102	76	8	.274
1989	KC.....	133	441	54	118	22	0	18	62	69	4	.268
		603	2122	316	601	120	13	106	375	295	26	.283

Gary Thurman

Birth Date: 11/12/64
Bats: Right
Throws: Right
1989 Club:
Kansas City Royals
Contest Code #: 680

Rating: 2

Gary Thurman's troubles hitting major-league pitching continue. The Indianapolis native, who turned down a scholarship at the U. of Miami to turn pro in 1983, always hit on the farm (.302 at Ft. Myers in 1985, .312 at Memphis in 1986), but in trials the last two seasons at Kansas City, even .200 has been out of reach.

The Royals would love nothing better than getting the 5'10", 175-pounder into the lineup—just for his speed. He stole 70 bases in 134 games at Ft. Myer and 58 in 115 games at Omaha, both league-leading figures. But you can't steal first, and until Thurman learns how to do that, speed will not become a factor.

Year	Team	G	AB	R	H	2B	3B	HR	RBI	BB	SB	AVG
1987	KC.....	27	81	12	24	2	0	0	5	8	7	.296
1988	KC.....	35	66	6	11	1	0	0	2	4	5	.167
1989	KC.....	71	87	24	17	2	1	0	5	15	16	.195
		133	234	42	52	5	1	0	12	27	28	.222

Greg Vaughn

Birth Date: 7/3/65
Bats: Right
Throws: Right
1989 Club:
Milwaukee Brewers
Contest Code #: 681

Rating: 2

For a guy with only 38 games of big-league experience, Greg Vaughn got a lot of attention in Milwaukee during the off-season. The twenty-four-year-old got a shot with the big club when Rob Deer went down with a sore knee last August. Vaughn came through pretty well.

Scouts are impressed with the native Californian's power. He belted 28 homers (105 RBI's) at El Paso in 1988 and 26 homers (92 RBI's) in 110 games with Denver in 1989 before the call to Milwaukee. With the Brew Crew, he had five homers and 23 RBI's in only 38 games, including a 2-homer game against the A's (and pitchers Dave Stewart and Dennis Eckersley). Not too shabby. Though Vaughn isn't nearly as wonderful on defense, the Brewers don't figure to use him as a DH at his tender age.

Year	Team	G	AB	R	H	2B	3B	HR	RBI	BB	SB	AVG
1989	Mil.....	38	113	18	30	3	0	5	23	13	4	.265
		38	113	18	30	3	0	5	23	13	4	.265

Gary Ward

Birth Date: 12/6/53
Bats: Right
Throws: Right
1989 Club:
New York Yankees &
Detroit Tigers
Contest Code #: 682

Rating: 3

You don't hang around the majors for nine years or so without doing something right. And if nothing else, Gary Ward can hit a baseball. That's why the Detroit Tigers picked him up last April (8 games, .294 BA) when Yankee boss Steinbrenner banished the thirty-six-year-old from the Bronx. The Tigers were pleased with Ward's versatility and power. He played in all three outfield spots, put in a little time at first base, DH'ed in 15 games, and pinch-hit on the other days. Though his numbers were borderline ordinary, let's face it: A fill-in type who can hit .253 with 30 RBI's in 113 games is a handy guy to have around.

Year	Team	G	AB	R	H	2B	3B	HR	RBI	BB	SB	AVG
1979	Min	10	14	2	4	0	0	0	1	3	0	.286
1980	Min	13	41	11	19	6	2	1	10	3	0	.463
1981	Min	85	295	42	78	7	6	3	29	28	5	.264
1982	Min	152	570	85	165	33	7	28	91	37	13	.289
1983	Min	157	623	76	173	34	5	19	88	44	8	.278
1984	Tex	155	602	97	171	21	7	21	79	55	7	.284
1985	Tex	154	593	77	170	28	7	15	70	39	26	.287
1986	Tex	105	380	54	120	15	2	5	51	31	12	.316
1987	NYA....	146	529	65	131	22	1	16	78	33	9	.248
1988	NYA....	91	231	26	52	8	0	4	24	24	0	.225
1989	NYA....	8	17	3	5	1	0	0	1	3	0	.294
1989	Det	105	275	24	69	10	2	9	29	21	1	.251
		1181	4170	562	1157	185	39	121	551	321	81	.277

Claudell Washington

Birth Date: 8/31/54
Bats: Left
Throws: Left
1989 Club:
California Angels
Contest Code #: 683

Rating: 4

As the Yankees cranked along toward the bottom of the AL East last summer, the word went out in the Bronx: "We should never have let Claudell Washington go." That's high praise for a well-traveled thirty-five-year-old outfielder who has already worn the double-knits of seven big-league clubs. And why not? A wild man in his early days, the California native has settled down and is a positive influence on any ball club that pays his salary.

Last season was fairly typical for Washington. A career .280 hitter, he swatted the ball at a .273 clip, with 13 homers, 13 steals, and 42 RBI's. He can still play all three outfield positions and play them well. He has a quick bat, can run, can steal—all traits of a solid baseball citizen. Even at an age when he should be backsliding, Washington retains all the tools that have produced a good, if not memorable, career.

Year	Team	G	AB	R	H	2B	3B	HR	RBI	BB	SB	AVG
1974	Oak	73	221	16	63	10	5	0	19	13	6	.285
1975	Oak	148	590	86	182	24	7	10	77	32	40	.308
1976	Oak	134	490	65	126	20	6	5	53	30	37	.257
1977	Tex	129	521	63	148	31	2	12	68	25	21	.284
1978	ChA	86	314	33	83	16	5	6	31	12	5	.264
1978	Tex	12	42	1	7	0	0	0	2	1	0	.167
1979	ChA	131	471	79	132	33	5	13	66	28	19	.280
1980	ChA	32	90	15	26	4	2	1	12	5	4	.289
1980	NYN ...	79	284	38	78	16	4	10	42	20	17	.275
1981	Atl	85	320	37	93	22	3	5	37	15	12	.291
1982	Atl	150	563	94	150	24	6	16	80	50	33	.266
1983	Atl	134	496	75	138	24	8	9	44	35	31	.278
1984	Atl	120	416	62	119	21	2	17	61	59	21	.286
1985	Atl	122	398	62	110	14	6	15	43	40	14	.276
1986	NYA....	54	135	19	32	5	0	6	16	7	6	.237
1986	Atl	40	137	17	37	11	0	5	14	14	4	.270
1987	NYA....	102	312	42	87	17	0	9	44	27	10	.279
1988	NYA....	126	455	62	140	22	3	11	64	24	15	.308
1989	Cal.....	110	418	53	114	18	4	13	42	27	13	.273
		1867	6673	919	1865	332	68	163	815	464	308	.279

Devon White

Birth Date: 12/29/62
Bats: Both
Throws: Right
1989 Club:
California Angels
Contest Code #: 684

Rating: 4

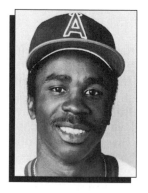

The word on Devon White remains "potential." Here's one of the most talented players in the big time. Yet he still hasn't made the most of it. Jamaica-born White can absolutely fly—on the base paths and in the field. He stole 44 bases in 1989, easily his career high. There could be lots more in his future. On defense, he runs down anything in the county. There aren't many better center fielders.

Otherwise, the questions remain. An impatient hitter, White doesn't draw enough walks (only 31 last year) and strikes out far too often (131). Even his hitting (.245) slipped back a notch from his career .260 mark. He has occasional power (12 homers, half of his rookie-year total of 24) and can make things happen on the field. The word on White is "moody, even temperamental at times," which isn't a good sign. Still, the twenty-seven-year-old is enormously talented, which means that he'll be around for a long time. Stay tuned.

Year	Team	G	AB	R	H	2B	3B	HR	RBI	BB	SB	AVG
1985	Cal.....	21	7	7	1	0	0	0	0	1	3	.143
1986	Cal.....	29	51	8	12	1	1	1	3	6	6	.235
1987	Cal.....	159	639	103	168	33	5	24	87	39	32	.263
1988	Cal.....	122	455	76	118	22	2	11	51	23	17	.259
1989	Cal.....	156	636	86	156	18	13	12	56	31	44	.245
		487	1788	280	455	74	21	48	197	100	102	.254

Kenny Williams

Birth Date: 4/6/64
Bats: Right
Throws: Right
1989 Club:
Detroit Tigers
Contest Code #: 685

Rating: 2

Kenny Williams' major-league career was best described by Don Quixote's sidekick, Sancho Panza. "More misadventures," shouted Panza as he and the Don went out to seek more windmills to tilt with. Williams, who came to the Tigers from the White Sox (for pitcher Eric King) in a nondescript deal, has bounced all over the place. Just a couple of seasons ago, Williams tried to become a third baseman and, in fact, opened the White Sox's 1988 season at the hot corner. That experiment ended fairly quickly.

Nagging injuries have limited his effectiveness after a promising .281 rookie season in 1987. Last year, a pulled muscle shelved him for five weeks, sandwiched by a 94-game season in which he hit .205 with 6 homers and 23 RBI's. When your season highlight is a 2-run double on opening day, it hasn't been much of a year.

Year	Team	G	AB	R	H	2B	3B	HR	RBI	BB	SB	AVG
1986	ChA....	15	31	2	4	0	0	1	1	1	1	.129
1987	ChA....	116	391	48	110	18	2	11	50	10	21	.281
1988	ChA....	73	220	18	35	4	2	8	28	10	6	.159
1989	Det	94	258	29	53	5	1	6	23	18	9	.205
		298	900	97	202	27	5	26	102	39	37	.224

Mookie Wilson

Birth Date: 2/9/56
Bats: Both
Throws: Right
1989 Club:
New York Mets &
Toronto Blue Jays
Contest Code #: 686

Rating: 3

Has Mookie Wilson begun a long siege of wanderlust? Perhaps. Long a fixture in centerfield for the New York Mets, neither Wilson nor his eventual partner, Lenny Dykstra, were happy platooning in New York—where they were known, collectively, as Mookstra. The outcome: New York dealt them both in a month and a half: Dykstra to Philadelphia and Wilson to Toronto.

The change of scenery revived the 5'10", 174-pound Wilson, who shook things up in Toronto. His 14-game hit streak immediately following his arrival at the Skydome missed his career longest by 1 game and was the impetus for his .298 average in his 54 games with the Jays.

Mookie has always been a decent fielder who takes fullest advantage of his speed (which also produced 12 steals in 13 tries in Toronto). His arm is, at best, marginal. Despite his impact, his new teammates awarded him a partial playoff share based on his fractional season, which didn't please the veteran. He filed for free-agency during the post-season filing period.

Year	Team	G	AB	R	H	2B	3B	HR	RBI	BB	SB	AVG
1980	NYN ...	27	105	16	26	5	3	0	4	12	7	.248
1981	NYN ...	92	328	49	89	8	8	3	14	20	24	.271
1982	NYN ...	159	639	90	178	25	9	5	55	32	58	.279
1983	NYN ...	152	638	91	176	25	6	7	51	18	54	.276
1984	NYN ...	154	587	88	162	28	10	10	54	26	46	.276
1985	NYN ...	93	337	56	93	16	8	6	26	28	24	.276
1986	NYN ...	123	381	61	110	17	5	9	45	32	25	.289
1987	NYN ...	124	385	58	115	19	7	9	34	35	21	.299
1988	NYN ...	112	378	61	112	17	5	8	41	27	15	.296
1989	NYN ...	80	249	22	51	10	1	3	18	10	7	.205
1989	Tor.....	54	238	32	71	9	1	2	17	3	12	.298
		1170	4265	624	1183	179	63	62	359	243	293	.277

Willie Wilson

Birth Date: 7/9/55
Bats: Both
Throws: Right
1989 Club:
Kansas City Royals
Contest Code #: 687

Rating: 4

Sad to say, Willie Wilson's career is on a downward curve. The 1982 AL batting champ (.332) chugged along at a .253 clip in 1989, his worst performance since his rookie year in 1978. When his option came up at season's end, the Royals announced that they would not pick it up. Sad.

Though his speed remains his number-one asset, Wilson is no longer the base-stealing threat he once was. His 1989 total (24) wasn't bad for most mortals, but this is Willie Wilson who has stolen 43 or more bases seven times in his career. His defense remains sound; he can still run down just about any ball in center field. At the plate, he makes decent contact, but his power—never much—is now virtually nonexistent.

Back in 1974, Wilson was the nation's most highly sought-after high-school running back. Kansas City's money persuaded him to reject the U. of Maryland's football scholarship to play pro baseball. If Bo Jackson had been around then, there's no telling what Willie might have done. Meanwhile, there's more baseball left in Wilson, even if it's not vintage Willie.

Year	Team	G	AB	R	H	2B	3B	HR	RBI	BB	SB	AVG
1976	KC	12	6	0	1	0	0	0	0	0	2	.167
1977	KC	13	34	10	11	2	0	0	1	1	6	.324

1978	KC	127	198	43	43	8	2	0	16	16	46	.217
1979	KC	154	588	113	185	18	13	6	49	28	83	.315
1980	KC	161	705	133	230	28	15	3	49	28	79	.326
1981	KC	102	439	54	133	10	7	1	32	18	34	.303
1982	KC	136	585	87	194	19	15	3	46	26	37	.332
1983	KC	137	576	90	159	22	8	2	33	33	59	.276
1984	KC	128	541	81	163	24	9	2	44	39	47	.301
1985	KC	141	605	87	168	25	21	4	43	29	43	.278
1986	KC	156	631	77	170	20	7	9	44	31	34	.269
1987	KC	146	610	97	170	18	15	4	30	32	59	.279
1988	KC	147	591	81	155	17	11	1	37	22	35	.262
1989	KC	112	383	58	97	17	7	3	43	27	24	.253
		1672	6492	1011	1879	228	130	38	467	330	588	.289

Dave Winfield

Birth Date: 10/3/51
Bats: Right
Throws: Right
1989 Club:
New York Yankees
Contest Code #: 688

Rating: 3

The Yankees' annual off-season bickering began early. The New Yorkers' front office announced that Jesse Barfield would be the rightfielder in 1990. Then the head of the David M. Winfield Foundation announced that he would be the Yankees' man in right starting the new decade.

Barfield is the incumbent. Winfield is the traditional candidate. There's no telling how much the Bronx Bombers missed their superstar who lost the entire 1989 season to a back injury. The former Minnesota basketball ace (Dave is 6′6″ and 220) ranks in the top ten among active players in just about every offensive category. One of the few major-leaguers who has never played an inning of minor-league ball, Winfield came to the Padres right out of Minnesota. He signed with the Yankees as a free-agent in 1981 and has hit .291 and knocked in 812 runs in the succeeding eight seasons.

If David is healthy, look for his strong arm to return to right field. Sorry, Jesse. If not, Dave has had one sensational career.

Year	Team	G	AB	R	H	2B	3B	HR	RBI	BB	SB	AVG
1973	SD	56	141	9	39	4	1	3	12	12	0	.277
1974	SD	145	498	57	132	18	4	20	75	40	9	.265
1975	SD	143	509	74	136	20	2	15	76	69	23	.267
1976	SD	137	492	81	139	26	4	13	69	65	26	.283
1977	SD	157	615	104	169	29	7	25	92	58	16	.275
1978	SD	158	587	88	181	30	5	24	97	55	21	.308
1979	SD	159	597	97	184	27	10	34	118	85	15	.308
1980	SD	162	558	89	154	25	6	20	87	79	23	.276
1981	NYA	105	388	52	114	25	1	13	68	43	11	.294
1982	NYA	140	539	84	151	24	8	37	106	45	5	.280
1983	NYA	152	598	99	169	26	8	32	116	58	15	.283
1984	NYA	141	567	106	193	34	4	19	100	53	6	.340
1985	NYA	155	633	105	174	34	6	26	114	52	19	.275
1986	NYA	154	565	90	148	31	5	24	104	77	6	.262
1987	NYA	156	575	83	158	22	1	27	97	76	5	.275
1988	NYA	149	559	96	180	37	2	25	107	69	9	.322
		2269	8421	1314	2421	412	74	357	1438	936	209	.287

Matt Winters

Birth Date: 3/18/60
Bats: Left
Throws: Right
1989 Club:
Kansas City Royals
Contest Code #: 689

Rating: 2

Patience finally paid off for Matt Winters last season. After eleven—count 'em, eleven—years in the minors, Matt Winters finally got to see the inside of a major-league dugout last season. The twenty-nine-year-old rookie got into 42 Royals games, hitting .234, with 9 RBI's and his first 2 big-league homers. At the minor-league level, Winters almost always succeeded. His odyssey took him through Oneonta (NY), Fort Lauderdale (FL), Greensboro (NC), Nashville (TN), Columbus (OH), Albany (NY), Buffalo (NY), Memphis (TN), and Omaha (NE) before landing in Kansas City (MO). Oh yes, there were return trips throughout the journey. Now he hopes to stay where the only buses you see take you to and from the airport. Problem is, he doesn't seem to have enough to stay. The bat is a question mark, his defense is so-so, and his arm and speed are barely borderline.

Year	Team	G	AB	R	H	2B	3B	HR	RBI	BB	SB	AVG
1989	KC.....	42	107	14	25	6	0	2	9	14	0	.234
		42	107	14	25	6	0	2	9	14	0	.234

Mike Young

Birth Date: 3/20/60
Bats: Both
Throws: Right
1989 Club:
Cleveland Indians
Contest Code #: 690

Rating: 1

At this point, Mike Young is strictly hanging on. He probably doesn't send his laundry out, unless the valet can assure six-hour service. Young moved through Philadelphia and Milwaukee in 1988, then on to Cleveland in 1989, where he got to play in only 32 games (59 at-bats) for the big-league club in 1989. A ten-year professional, the 6'2", 195-pounder has paid his dues, with stops all along the minor-league trail. Dues paying, however, doesn't always pay off. Young hit only a buck eighty-six for the Indians last season, with one home run his only extra-base hit. Next stop? Who knows? If he can keep his head on straight, he can contribute to his ball club.

Year	Team	G	AB	R	H	2B	3B	HR	RBI	BB	SB	AVG
1982	Bal	6	2	2	0	0	0	0	0	0	0	.000
1983	Bal	25	36	5	6	2	1	0	2	2	1	.167
1984	Bal	123	401	59	101	17	2	17	52	58	6	.252
1985	Bal	139	450	72	123	22	1	28	81	48	1	.273
1986	Bal	117	369	43	93	15	1	9	42	49	3	.252
1987	Bal	110	363	46	87	10	1	16	39	46	10	.240
1988	Mil.....	8	14	2	0	0	0	0	0	2	0	.000
1988	Phi	75	146	13	33	14	0	1	14	26	0	.226
1989	Cle.....	32	59	2	11	0	0	1	5	6	1	.186
		635	1840	244	454	80	6	72	235	237	22	.247

Robin Yount

Birth Date: 9/16/55
Bats: Right
Throws: Right
1989 Club:
Milwaukee Brewers
Contest Code #: 691

Rating: 5

By the end of April, Robin Yount will have played in his 2300th Milwaukee Brewer game. But at age thirty-four—only thirty-four—he still plays with the enthusiasm of a rookie. Yount became the Brew Crew shortstop at age eighteen, after only a half season or so in the minors. An outstanding shortstop through 1984, Robin was switched to center field in 1985 and has become a polished outfielder as well. Yount's .318 mark last season (with 21 homers, 103 RBI's, and 19 stolen bases) marked his fourth straight year over .300 and earned the American League's Most Valuable Player award. It also earned him a new, three-year contract with the Brewers at $3.2 million annually. At a time when some veteran players would be looking for an occasional day off, Yount has played in 480 of the Brewers' 486 games the last three seasons. If Yount stays healthy, and he has in all but two of his 16 major-league seasons, he could well become the majors' all-time leader in games-played by the time he hangs up his glove.

Year	Team	G	AB	R	H	2B	3B	HR	RBI	BB	SB	AVG
1974	Mil.....	107	344	48	86	14	5	3	26	12	7	.250
1975	Mil.....	147	558	67	149	28	2	8	52	33	12	.267
1976	Mil.....	161	638	59	161	19	3	2	54	38	16	.252
1977	Mil.....	154	605	66	174	34	4	4	49	41	16	.288
1978	Mil.....	127	502	66	147	23	9	9	71	24	16	.293
1979	Mil.....	149	577	72	154	26	5	8	51	35	11	.267
1980	Mil.....	143	611	121	179	49	10	23	87	26	20	.293
1981	Mil.....	96	377	50	103	15	5	10	49	22	4	.273
1982	Mil.....	156	635	129	210	46	12	29	114	54	14	.331
1983	Mil.....	149	578	102	178	42	10	17	80	72	12	.308
1984	Mil.....	160	624	105	186	27	7	16	80	67	14	.298
1985	Mil.....	122	466	76	129	26	3	15	68	49	10	.277
1986	Mil.....	140	522	82	163	31	7	9	46	62	14	.312
1987	Mil.....	158	635	99	198	25	9	21	103	76	19	.312
1988	Mil.....	162	621	92	190	38	11	13	91	63	22	.306
1989	Mil.....	160	614	101	195	38	9	21	103	63	19	.318
		2291	8907	1335	2602	481	111	208	1124	737	226	.292

PITCHERS

Jim Abbott

Birth Date: 9/19/67
Throws: Left
1989 Club:
California Angels
Contest Code #: 701

Rating: 4

Any questions about Jim Abbott's ability to pitch (and win) at the major level are gone. The former U. of Michigan and U. S. Olympic Team ace, the object of the nation's attention much of last season, passed all his tests with flying colors. American League rivals quickly learned that a one-armed pitcher with Abbott's talent is as good as most solid two-armed pitchers. He's an inspiration to everyone who knows or watches him.

Our scouts describe Abbott in one word: "amazing." His fastball borders on outstanding, and his slider or cut fastball is highly effective. He pitches with the intelligence of a veteran, and his control is superb. His ability to paint the black makes him tough on every hitter, and he is in total command of his pitches. He tossed a pair of shutouts among four complete games last season, earning a 12–12 mark with a 3.92 ERA. At age twenty-two, his future is absolutely brilliant.

Year	Team	W	L	SV	ERA	IP	H	BB	K
1989	Cal	12	12	0	3.92	181.1	190	74	115
		12	12	0	3.92	181.1	190	74	115

Jim Acker

Birth Date: 9/24/58
Throws: Right
1989 Club:
Atlanta Braves &
Toronto Blue Jays
Contest Code #: 702

Rating: 3

The plethora of off-season free agents had major-league general managers scratching their heads, entertaining the agents, and patting their wallets. The Toronto Blue Jays, whose roster was littered with uncontracted talent, made newly acquired Jim Acker one of their primary targets for retention—and they pulled it off. Acker, who came to the Jays for the pennant chase after some distinguished work with the Atlanta Braves, impressed everyone in Ontario with his setup work for ace closer Tom Henke. In 14 appearances, the big right-hander was 2–1 with a handsome 1.59 ERA, striking out 24 in 28⅓ innings. What did it take to keep Acker in Canada? Easy, a two-year deal calling for a $300,000 signing bonus, $550,000 for the coming season, and $900,000 in 1991. Even with the current rate of exchange, Mr. Acker has done well.

Year	Team	W	L	SV	ERA	IP	H	BB	K
1983	Tor.......	5	1	1	4.33	97.2	103	38	44
1984	Tor.......	3	5	1	4.37	72.0	79	25	33
1985	Tor.......	7	2	10	3.23	86.1	86	43	42
1986	Tor.......	2	4	0	4.35	60.0	63	22	32
1986	Atl.......	3	8	0	3.79	95.0	100	26	37
1987	Atl.......	4	9	14	4.16	114.2	109	51	68
1988	Atl.......	0	4	0	4.71	42.0	45	14	25
1989	Atl.......	0	6	2	2.67	97.2	84	20	68
1989	Tor.......	2	1	0	1.59	28.1	24	12	24
		26	40	28	3.78	693.2	693	251	373

Rick Aguilera

Birth Date: 12/31/61
Throws: Right
1989 Club:
New York Mets &
Minnesota Twins
Contest Code #: 703

Rating: 3

What Rick Aguilera figured as a comeback season with the New York Mets wound up as a go-away season with the Minnesota Twins. The normally steady right-hander, who bounced back from arm woes which produced a lengthy stay on the DL and an 0–4 season in 1988, could never crack the Mets' stellar rotation.

Thus it could have been a blessing when Minnesota plucked him out of the package of pitchers who arrived in exchange for Frank Viola. The Mets figure that Cy Young alumnus Viola will be a superstar for the next five to eight years. If he isn't, Aguilera alone could embarrass them. Despite a slow start in the AL, the big (6′5″, 200 pounds) righty found a groove in September. Though his record was only 3–5 for the Twins, his 3.21 ERA and 3 complete games in 11 starts were impressive. So were his 57 strikeouts and only 17 walks in 75⅔ innings.

Year	Team	W	L	SV	ERA	IP	H	BB	K
1985	NYN	10	7	0	3.24	122.1	118	37	74
1986	NYN	10	7	0	3.88	141.2	145	36	104
1987	NYN	11	3	0	3.60	115.0	124	33	77
1988	NYN	0	4	0	6.93	24.2	29	10	16
1989	NYN	6	6	7	2.34	69.1	59	21	80
1989	Min	3	5	0	3.21	75.2	71	17	57
		40	32	7	3.53	548.2	546	154	408

Doyle Alexander

Birth Date: 9/4/50
Throws: Right
1989 Club:
Detroit Tigers
Contest Code #: 704

Rating: 2

When Roger Craig went 10–24 for the early, laughable New York Mets, baseball folks said that for Craig to keep his spot in the rotation despite 24 losses, he must be some pitcher. Now take the case of Detroit's Doyle Alexander. At age thirty-nine last season, he went 6–18 with a 4.44 ERA. Yet Sparky Anderson handed him the ball thirty-three times. He must be some pitcher.

Not anymore. The awkward-looking right-hander has slowed up measurably in recent years, and his fastball is short and getting shorter. He knows how to pitch; who wouldn't after twenty-two years as a pro, nineteen in the majors? His slider is still pretty decent, and Doyle is working on a knuckleball. Those fellas can last forever. A one-time—listen to this—forty-fourth-round draft choice by the Dodgers, Alexander has been with L.A., Baltimore, the Yankees, Texas, Atlanta, San Francisco, the Yankees again, Toronto, Atlanta again, and Detroit. Where and when it will all end is anyone's guess.

Year	Team	W	L	SV	ERA	IP	H	BB	K
1971	LA........	6	6	0	3.82	92.0	105	18	30
1972	Bal	6	8	2	2.46	106.0	78	30	49
1973	Bal	12	8	0	3.86	175.0	169	52	63
1974	Bal	6	9	0	4.03	114.0	127	43	40
1975	Bal	8	8	1	3.05	133.0	127	47	46
1976	Bal	3	4	0	3.52	64.0	58	24	17
1976	NYA......	10	5	0	3.28	137.0	114	39	41
1977	Tex	17	11	0	3.65	237.0	221	82	82
1978	Tex	9	10	0	3.86	191.0	198	71	81
1979	Tex	5	7	0	4.46	113.0	114	69	50
1980	Atl.......	14	11	0	4.19	232.0	227	74	114
1981	SF.......	11	7	0	2.90	152.0	156	44	77
1982	NYA......	1	7	0	6.08	66.2	81	14	26
1983	NYA......	0	2	0	6.35	28.1	31	7	17

1983	Tor.......	7	6	0	3.93	116.2	126	26	46
1984	Tor.......	17	6	0	3.13	261.2	238	59	139
1985	Tor.......	17	10	0	3.45	260.2	268	67	142
1986	Tor.......	5	4	0	4.46	111.0	120	20	65
1986	Atl.......	6	6	0	3.84	117.1	135	17	74
1987	Det	9	0	0	1.53	88.1	63	26	44
1987	Atl	5	10	0	4.13	117.2	115	27	64
1988	Det	14	11	0	4.32	229.0	260	46	126
1989	Det	6	18	0	4.44	223.0	245	76	95
		194	174	3	3.76	3366.1	3376	978	1528

Allan Anderson

Birth Date: 1/7/64
Throws: Left
1989 Club:
Minnesota Twins
Contest Code #: 705

Rating: 4

Ohio native Allan Anderson has impressed baseball insiders and Twins fans since popping onto the big-league scene early in 1988. The 6', 186-pound left-hander has won 33 games in his two seasons, easily leading the ball club with 17 wins (and 10 losses) last year.

Anderson, who once threw back-to-back no-hitters at Lancaster (OH) High School, makes his living with average to above-average stuff, featuring an outstanding straight change. He obviously got good schooling in the Twins' minor-league organization because he knows how to pitch. Most important, he doesn't get himself into trouble; he throws strikes. That doesn't mean that he rings up a lot of strikeouts, but he doesn't beat himself.

Possibly the biggest surprise about Anderson's success at the major-league level is that he didn't win in the minors. At AA and AAA from 1985 to 1987, Anderson went 7–11, 2–5, and 4–8—and his ERA never approached the levels he has achieved in Minnesota.

Year	Team	W	L	SV	ERA	IP	H	BB	K
1986	Min......	3	6	0	5.55	84.1	106	30	51
1987	Min......	1	0	0	10.95	12.1	20	10	3
1988	Min......	16	9	0	2.45	202.1	199	37	83
1989	Min......	17	10	0	3.80	196.2	214	53	69
		37	25	0	3.72	495.2	539	130	206

Luis Aquino

Birth Date: 5/19/65
Throws: Right
1989 Club:
Kansas City Royals
Contest Code #: 706

Rating: 3

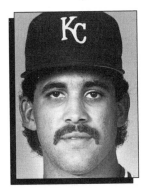

It took a while, but it looks as though Luis Aquino is in the majors to stay. Beginning at age seventeen, he began kicking around the Toronto farm system (Bradenton, Florence, Kinston, Knoxville, Syracuse) for 5½ seasons before the Jays dealt him to the Royals (for outfielder Juan Beniquez) midway through the 1987 season. A late 1988 trial convinced Kaycee to give him a full shot in 1989 at the still tender age of twenty-three, and it seems to be paying off for the native of Puerto Rico.

Scouts like Aquino's sneaky fastball, made all the more effective because of his deceptive motion. Though he made 16 starts for the 1989 Royals (two complete games), he seems destined to see only spot duty as a starter. Long relief seems to be the spot for him. Overall he saw action in 34 games, finishing up in 5 of his relief appearances. His 2:1 strikeouts-to-walks ratio (68–35) demonstrates his adequate control.

Year	Team	W	L	SV	ERA	IP	H	BB	K
1986	Tor.......	1	1	0	6.35	11.1	14	3	5
1988	KC.......	1	0	0	2.79	29.0	33	17	11
1989	KC.......	6	8	0	3.50	141.1	148	35	68
		8	9	0	3.57	181.2	195	55	84

Scott Bailes

Birth Date: 12/18/62
Throws: Left
1989 Club:
Cleveland Indians
Contest Code #: 707

Rating: 2

The Cleveland Indians' Scott Bailes is a pretty average pitcher. His 5–9 record in 1989 more or less mirrored his team's 73–89 mark. His 4.28 ERA actually was his major-league career-best but it's, well, pretty average. The scouts say his fastball is average. His curve ball is average. After four seasons with the Indians, Scott is an average pitcher.

The folks who run the Indians feel that the Ohio native can get better. His major problem is lack of location. Pitchers who have location become better than average. If he gets it and perfects the change-up that he's working on, he'll make it.

The one-time Southwest Missouri State star was drafted and signed by the Pittsburgh Pirates in 1982 and was dealt to the Indians in 1985 as the legendary "player to be named later" in a deal that sent Johnnie Lemaster to Pittsburgh. After three straight losing seasons in Cleveland, the pressure on Bailes must be mounting.

Year	Team	W	L	SV	ERA	IP	H	BB	K
1986	Cle	10	10	7	4.95	112.2	123	43	60
1987	Cle	7	8	6	4.64	120.1	145	47	65
1988	Cle	9	14	0	4.90	145.0	149	46	53
1989	Cle	5	9	0	4.28	113.2	116	29	47
		31	41	13	4.70	491.2	533	165	225

Jeff Ballard

Birth Date: 8/13/63
Throws: Left
1989 Club:
Baltimore Orioles
Contest Code #: 708

Rating: 3

It didn't take long for Jeff Ballard to make a big-league impression. One of Stanford's all-time pitching leaders, he hit four stops on the Baltimore farm before making the big club to stay six weeks into the 1988 season. Now he's the ace of the staff.

Chances are he isn't as good as he looked in 1989 when he went 18–8 with a 3.43 ERA (including 1 of only 3 Oriole shutouts during their spectacular season). He's not much of a power pitcher, as his 62 strikeouts in 215⅓ innings clearly show. But he has decent control and outstanding breaking stuff. The scouts are tremendously impressed with his slurve (slider-curve) that buckles hitters' knees.

Still, with any club—especially a first-division outfit—Ballard will be a key member of the rotation. Along with Bob Milacki, Jeff will be out there every five days, which means he should be ringing up numbers in 1990—and beyond.

Year	Team	W	L	SV	ERA	IP	H	BB	K
1987	Bal	2	8	0	6.59	69.2	100	35	27
1988	Bal	8	12	0	4.40	153.1	167	42	41
1989	Bal	18	8	0	3.43	215.1	240	57	62
		28	28	0	4.27	438.1	507	134	130

Scott Bankhead

Birth Date: 7/31/63
Throws: Right
1989 Club:
Seattle Mariners
Contest Code #: 709

Rating: 3

Whether he realizes it or not, Seattle pitcher Scott Bankhead has issued a challenge to Jeff Smulyan and the rest of the new Mariner owners. Under previous owner George Argyros, the M's best pitchers, Mark Langston and Mike Moore, have forced their way out of the Kingdome. Now Bankhead has begun to take over the leadership role. With the injuries (shoulder, ribs, etc.) behind him, Bankhead is beginning to put it all together.

The former North Carolina Tarheel owns an outstanding fastball, and his slider is just a tad behind. He's working on a change-up, to complete his array of pitches. Good control has been a key ingredient in his game. The 5'10", 185-pound right-hander was 14–6 for the 73–89 Mariners in 1989. His 33 starts included 3 complete games, 2 of them shutouts.

Bankhead came to Seattle from Kansas City in the Danny Tartabull trade in December 1986. If he stays healthy, he should be the M's staff leader.

Year	Team	W	L	SV	ERA	IP	H	BB	K
1986	KC.......	8	9	0	4.61	121.0	121	37	94
1987	Sea......	9	8	0	5.42	149.1	168	37	95
1988	Sea.....	7	9	0	3.07	135.0	115	38	102
1989	Sea......	14	6	0	3.34	210.1	187	63	140
		38	32	0	4.03	615.2	591	175	431

Juan Berenguer

Birth Date: 11/30/54
Throws: Right
1989 Club:
Minnesota Twins
Contest Code #: 710

Rating: 4

The well-traveled Señor Berenguer, like fine wine, seems to get better with age. The burly (5'11", 225 pounds) Panamanian first reached the majors in a trial with the Mets in 1978. Five years later, after stops in Kansas City, Toronto, and Detroit, his overall record was 3–17. He became a pitcher with the Tigers in 1983 (9–5) and, after another one-season stop with San Francisco, found his role in the Minnesota bullpen in that championship season (1987).

Last year was his best. His 9–3 record in 60 appearances (106 innings), combined with a 3.48 ERA, really got the job done. Even at age thirty-five, the right-hander still throws very hard. Control remains a problem, as it is with most hard throwers. But he's super-tough, challenging every hitter he faces. There's no indication that he's lost anything. He could go on for years.

Year	Team	W	L	SV	ERA	IP	H	BB	K
1978	NYN	0	2	0	8.31	13.0	17	11	8
1979	NYN	1	1	0	2.90	31.0	28	12	25
1980	NYN	0	1	0	6.00	9.0	9	10	7
1981	KC.......	0	4	0	8.55	20.0	22	16	20
1981	Tor.......	2	9	0	4.31	71.0	62	35	29
1982	Det.......	0	0	0	6.76	6.2	5	9	8
1983	Det	9	5	1	3.14	157.2	110	71	129
1984	Det	11	10	0	3.48	168.1	146	79	118
1985	Det	5	6	0	5.59	95.0	96	48	82
1986	SF.......	2	3	4	2.70	73.1	64	44	72
1987	Min......	8	1	4	3.94	112.0	100	47	110
1988	Min......	8	4	2	3.96	100.0	74	61	99
1989	Min......	9	3	3	3.48	106.0	96	47	93
		55	49	14	3.93	963.0	829	490	800

Bud Black

Birth Date: 6/30/57
Throws: Left
1989 Club:
Cleveland Indians
Contest Code #: 711

Rating: 4

After eight years in the majors, former Kansas City Royal Bud Black continues to improve. That's how thirty-two-year old pitchers stay in the bigs. The 6'2", 185-pound lefty is crafty. He changes speeds as well as any Indian moundsman. His slider and curve are decent, and the velocity on his fastball is usually in the average range. Scouts are impressed with his control; he walked 52 batters in 222⅓ innings last season.

Black, who won 37 games for the Royals in 1983–85, came to Cleveland (for 1B–DH Pat Tabler) in June 1988. An elbow injury limited his service that season, but a healthy Black went 12–11 with a 3.36 ERA in 1989. The one-time San Diego State star, whose father was a professional hockey player, is now 70–71 for his major-league career, which began with 2 relief appearances for the Seattle Mariners late in the 1981 season.

Year	Team	W	L	SV	ERA	IP	H	BB	K
1981	Sea......	0	0	0	0.00	1.0	2	3	0
1982	KC.......	4	6	0	4.59	88.1	92	34	40
1983	KC.......	10	7	0	3.79	161.1	159	43	58
1984	KC.......	17	12	0	3.12	257.0	226	64	140
1985	KC.......	10	15	0	4.33	205.2	216	59	122
1986	KC.......	5	10	9	3.20	121.0	100	43	68
1987	KC.......	8	6	1	3.60	122.1	126	35	61
1988	KC.......	2	1	0	4.91	22.0	23	11	19
1988	Cle	2	3	1	5.03	59.0	59	23	44
1989	Cle	12	11	0	3.36	222.1	213	52	88
		70	71	11	3.72	1260.0	1216	367	640

Bert Blyleven

Birth Date: 4/6/51
Throws: Right
1989 Club:
California Angels
Contest Code #: 712

Rating: 4

Thanks to a spectacular 1989, Bert earned at least another go-around with the California Angels despite the fact that he'll be thirty-nine when the 1990 season begins. The Netherlands native has enjoyed a remarkable big-league career which began in 1970 (at age nineteen) with the Twins. In two stints with Minnesota, along with briefer stops in Texas, Pittsburgh, Cleveland, and now California, Blyleven has won 271 games—putting him within striking distance of the magic three hundred.

After a 10–17 season with Minnesota in 1988, that didn't seem possible. California picked him up for a song in the off-season, gave him the ball, and reaped all the rewards. His great curve ball, which deserted him in 1988, came back in 1989 and keyed a sparkling 17–5 record with an equally sparkling 2.73 ERA. His slider is good, and his aggressiveness is first-rate. He really challenges the hitter. The biggest concern is that his fastball is now a little short—and enemy batters can turn that short fastball or a hanging curve ball around quickly.

Year	Team	W	L	SV	ERA	IP	H	BB	K
1970	Min......	10	9	0	3.18	164.0	143	47	135
1971	Min......	16	15	0	2.82	278.0	267	59	224
1972	Min......	17	17	0	2.73	287.0	247	69	228
1973	Min......	20	17	0	2.52	325.0	296	67	258
1974	Min......	17	17	0	2.66	281.0	244	77	249
1975	Min......	15	10	0	3.00	276.0	219	84	233
1976	Min......	4	5	0	3.13	95.0	101	35	75
1976	Tex	9	11	0	2.76	202.0	182	46	144
1977	Tex	14	12	0	2.72	235.0	181	69	182
1978	Pit.......	14	10	0	3.02	244.0	217	66	182

1979	Pit.......	12	5	0	3.61	237.0	238	92	172
1980	Pit.......	8	13	0	3.82	217.0	219	59	168
1981	Cle	11	7	0	2.89	159.0	145	40	107
1982	Cle	2	2	0	4.87	20.1	16	11	19
1983	Cle	7	10	0	3.91	156.1	160	44	123
1984	Cle	19	7	0	2.87	245.0	204	74	170
1985	Cle	9	11	0	3.26	179.2	163	49	129
1985	Min......	8	5	0	3.00	114.0	101	26	77
1986	Min......	17	14	0	4.01	271.2	262	58	215
1987	Min......	15	12	0	4.01	267.0	249	101	196
1988	Min......	10	17	0	5.43	207.1	240	51	145
1989	Cal	17	5	0	2.73	241.0	225	44	131
		271	231	0	3.22	4702.1	4319	1268	3562

Mike Boddicker

Birth Date: 8/23/57
Throws: Right
1989 Club:
Boston Red Sox
Contest Code #: 713

Rating: 3

ike Boddicker keeps making the 1988 trade that brought him from Baltimore to Boston look good. After going 7–3 in the final two months of the 1988 season with the Sox, he came right back with a 15–11 mark (4.00 ERA) in 1989. He's smart enough to keep it going in 1990.

At age thirty-two, Boddicker still has some productive years ahead. The 5'11", 186-pounder was never overpowering and still isn't. He makes his living off the breaking ball, and his circle change-up is easily his most effective pitch. Combined with superb control (71 walks in 211 ⅔ innings last season), he's always in the hunt. Just as impressive, his 145 strikeouts trailed only Roger Clemens among Sox pitchers. Though his fastball has gone back in the last couple of years, Boddicker makes up for it with bulldog tenacity. He's a superb competitor every time he walks to the mound.

Year	Team	W	L	SV	ERA	IP	H	BB	K
1980	Bal	0	1	0	6.43	7.0	6	5	4
1981	Bal	0	0	0	4.50	6.0	6	2	2
1982	Bal	1	0	0	3.51	25.2	25	12	20
1983	Bal	16	8	0	2.77	179.0	141	52	120
1984	Bal	20	11	0	2.79	261.1	218	81	128
1985	Bal	12	17	0	4.07	203.1	227	89	135
1986	Bal	14	12	0	4.70	218.1	214	74	175
1987	Bal	10	12	0	4.18	226.0	212	78	152
1988	Bal	6	12	0	3.86	147.0	149	51	100
1988	Bos	7	3	0	2.63	89.0	85	26	56
1989	Bos	15	11	0	4.00	211.2	217	71	145
		101	87	0	3.70	1574.1	1500	541	1037

Chris Bosio

Birth Date: 4/3/63
Throws: Right
1989 Club:
Milwaukee Brewers
Contest Code #: 714

Rating: 4

hough right-hander Chris Bosio wasn't overly impressive in a 7–15 debut in 1988, the Brewers knew that he'd have to deliver for them to get into the 1989 title hunt. Did he ever!

Seemingly a complete pitcher at age twenty-seven, Bosio is tough in the first inning and even tougher in succeeding frames. Bosio was the Brewers' top winner (15, with 10 losses) in 1989, tossing a team-high 8 complete games. The big 6'3", 210-pounder has a tremendous slider and he's always around the plate, which separates ordinary young pitchers from good ones. (Bosio fanned 173 last season, a record for Brewer right-handers, while walking only 48.)

Especially tough in money games, Bosio was the workhorse of the Milwaukee staff in 1989 (234⅔ innings), which may have contributed to a tired arm in September when he made only 4 starts, none in the last two weeks.

Year	Team	W	L	SV	ERA	IP	H	BB	K
1986	Mil	0	4	0	7.01	34.2	41	13	29
1987	Mil	11	8	2	5.24	170.0	187	50	150
1988	Mil	7	15	6	3.36	182.0	190	38	84
1989	Mil	15	10	0	2.95	234.2	225	48	173
		33	37	8	3.93	621.1	643	149	436

Kevin Brown

Birth Date: 3/14/65
Throws: Right
1989 Club:
Texas Rangers
Contest Code #: 715

Rating: 4

What a pleasant surprise Kevin Brown provided to his manager, Bobby Valentine. The right-hander from McIntyre, GA, tied the Ranger club record (Edwin Correa, 1986) with 12 wins, including a nifty 2-hitter against the Yankees last May. In fact, he was 11–6 (with a 2.85 ERA) before losing 3 of his last 4 (7.40), though his season ended prematurely on September 8.

The scouts are tremendously impressed with the twenty-five-year-old who won his first major-league game in 1986, his first year as a pro. He has great stuff, featuring an excellent fastball and slider. His overall 3.35 ERA was second among Texas starters and best among all major-league rookies. Opposing batters have lots of trouble taking him deep. Kevin allowed home runs in only 6 of his 28 starts last season—none in his last 7 games.

Year	Team	W	L	SV	ERA	IP	H	BB	K
1986	Tex	1	0	0	3.60	5.0	6	0	4
1988	Tex	1	1	0	4.24	23.1	33	8	12
1989	Tex	12	9	0	3.35	191.0	167	70	104
		14	10	0	3.45	219.1	206	78	120

Todd Burns

Birth Date: 7/6/63
Throws: Right
1989 Club:
Oakland Athletics
Contest Code #: 716

Rating: 4

Todd Burns' hard-nosed attitude and knowledge of pitching craft have enabled him to overcome basically limited stuff and remain as a valued member of the Oakland Athletics' pitching staff. The twenty-six-year-old has a better-than-decent curveball and slider and, really, not much else. But he's an outstanding competitor who really knows how to pitch. Best of all, he seems to thrive when the going gets really tough.

The one-time Oral Roberts U. star was a seventh-round draft choice by Oakland in 1984. After 4½ minor-league seasons, he arrived with the parent club in mid-1988, then threw in a 6–5 season and a sparkling 2.24 ERA in 50 appearances (96⅓ innings) for the 1989 world champs. Burns was ready for every role presented to him by manager Tony LaRussa. His 50 outings included a pair of starts and 8 saves.

Year	Team	W	L	SV	ERA	IP	H	BB	K
1988	Oak......	8	2	1	3.16	102.2	93	34	57
1989	Oak......	6	5	8	2.24	96.1	66	28	49
		14	7	9	2.71	199.0	159	62	106

Greg Cadaret

Birth Date: 2/27/62
Throws: Left
1989 Club:
Oakland Athletics &
New York Yankees
Contest Code #: 717

Rating: 2

When the Yankees finally decide to use lefty Greg Cadaret strictly in relief, they'll have themselves one fine pitcher. New York used Cadaret as both a starter and reliever after he came to the Bronx in the Rickey Henderson trade last summer. The Detroit native never really adjusted to a starting role, which didn't help matters.

The book on Cadaret indicates that his fastball is much more effective when he comes on late in the game. That sets up his other pitches, including a pretty fair forkball. Not that Greg did badly as a starter last year. He pitched 3 complete games—in only 13 starts. That probably puts him among the top 10 percent of AL pitchers. Still, Cadaret has been a reliever since 1987 in Huntsville (AL), the A's AA farm team. His first two years in the majors, he went 11–4 with a 3.48 ERA. If he can duplicate those numbers for the Yanks, even Boss George will be delighted.

Year	Team	W	L	SV	ERA	IP	H	BB	K
1987	Oak......	6	2	0	4.54	39.2	37	24	30
1988	Oak......	5	2	3	2.89	71.2	60	36	64
1989	Oak......	0	0	0	2.28	27.2	21	19	14
1989	NYA......	5	5	0	4.58	92.1	109	38	66
		16	9	3	3.77	231.1	227	117	174

Tom Candiotti

Birth Date: 8/31/57
Throws: Right
1989 Club:
Cleveland Indians
Contest Code #: 718

Rating: 3

When a pitcher earns the label "knuckleballer," fans get the impression that's all he has. In a lot of cases, that's true. This does not include Cleveland's right-hander Tom Candiotti. His knuckler ranks as outstanding, but it's only one pitch in his four-pitch arsenal. The 6'2", 205-pounder also features a plus-rated curveball, a fair slider, and a fastball classified as borderline—though the native Californian makes excellent use of the pitch.

Candiotti's arrival with the Indians in 1986 ended a trek through a variety of minor-league organizations. A star at St. Mary's (CA), Candiotti was picked up from Victoria (Independent) by the Kaycee Royals in January 1980. The following December, he moved to the Milwaukee farm group. He made 18 appearances for the parent Brewers in 1983 and 1984, before moving to Cleveland. His all-time best ERA (3.10) highlighted a 13–10 record in 1989, including four complete games.

Year	Team	W	L	SV	ERA	IP	H	BB	K
1983	Mil	4	4	0	3.23	55.2	62	16	21
1984	Mil	2	2	0	5.29	32.1	38	10	23
1986	Cle	16	12	0	3.57	252.1	234	106	167
1987	Cle	7	18	0	4.78	201.2	193	93	111
1988	Cle	14	8	0	3.28	216.2	225	53	137
1989	Cle	13	10	0	3.10	206.0	188	55	124
		56	54	0	3.69	964.2	940	333	583

Chuck Cary

Birth Date: 3/3/60
Throws: Left
1989 Club:
New York Yankees
Contest Code #: 719

Rating: 2

In his tenth year of professional baseball, Chuck Cary faces a major challenge. The Yankees need him. He hurled 99⅓ innings for them last year, his busiest season among five part-years in his major-league career. The Yankees' biggest shortcoming is pitching. Cary can fit the bill. Will he? There aren't a lot of questions about his stuff. Scouts believe that it's good enough across the board to work in the big leagues.

The thirty-year-old lefty, originally a Detroit Tiger signee, spent 4½ seasons in the Bengal organization before arriving at Tiger Stadium in mid-1985. After the 1986 season, he was dealt to the Braves, for whom he worked 20 games over two campaigns. Last year's 4–4 Yankee mark featured a 3.26 ERA. A basic power pitcher, Cary occasionally suffers from control problems.

Year	Team	W	L	SV	ERA	IP	H	BB	K
1985	Det	0	1	2	3.42	23.2	16	8	22
1986	Det	1	2	0	3.41	31.2	33	15	21
1987	Atl	1	1	1	3.78	16.2	17	4	15
1988	Atl	0	0	0	6.48	8.1	8	4	7
1989	NYA	4	4	0	3.26	99.1	78	29	79
		6	8	3	3.51	179.2	152	60	144

John Cerutti

Birth Date: 4/28/60
Throws: Left
1989 Club:
Toronto Blue Jays
Contest Code #: 720

Rating: 3

If John Cerutti learned anything in six years in the Toronto Blue Jay minor-league system, it was knowing how to pitch. That's why he was handed the ball 31 times last year. He had never made more than 21 starts in a season before.

The 6'2", 200-pounder's savvy makes him a valued member of the Jay rotation. His fastball is probably not as fast as it needs to be. His curve and slider are just about average. But his knowledge makes him tough for enemy batters to deal with. His pinpoint control doesn't hurt, either.

Cerutti's cerebral approach to pitching shouldn't surprise anyone. Before turning pro, John pitched for Amherst College, which accepts no dummies. His talent and knowledge combined for an 11–11 mark in 1989, with a handsome 3.07 ERA and 3 complete games (one of them a shutout). Baseball will always find a spot for a thinking man's pitcher.

Year	Team	W	L	SV	ERA	IP	H	BB	K
1985	Tor.	0	2	0	5.41	6.2	10	4	5
1986	Tor.	9	4	1	4.15	145.1	150	47	89
1987	Tor.	11	4	0	4.40	151.1	144	59	92
1988	Tor.	6	7	1	3.13	123.2	120	42	65
1989	Tor.	11	11	0	3.07	205.1	214	53	69
		37	28	2	3.67	632.1	638	205	320

Terry Clark

Birth Date: 10/10/60
Throws: Right
1989 Club:
California Angels
Contest Code #: 721

Rating: 3

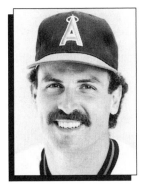

At age twenty-nine, and with only 19 major-league games under his belt, Terry Clark must be wondering where he's headed. A one-time St. Louis Cardinal farmhand, the Los Angeles native came to the Angels as a free agent before the 1986 season. It took him another 3 seasons to get a shot in Anaheim. It looked as though Clark could find a place in the Angels' plans after making 15 starts (with 2 complete games and 1 shutout) in his 1988 debut. His 6–6 record was acceptable; his 5.07 ERA wasn't.

Then it was back to the boonies in 1989, with only 4 Angel appearances (2 starts, 2 in relief). The ERA remained in the same territory (4.91); the record was only 0-2. The future doesn't look pretty.

Year	Team	W	L	SV	ERA	IP	H	BB	K
1988	Cal	6	6	0	5.07	94.0	120	31	39
1989	Cal	0	2	0	4.91	11.0	13	3	7
		6	8	0	5.06	105.0	133	34	46

Roger Clemens

Birth Date: 8/4/62
Throws: Right
1989 Club:
Boston Red Sox
Contest Code #: 722

Rating: 5

Once the American League's premier pitcher, the Rocket Man has slipped a little. But on any given day, he's still as tough as they come.

His 1989 numbers weren't bad for most mortals: 17–11 W-L record, 3.13 ERA, 8 complete games, 230 strikeouts (and only 93 walks) in 253⅓ innings. But compared to the vintage Clemens of 1986 through 1988, they brought concern to Sox fans throughout New England. After all, this is the guy who went 24–4 (with a league-leading 2.48 ERA) for the 1986 AL kings and 20–9 (18 complete games) in 1987. Even in 1988, when he slipped to 18–12, he led the junior circuit with 291 strikeouts and 8 shutouts. The fastball, Clemens' money pitch, is still impressive—sometimes. "Sporadic," the scouts are saying. But now he's perfecting his slider, which can be downright nasty.

While the folks in Boston are becoming depressed, they should know that the rival teams still consider The Rocket Man an impact pitcher.

Year	Team	W	L	SV	ERA	IP	H	BB	K
1984	Bos	9	4	0	4.32	133.1	146	29	126
1985	Bos	7	5	0	3.30	98.1	83	37	74
1986	Bos	24	4	0	2.48	254.0	179	67	238
1987	Bos	20	9	0	2.97	281.2	248	83	256
1988	Bos	18	12	0	2.93	264.0	217	62	291
1989	Bos	17	11	0	3.13	253.1	215	93	230
		95	45	0	3.06	1284.2	1088	371	1215

Keith Comstock

Birth Date: 12/23/55
Throws: Left
1989 Club:
Seattle Mariners
Contest Code #: 723

Rating: 2

Keith Comstock must be wondering where his next baseball adventure will take him. The 6', 175-pound lefthander has toiled in every possible setting since signing with the California Angels organization in 1976. Now, at age thirty-four, he has worked at every minor-league level, with four major-league teams and, for two seasons, with the Yomiuri Gliants in Japan.

Comstock, who features a nasty screwball, opened last season with San Diego's Las Vegas AAA franchise. Oddly, after running up a 7-1 record with a more than reasonable 3.17 ERA, the Padres turned him loose. Picked up by Seattle, he spent a couple of weeks at AAA Calgary (2-1, 1.29 ERA), then moved up to the parent club on July 7. In 31 games, he allowed the opponents to score only four times and, oddly enough for a screwballer, did better against righty hitters (.212) than lefties (.333).

Year	Team	W	L	SV	ERA	IP	H	BB	K
1984	Min	0	0	0	8.53	6.1	6	4	2
1987	SD	0	1	0	5.50	36.0	33	21	38
1987	SF	2	0	1	3.05	20.2	19	10	21
1988	SD	0	0	0	6.75	8.0	8	3	9
1989	Sea	1	2	0	2.81	25.2	26	10	22
		3	3	1	4.56	96.2	92	48	92

Steve Crawford

Birth Date: 4/29/58
Throws: Right
1989 Club:
Kansas City Royals
Contest Code #: 724

Rating: 2

Who was the surprise player of 1989? Steve Crawford of the Kansas City Royals drew more than one vote. Unemployed in March 1989, Crawford signed on with the Royals, was invited to their camp as a non-roster player, was offered—and accepted—a spot with Class AAA Omaha, went 3-1 with a 2.93 ERA and 2 saves, and pitched his way back to the big time by July 4.

He took full advantage of the opportunity. The six-and-one-half-year major-league veteran did slightly better in Kaycee than he did in Omaha. The record was 3-1 again, with a 2.83 ERA in 25 games. The big guy—he's 6'6" and 240 pounds—struck out 33 in 54 innings, allowed opponents to hit only .242, and went 16⅔ innings (from July 28 through August 20) without allowing a run.

Year	Team	W	L	SV	ERA	IP	H	BB	K
1980	Bos	2	0	0	3.66	32.0	41	8	10
1981	Bos	0	5	0	4.97	58.0	69	18	29
1982	Bos	1	0	0	2.00	9.0	14	0	2
1984	Bos	5	0	1	3.34	62.0	69	21	21
1985	Bos	6	5	12	3.76	91.0	103	28	58
1986	Bos	0	2	4	3.92	57.1	69	19	32
1987	Bos	5	4	0	5.33	72.2	91	32	43
1989	KC	3	1	0	2.83	54.0	48	19	33
		22	17	17	3.98	436.0	504	145	228

Chuck Crim

Birth Date: 7/23/61
Throws: Right
1989 Club:
Milwaukee Brewers
Contest Code #: 725

Rating: 3

They say that you should always give a big job to a busy man. Maybe that's why Tom Trebelhorn calls Chuck Crim's number in almost any game situation in the seventh or eighth inning. Crim has appeared in—in order—53, 70, and 76 games in his three years with the Milwaukee Brewers.

Consistency is the name of the California veteran's game. He has two excellent pitches—a nasty slider and a sharp curve—and his control is outstanding. Those are the ingredients of a top setup man—and with Dan Plesac behind him in the bullpen, Milwaukee is in great shape in the late innings.

Year	Team	W	L	SV	ERA	IP	H	BB	K
1987	Mil	6	8	12	3.67	130.0	133	39	56
1988	Mil	7	6	9	2.91	105.0	95	28	58
1989	Mil	9	7	7	2.83	117.2	114	36	59
		22	21	28	3.16	352.2	342	103	173

Storm Davis

Birth Date: 12/26/61
Throws: Right
1989 Club:
Oakland Athletics
Contest Code #: 726

Rating: 4

You couldn't prove it by his 4.36 ERA, but Storm Davis easily enjoyed his best big-league season in 1989. The one-time Baltimore Oriole (54–40 in 4½ seasons as a Bird starter), Davis came to the A's in 1987 after a half season with the San Diego Padres. In two seasons in Oakland, Davis went 35–14 as a valued member of the starting rotation. He'll pitch for Kansas City in 1990.

The only weakness in Davis' game is his infrequent ability to finish what he starts. The book on the 6'4″, 200-pounder reads "six-inning pitcher." Davis, who's no relation to his high-school teammate, Houston first sacker Glenn Davis (Storm's father was the coach), has a fine slider and cut fastball, both of which seem to act the same way. His fastball is rated above average, and the key to his game is control.

Year	Team	W	L	SV	ERA	IP	H	BB	K
1982	Bal	8	4	0	3.49	100.2	96	28	67
1983	Bal	13	7	0	3.59	200.1	180	64	125
1984	Bal	14	9	1	3.12	225.0	205	71	105
1985	Bal	10	8	0	4.53	175.0	172	70	93
1986	Bal	9	12	0	3.62	154.0	166	49	96
1987	SD	2	7	0	6.18	62.2	70	36	37
1987	Oak	1	1	0	3.26	30.1	28	11	28
1988	Oak	16	7	0	3.70	201.2	211	91	127
1989	Oak	19	7	0	4.36	169.1	187	68	91
		92	62	1	3.86	1319.0	1315	488	769

Mark Davis

Birth Date: 10/19/60
Throws: Left
1989 Club:
San Diego Padres
Contest Code #: 727

Rating: 5

Through most of the 1980s fantasy-league owners who had Mark Davis on their pitching staffs ate their hearts out. Davis, armed with a 95-mile-an-hour fastball and one of the league's best curveballs, simply wasn't getting the job done as a starter with the Phillies and Giants.

But Davis finally fulfilled his promise after being traded in 1987 by the Giants with third baseman Chris Brown and pitchers Keith Comstock and Mark Grant for outfielder Kevin Mitchell and pitchers Dave Dravecky and Craig Lefferts. The Padres decided to use Davis as their closer, and in 1988 he earned 28 saves in 34 opportunities.

Last year Davis won the National League's Cy Young Award, baseball's premier pitching prize. He allowed a piddling 19 earned runs in 92⅔ innings, with a major-league leading 44 saves. How important was Davis to the Padres? He won or saved 56 percent of the team's 86 victories. He could make the difference for Kansas City this year.

Year	Team	W	L	SV	ERA	IP	H	BB	K
1980	Phi	0	0	0	2.57	7.0	4	5	5
1981	Phi	1	4	0	7.74	43.0	49	24	29
1983	SF	6	4	0	3.49	111.0	93	50	83
1984	SF	5	17	0	5.36	174.2	201	54	124
1985	SF	5	12	7	3.54	114.1	89	41	131
1986	SF	5	7	4	2.99	84.1	63	34	90
1987	SF	4	5	0	4.71	70.2	72	28	51
1987	SD	5	3	2	3.18	62.1	51	31	47
1988	SD	5	10	28	2.01	98.1	70	42	102
1989	SD	4	3	44	1.85	92.2	66	31	92
		40	65	85	3.76	858.1	758	340	754

John Dopson

Birth Date: 7/14/63
Throws: Right
1989 Club:
Boston Red Sox
Contest Code #: 728

Rating: 3

Will the real John Dopson please stand up? Is it the Dopson who went 3–11 with the Expos (albeit with a 3.04 ERA) in 1988? Or is it the Dopson who pleased the Boston faithful with a 12–8 mark and a not-bad-for-Fenway 3.99 ERA in 1989?

Maybe it's a third Dopson we haven't seen yet. The Baltimore native spent seven years in the Montreal organization (he was a second-round draft choice in 1982) before coming to the Sox in a December 1988 trade that saw Spike Owen and Dan Gakeler move to Canada for Dopson and Luis Rivera. Dopson's minor-league performance was fairly consistent, if not spectacular. He didn't win consistently at the AAA level, though a variety of injuries (he had shoulder surgery in 1986, which shelved him until early 1987) didn't help.

Never much of a power pitcher, John will have to work on his control to make certain that the 1989 Dopson remains the real Dopson.

Year	Team	W	L	SV	ERA	IP	H	BB	K
1985	Mon	0	2	0	11.08	13.0	25	4	4
1988	Mon	3	11	0	3.04	168.2	150	58	101
1989	Bos	12	8	0	3.99	169.1	166	69	95
		15	21	0	3.79	351.0	341	131	200

Richard Dotson

Birth Date: 1/10/59
Throws: Right
1989 Club:
New York Yankees &
Chicago White Sox
Contest Code #: 729

Rating: 2

After just a season-plus with the New York Yankees, right-hander Richard Dotson came home to the Chicago White Sox last summer. How long the off-season free agent planned to stay was questionable.

The insiders' report on Dotson isn't all that encouraging. Both his fastball and slider rank in the borderline category, though the slider is possibly a smidgen better than the fastball. His straight change is effective much of the time. Still, he looks as if he has seen better days.

There have been better days. Dotson was 22–7 for the Sox in 1983 (teammate LaMarr Hoyt won the Cy Young Award, and the Sox won the AL-West title), one of only four winning seasons for the ten-year-plus veteran. Last year, his combined numbers were 5–12 and a 4.46 ERA. That put him two games over .500 for his career, which seems on the way down.

Year	Team	W	L	SV	ERA	IP	H	BB	K
1979	ChA......	2	0	0	3.75	24.0	28	6	13
1980	ChA......	12	10	0	4.27	198.0	185	87	109
1981	ChA......	9	8	0	3.77	141.0	145	49	73
1982	ChA......	11	15	0	3.84	196.2	219	73	109
1983	ChA......	22	7	0	3.22	240.0	209	106	137
1984	ChA......	14	15	0	3.59	245.2	216	103	120
1985	ChA......	3	4	0	4.47	52.1	53	17	33
1986	ChA......	10	17	0	5.48	197.0	226	69	110
1987	ChA......	11	12	0	4.17	211.1	201	86	114
1988	NYA......	12	9	0	5.00	171.0	178	72	77
1989	NYA......	2	5	0	5.57	51.2	69	17	14
1989	ChA......	3	7	0	3.88	99.2	112	41	55
		111	109	0	4.16	1828.1	1841	726	964

Tim Drummond

Birth Date: 12/24/64
Throws: Right
1989 Club:
Minnesota Twins
Contest Code #: 730

Rating: 1

After three straight successful years at AAA, Tim Drummond may be ready to become a major-league setup man. Drummond, who came to the Minnesota Twins in the Frank Viola deal last summer, worked at Tidewater (5–1, 3.27, 35 appearances) and Portland (1–1, 3.27, 10 appearances, 1 save) last summer before reporting to Minny on August 28. He got into 8 Twins games in September (his first major-league action since 6 games with the 1987 Pittsburgh Pirates) but wasn't involved in any decisions—though he did pick up his first big-league save.

It may be too early to tell, but the Maryland native seems to be able to pitch. He has overcome control problems which slowed him down early in his career.

Year	Team	W	L	SV	ERA	IP	H	BB	K
1987	Pit.......	0	0	0	4.50	6.0	5	3	5
1989	Min......	0	0	1	3.86	16.1	16	8	9
		0	0	1	4.03	22.1	21	11	14

Brian DuBois

Birth Date: 4/18/67
Throws: Left
1989 Club:
Detroit Tigers
Contest Code #: 731

Rating: 1

If you only look at won-lost, you think that Brian DuBois needs a lot more minor-league preparation. If you look deeper, you have to believe that this is a talented young left-hander. DuBois went from Class-A Hagerstown in the Baltimore organization to the majors with Detroit in just over one year. Acquired by the Tigers in a deal that sent Keith Moreland to the Orioles in late July, DuBois (say it Du-BOYS) made 5 starts for Detroit and wound up 0–4.

But look more closely. His ERA was a stellar 1.75. In his first start, he allowed 2 first-inning runs to the Yankees and lost 2–0. He lost another 2–0 game to Toronto, despite 7 innings of 4-hit pitching. In his lone relief appearance, he pitched 5 shutout innings and gained his first save. His pickoff move is awesome. He picked off Wade Boggs, Kevin Seitzer, and two others in his 6 games.

Year	Team	W	L	SV	ERA	IP	H	BB	K
1989	Det	0	4	1	1.75	36.0	29	17	13
		0	4	1	1.75	36.0	29	17	13

Michael Dunne

Birth Date: 10/27/62
Throws: Right
1989 Club:
Pittsburgh Pirates &
Seattle Mariners
Contest Code #: 732

Rating: 3

You can't help but wonder what's going on inside Mike Dunne's head. Off a spectacular major-league debut in 1987, he has now put together two relatively poor, somewhat confusing seasons.

A former St. Louis Cardinal farmhand, Dunne came to the Pittsburgh Pirates in the Tony Pena deal. Summoned to Three Rivers on June 1, 1987, he tore up the NL, going 13–6 with a sparkling 3.03 ERA.

A new phenom? Perhaps. Then it went south. Dunne stumbled to 7–11 for the second-place Bucs in 1988, went 1–1 (with a hideous 7.53 ERA) in his first three 1989 starts with Pittsburgh, then was dealt to Seattle in the infamous Rey Quinones trade. Though Seattle got the best of it, Dunne was an unimpressive 2–9 in 15 starts with the Mariners with an equally unimpressive 5.27 ERA. Will we ever see the 1987 model Dunne again?

Year	Team	W	L	SV	ERA	IP	H	BB	K
1987	Pit	13	6	0	3.03	163.1	143	68	72
1988	Pit	7	11	0	3.92	170.0	163	88	70
1989	Pit	1	1	0	7.54	14.1	21	9	4
1989	Sea	2	9	0	5.27	85.1	104	37	38
		23	27	0	3.97	433.0	431	202	184

Mike Dyer

Birth Date: 9/8/66
Throws: Right
1989 Club:
Minnesota Twins
Contest Code #: 733

Rating: 1

Thanks to the Frank Viola trade which brought 5 new arms to the Minnesota Twins, the Twins' off-season forty-man roster included 19 pitchers. Obviously the competition for pitching jobs will be fierce. Mike Dyer had a decent shot last summer, making 12 starts and 16 appearances for the Humphreydomers after 15 starts for Class-AAA Portland.

The results were decidedly mixed. In both spots, his ERA was in the mid-to-high 4's, 4.43 in the Pacific Coast League and 4.82 in the American League. He didn't win in either place, 3–6 at Portland and 4–7 at Minnesota.

At age twenty-three, Mike has plenty of time to make it. If he can get a handle on on-going control problems, he might do it.

Year	Team	W	L	SV	ERA	IP	H	BB	K
1989	Min......	4	7	0	4.82	71.0	74	37	37
		-4	7	0	4.82	71.0	74	37	37

Dennis Eckersley

Birth Date: 10/3/54
Throws: Right
1989 Club:
Oakland Athletics
Contest Code #: 734

Rating: 5

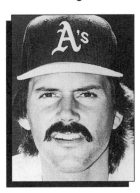

Every championship club needs that closer who can lock up the "W" any time he gets the ball. For the world-champion Oakland Athletics, that means Dennis Eckersley. The well-traveled (Cleveland, Boston, Chicago Cubs, and Oakland in fourteen big-league seasons) right-hander racked up 33 saves for the A's last year, giving him a three-year total of 94 with Oakland. When you consider that Eck had started 335 games in the previous eleven seasons with no saves since 1976, it hasn't been a bad transformation.

The 6'2", 195-pounder has a great assortment of pitches and even better control. His fastball rates above average with above-average location, and his slider is brutal. What makes the whole package effective, however, is Eck's control—which allowed only 3 walks during all of last season (57⅔ innings). He also struck out 55. His 4–0 record and 33 saves were accomplished with a stingy 1.56 ERA.

Year	Team	W	L	SV	ERA	IP	H	BB	K
1976	Cle	13	12	1	3.44	199.0	155	78	200
1977	Cle	14	13	0	3.53	247.0	214	54	191
1978	Bos	20	8	0	2.99	268.0	258	71	162
1979	Bos	17	10	0	2.99	247.0	234	59	150
1980	Bos	12	14	0	4.27	198.0	188	44	121
1981	Bos	9	8	0	4.27	154.0	160	35	79
1982	Bos	13	13	0	3.73	224.1	228	43	127
1983	Bos	9	13	0	5.61	176.1	223	39	77
1984	Bos	4	4	0	5.01	64.2	71	13	33
1984	ChN	10	8	0	3.03	160.1	152	36	81
1985	ChN	11	7	0	3.08	169.1	145	19	117
1986	ChN	6	11	0	4.57	201.0	226	43	137
1987	Oak	6	8	16	3.03	115.2	99	17	113
1988	Oak	4	2	45	2.35	72.2	52	11	70
1989	Oak	4	0	33	1.56	57.2	32	3	55
		152	131	95	3.64	2555.0	2437	565	1713

Steve Farr

Birth Date: 12/12/56
Throws: Right
1989 Club:
Kansas City Royals
Contest Code #: 735

Rating: 3

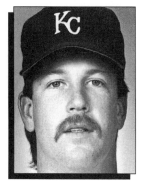

Steve Farr has found a home. It's the bullpen bench, and he usually calls it home until late in the game when the Royals need a save or a setup.

For a while, it didn't look as though Steve would ever find that home. One of those rare birds (a star athlete at Hyattsville, MD's Demetha High School who didn't play basketball), the 5′11″, 200-pounder signed with the Pirates in 1976 and hung around their farm system through early 1983. Dealt to Cleveland, he finally earned a major-league shot in 1984—and dropped the ball, going 3–11 for the Tribe with a don't-write-home-about 4.58 ERA. That earned him his release and one more minor-league stint, with Kaycee's top Omaha farm club —where his 10–4 record and league-leading 2.02 ERA gave him one last chance. He took it, and the rest is history.

Given a chance to be the Royals' closer in 1988, Farr responded with a 5–4 mark, a 2.50 ERA, and 20 saves. In 1989, he teamed with Jeff Montgomery to form one of the best one-two closing punches in the AL. A tough competitor, Farr is a breaking-ball pitcher who's never afraid to take the ball and head to the mound. In a word, he's a staff-saver.

Year	Team	W	L	SV	ERA	IP	H	BB	K
1984	Cle	3	11	1	4.58	116.0	106	46	83
1985	KC........	2	1	1	3.11	37.2	34	20	36
1986	KC........	8	4	8	3.13	109.1	90	39	83
1987	KC........	4	3	1	4.15	91.0	97	44	88
1988	KC........	5	4	20	2.50	82.2	74	30	72
1989	KC........	2	5	18	4.12	63.1	75	22	56
		24	28	49	3.67	500.0	476	201	418

John Farrell

Birth Date: 8/4/62
Throws: Right
1989 Club:
Cleveland Indians
Contest Code #: 736

Rating: 3

After a 14–10 record in 1988, John Farrell expected to be the big man in Cleveland's 1989 rotation. It didn't happen. It's strange but the New Jersey native got off to a superstart in 1988, then faded at the finish. In 1989, it was just the opposite: slow start, fast finish.

Cleveland management thinks that the late-1989 Farrell is the real thing. He has the tools. His rising fastball has plenty of pop. His other pitches are coming, too. His hard slider is almost there, and his change-up isn't bad. Control, long a Farrell problem, has come a long way and is now rated above average.

A second-generation Indian—his father was a Cleveland minor-leaguer in the mid-1950s—Farrell was 9–14 with a 3.63 ERA last season. Most impressive, he had 7 complete games, tops among Indian starters—especially knowing that Doug Jones was always ready to step out of the bullpen to finish. After only two and a fraction big-league seasons, Farrell is still getting better.

Year	Team	W	L	SV	ERA	IP	H	BB	K
1987	Cle	5	1	0	3.39	69.0	68	22	28
1988	Cle	14	10	0	4.24	210.1	216	67	92
1989	Cle	9	14	0	3.63	208.0	196	71	132
		28	25	0	3.86	487.1	480	160	252

Tom Filer

Birth Date: 12/1/56
Throws: Right
1989 Club:
Milwaukee Brewers
Contest Code #: 737

Rating: 1

Tom Filer has gotten to the stage of his career when he can go through the enemy's lineup effectively— once. After that they catch up with him quickly. The veteran right-hander's stuff is now extremely short, compounded by a series of arm problems. Tendinitis in the right shoulder forced the 6'1", 198-pounder to open the 1989 season on the DL, then spend two months at Class-AAA Denver (5–1, 2.80 ERA) where he worked his way back to the big club.

A 4-game win-streak from July 23 to August 18 enabled Tom to finish 1989 at 7–3 with a 3.61 ERA. But only 3 times in 13 starts was he able to last 7 innings or more— a clear indication of his lack of on-the-mound stamina. The book on Filer indicates that he's a marginal major-league talent.

Year	Team	W	L	SV	ERA	IP	H	BB	K
1982	ChN......	1	2	0	5.53	40.2	50	18	15
1985	Tor.......	7	0	0	3.88	48.2	38	18	24
1988	Mil	5	8	0	4.43	101.2	108	33	39
1989	Mil	7	3	0	3.61	72.1	74	23	20
		20	13	0	4.27	263.1	270	92	98

Chuck Finley

Birth Date: 11/16/62
Throws: Left
1989 Club:
California Angels
Contest Code #: 738

Rating: 4

After back-to-back 2–7 and 9–15 seasons, Chuck Finley had to be wondering about his major-league future. No more. The towering (6'6", 215 pounds) Louisiana native showed the world last year that he is a pitcher, a fine pitcher. His fastball is good. His forkball is even better. Enemy batters say that the bottom falls out of it, and that makes Finley one tough hombre.

Finley arrived on the big-league scene in 1986 as a reliever, without much success. Placed into the starting rotation in September 1987, Finley has now made 63 straight starts for the Angels. He has found his niche. The 16–9 record with a nifty 2.57 ERA were just one indication of Finley's growth and improvement. Add in his hits-to-innings-pitched ratio (171 hits in 199⅔ innings) and you have a better idea of how tough he has become. He's going to get even better.

Year	Team	W	L	SV	ERA	IP	H	BB	K
1986	Cal	3	1	0	3.30	46.1	40	23	37
1987	Cal	2	7	0	4.67	90.2	102	43	63
1988	Cal	9	15	0	4.17	194.1	191	82	111
1989	Cal	16	9	0	2.57	199.2	171	82	156
		30	32	0	3.58	531.0	504	230	367

Mike Flanagan

Birth Date: 12/16/51
Throws: Left
1989 Club:
Toronto Blue Jays
Contest Code #: 739

Rating: 3

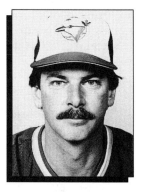

Mike Flanagan, the one-time Baltimore Oriole power pitcher, is now Toronto Blue Jay junkman Mike Flanagan. After fourteen years in the majors, Flanagan's fastball is nowhere near where it was in the mid-1970s when he won 15, 19, 23, and 16 in four straight Oriole seasons. Now the 6′, 195-pounder depends on changing speeds and painting corners, and he does it pretty well. The left-hander made 30 starts for the AL-East champions last year, getting 171⅔ innings under his belt. His 8–10 record (3.93 ERA) marked his first sub-.500 season in Toronto, where he arrived from Baltimore in 1987.

Getting Flanagan wasn't a bad idea for the Jays. Since their founding in 1977 the pitcher they had the most trouble beating was Mike Flanagan. As an Oriole, he beat them 17 times, more than any other AL pitcher.

Year	Team	W	L	SV	ERA	IP	H	BB	K
1975	Bal	0	1	0	2.70	10.0	9	6	7
1976	Bal	3	5	0	4.13	85.0	83	33	56
1977	Bal	15	10	1	3.64	235.0	235	70	149
1978	Bal	19	15	0	4.04	281.0	271	87	167
1979	Bal	23	9	0	3.08	266.0	245	70	190
1980	Bal	16	13	0	4.12	251.0	278	71	128
1981	Bal	9	6	0	4.19	116.0	108	37	72
1982	Bal	15	11	0	3.97	236.0	233	76	103
1983	Bal	12	4	0	3.30	125.1	135	31	50
1984	Bal	13	13	0	3.53	226.2	213	81	115
1985	Bal	4	5	0	5.13	86.0	101	28	42
1986	Bal	7	11	0	4.24	172.0	179	66	96
1987	Bal	3	6	0	4.94	94.2	102	36	50
1987	Tor.	3	2	0	2.37	49.1	46	15	43
1988	Tor.	13	13	0	4.18	211.0	220	80	99
1989	Tor.	8	10	0	3.93	171.2	186	47	47
		163	134	1	3.89	2616.2	2644	834	1414

Tony Fossas

Birth Date: 9/23/58
Throws: Left
1989 Club:
Milwaukee Brewers
Contest Code #: 740

Rating: 1

Given a shot at the majors thanks to an injury to right-hander Bill Wegman, Tony Fossas did a workmanlike job in three months as a Milwaukee Brewer. A ten-year minor-leaguer, Fossas won his first major-league game last June 15 against Toronto, followed with his first big-league save on August 20 against the Red Sox. In 51 appearances, Fossas inherited 54 base runners and allowed 10 to score, an impressive 19 percent record. And he permitted only 3 homers in 61 innings.

Still, the scouts report that all of Fossas' stuff is somewhat short and despite a delivery that tends to confuse the hitters, his long-term major-league prospects are marginal, at best.

Year	Team	W	L	SV	ERA	IP	H	BB	K
1988	Tex	0	0	0	4.77	5.2	11	2	0
1989	Mil	2	2	1	3.54	61.0	57	22	42
		2	2	1	3.65	66.2	68	24	42

Willie Fraser

Birth Date: 5/26/64
Throws: Right
1989 Club:
California Angels
Contest Code #: 741

Rating: 2

Willie Fraser is something of an anomaly. He has everything he needs to become a top pitcher, but he still hasn't really become a pitcher. The book on Fraser continues to read "thrower." His biggest problem is inconsistency. Once he overcomes those two shortcomings, he could be a front-liner.

A New York City native who played at Concordia College in the New York suburbs, Fraser owns a decent fastball and a more-than-decent fork ball. At times, he's overpowering. At others, he's ready for batting practice. (In August 1988, Yankee batters touched him for an Angel club-record five homers, though California won 15–6.)

Though he won 12 games as a starter in 1988, the Angels moved him to the bullpen in 1989, where the record slipped to 4–7—albeit with a 3.24 ERA. His control is decent (46 strikeouts and 23 walks in 91⅔ innings), and he can get people out. The rest of the trip is up to Willie.

Year	Team	W	L	SV	ERA	IP	H	BB	K
1986	Cal	0	0	0	8.31	4.1	6	1	2
1987	Cal	10	10	1	3.92	176.2	160	63	106
1988	Cal	12	13	0	5.41	194.2	203	80	86
1989	Cal	4	7	2	3.24	91.2	80	23	46
		26	30	3	4.45	467.1	449	167	240

Wes Gardner

Birth Date: 4/29/61
Throws: Right
1989 Club:
Boston Red Sox
Contest Code #: 742

Rating: 2

A one-time Met hotshot prospect, Gardner didn't show a thing in Boston last year, finishing the season on the twenty-one-day DL. Coming off a 1988 season which produced his first winning big-league record (8–6, 3.50 ERA) as a part-time starter, part-time reliever, 1989 was a bummer, with a 3–7 record and a rocky 5.97 ERA. With stints on the DL in three of his last four seasons, Gardner appears to be fragile as well as inconsistent.

The Natick, MA, native (who now lives in Arkansas) owns an average fastball, which doesn't strike much fear into enemy hearts. His best pitch is a slider, which can be effective at times. If Boston looks to keep Gardner in a starting role, it's probably a mistake. He seems best suited to a middle-relief or setup position.

Year	Team	W	L	SV	ERA	IP	H	BB	K
1984	NYN	1	1	1	6.40	25.1	34	8	19
1985	NYN	0	2	0	5.25	12.0	18	8	11
1986	Bos	0	0	0	9.00	1.0	1	0	1
1987	Bos	3	6	10	5.42	89.2	98	42	70
1988	Bos	8	6	2	3.50	149.0	119	64	106
1989	Bos	3	7	0	5.97	86.0	97	47	81
		15	22	13	4.83	363.0	367	169	288

Paul Gibson

Birth Date: 1/4/60
Throws: Left
1989 Club:
Detroit Tigers
Contest Code #: 743

Rating: 2

When you play for a last-place team, you have to do whatever you can to keep your sanity. Paul Gibson, the Detroit Tigers' top rookie in 1988 as an outstanding middle- and long-reliever, split his sophomore year between the starting staff and the bullpen. Similarly, the results were mixed. The Long Island native made 13 starts and 32 relief appearances, winning 4 and losing 8.

The left-hander didn't impress the scouts. Both his fastball and breaking ball are short. What has kept him in the big leagues so far is a straight change that is very effective.

The 6', 185-pounder (who looks smaller out on the mound) knocked around the minors for ten seasons before getting his shot with the Tigers in 1988. Released by the Cincinnati Reds in 1981, he signed on with Detroit and continued his minor-league odyssey until he finally arrived in Tiger Stadium.

Year	Team	W	L	SV	ERA	IP	H	BB	K
1988	Det	4	2	0	2.93	92.0	83	34	50
1989	Det	4	8	0	4.64	132.0	129	57	77
		8	10	0	3.94	224.0	212	91	127

Thomas (Flash) Gordon

Birth Date: 11/18/67
Throws: Right
1989 Club:
Kansas City Royals
Contest Code #: 744

Rating: 4

How many young big-league pitchers would turn down the chance to exchange futures with Flash Gordon? Not too many. The much-heralded twenty-two-year-old hit the big time a year ago and lived up to his advance billing. How many young players can make that claim? The minor-league player of the year in 1988 after three stops on the Kaycee minor-league chain (with a combined 16–5 record), Gordon was hailed as the next Royal superstar last spring.

No matter what manager John Wathan asked him to do, he did well: start, relieve, finish. He compiled a 17–9 record in 49 appearances, 16 of them starts. In 163 innings, he punched out 153 hitters while walking 86. The book on Gordon reads: "tremendous curveball, above-average fastball." American League hitters won't be thrilled to learn that he's also working on a straight change, which will give him an awesome arsenal.

There are some questions about his size (only 5'9", 160 pounds), which may create problems in terms of stamina and durability as his career progresses. But, that aside, this is one fine-looking young pitcher.

Year	Team	W	L	SV	ERA	IP	H	BB	K
1988	KC.......	0	2	0	5.17	15.2	16	7	18
1989	KC.......	17	9	1	3.64	163.0	122	86	153
		17	11	1	3.78	178.2	138	93	171

Goose Gossage

Birth Date: 7/5/51
Throws: Right
1989 Club:
New York Yankees
Contest Code #: 745

Rating: 2

Once upon a time, the mere sight of the large, powerful Goose Gossage ambling in from the Yankee bullpen was enough to crumble a batter's knees. Now the only one Gossage scares is his manager.

The Goose has been throwing heat in pro ball since 1970, in the majors since 1972. The act is old, the fastball is a foot or two short, and the Goose has been cooked. Mopping up with his beloved old Yankees late last summer, Gossage stormed around the mound long enough to confuse a couple of batters to rack up 1 win (no losses) and 1 save in 11 appearances (14⅓ innings). The 3.77 ERA wasn't much to write home about, and he doesn't have the speed to strike out a batter an inning as he used to. The Goose will be thirty-nine this summer. He may have created his last flap.

Year	Team	W	L	SV	ERA	IP	H	BB	K
1972	ChA	7	1	2	4.27	80.0	72	44	57
1973	ChA	0	4	0	7.38	50.0	57	37	33
1974	ChA	4	6	1	4.15	89.0	92	47	64
1975	ChA	9	8	26	1.84	142.0	99	70	130
1976	ChA	9	17	1	3.94	224.0	214	90	135
1977	Pit	11	9	26	1.62	133.0	78	49	151
1978	NYA	10	11	27	2.01	134.0	87	59	122
1979	NYA	5	3	18	2.64	58.0	48	19	41
1980	NYA	6	2	33	2.27	99.0	74	37	103
1981	NYA	3	2	20	0.77	47.0	22	14	48
1982	NYA	4	5	30	2.23	93.0	63	28	102
1983	NYA	13	5	22	2.27	87.1	82	25	90
1984	SD	10	6	25	2.90	102.1	75	36	84
1985	SD	5	3	26	1.82	79.0	64	17	52
1986	SD	5	7	21	4.45	64.2	69	20	63
1987	SD	5	4	11	3.12	52.0	47	19	44
1988	ChN	4	4	13	4.33	43.2	50	15	30
1989	SF	2	1	4	2.68	43.2	32	27	24
1989	NYA	1	0	1	3.77	14.1	14	3	6
		113	98	307	2.92	1636.0	1339	656	1379

Cecilio Guante

Birth Date: 2/2/60
Throws: Right
1989 Club:
Texas Rangers
Contest Code #: 746

Rating: 3

When you've got a premier closer, you want the set-up man who can get the ball to him. Cecilio Guante has been setting up some of the majors' best since arriving in the big leagues with Pittsburgh in 1982. Despite a late-season DL visit last summer, the Dominican did fairly well positioning the Rangers' Jeff Russell for his saves. In 50 games, he worked 69 innings, finishing 19 outings and saving 2. Most relievers don't get into stride until their late to mid-20s. Guante has been doing his thing since age 22, and there are some concerns about his arm, which has landed him on the DL in two of the last three summers. When he's healthy, however, he can get the job done.

Year	Team	W	L	SV	ERA	IP	H	BB	K
1982	Pit	0	0	0	3.33	27.0	28	5	26
1983	Pit	2	6	9	3.32	100.1	90	46	82
1984	Pit	2	3	2	2.61	41.1	32	16	30
1985	Pit	4	6	5	2.72	109.0	84	40	92
1986	Pit	5	2	4	3.35	78.0	65	29	63
1987	NYA	3	2	1	5.73	44.0	42	20	46
1988	NYA	5	6	11	2.88	75.0	59	22	61
1988	Tex	0	0	1	1.93	4.2	8	4	4
1989	Tex	6	6	2	3.91	69.0	66	36	69
		27	31	35	3.35	548.1	474	218	473

Mark Gubicza

Birth Date: 8/14/62
Throws: Right
1989 Club:
Kansas City Royals
Contest Code #: 747

Rating: 5

Though overshadowed by the AL's top pitcher of 1989, Bret Saberhagen, Gubicza continues to turn in stellar performances for Kansas City. He didn't come close to matching his 1988 season (20–8, 2.70 ERA), but he didn't miss by much. He went 15–11 with a none-too-shabby 3.04 earned-run mark. He also fanned 173 in 255 innings. He started 36 times and finished 8 of them—including a pair of shutouts. On a club without a Saberhagen, it would have been a brilliant season.

Scouts love Gubicza's tenacity on the mound. One calls him "an animal out there." Of course, all the intensity in the world won't help if you can't pitch, but Mark definitely can. He has excellent stuff with a good fastball and a slider that can only be termed nasty. Combined with an all-business attitude, it spells *impact pitcher*—which is exactly what Gubicza is.

Year	Team	W	L	SV	ERA	IP	H	BB	K
1984	KC.......	10	14	0	4.05	189.0	172	75	111
1985	KC.......	14	10	0	4.06	177.1	160	77	99
1986	KC.......	12	6	0	3.64	180.2	155	84	118
1987	KC.......	13	18	0	3.98	241.2	231	120	166
1988	KC.......	20	8	0	2.70	269.2	237	83	183
1989	KC.......	15	11	0	3.04	255.0	252	63	173
		84	67	0	3.51	1313.1	1207	502	850

Lee Guetterman

Birth Date: 11/22/58
Throws: Left
1989 Club:
New York Yankees
Contest Code #: 748

Rating: 3

The lefty member of the Yankees' bullpen pair (Dave Righetti was the right-hander), Lee Guetterman was a solid contributor in 1989, especially early in the season. He should continue in 1990.

At 6'8" and 225 pounds, Guetterman may well be a better rebounder than reliever, but his 5–5 record with 13 saves and a 2.45 ERA wasn't bad. An imposing and sometimes intimidating figure on the mound, he gets the most out of basically average stuff, though his change-up is a tremendous asset. His control is generally razor sharp.

In parts of three seasons with Seattle, Guetterman shuffled between starting and relief roles. He went 11–4 with the Mariners in 1987, making 17 starts among his 25 appearances. Traded to the Yankees the following season, he spent most of 1988 at AAA Columbus before spending the entire 1989 season in the Bronx.

Year	Team	W	L	SV	ERA	IP	H	BB	K
1984	Sea......	0	0	0	4.16	4.1	9	2	2
1986	Sea......	0	4	0	7.34	76.0	108	30	38
1987	Sea......	11	4	0	3.81	113.1	117	35	42
1988	NYA......	1	2	0	4.65	40.2	49	14	15
1989	NYA......	5	5	13	2.45	103.0	98	26	51
		17	15	13	4.30	337.1	381	107	148

Mark Guthrie

Birth Date: 9/22/65
Throws: Left
1989 Club:
Minnesota Twins
Contest Code #: 749

Rating: 2

Mark Guthrie, a twenty-four-year-old lefty, stepped through the Minnesota organization last season, from Class-AA Orlando to AAA Portland to the big club, with modest-to-better success along the way. A hard thrower, Guthrie fanned 103 and walked only 38 in 96 innings at Orlando, and continued to handcuff batters at the higher levels, as well. Surprisingly, his control seemed to deteriorate later in the season. At Minnesota, he went 2–4 in 8 starts and 5 relief appearances with a so-so 4.55 ERA.

At age twenty-four, he should have a major-league future.

Year	Team	W	L	SV	ERA	IP	H	BB	K
1989	Min......	2	4	0	4.55	57.1	66	21	38
		2	4	0	4.55	57.1	66	21	38

Drew Hall

Birth Date: 3/27/63
Throws: Left
1989 Club:
Texas Rangers
Contest Code #: 750

Rating: 2

Once Drew Hall gets a handle on his sometimes erratic control, he should be a fine addition to the Texas Rangers' staff. Hall, who came to Texas in the deal which sent Mitch Williams to Chicago, spent most of 1989 (all but three weeks in May) with the Rangers, with decent enough results (2–1, 3.70 ERA) in 58⅓ innings over 38 appearances.

The rangy 6'4", 220-pounder had three part-season trials with the Cubs before the trade in December 1988. His fastball isn't bad and his curve is pretty good. He gets into trouble when he loses his rhythm, which affects his delivery. Then his control goes downhill. Only two Ranger pitchers had a lower opponents' batting average than Hall's .207 (42 for 203). And he finished strongly. All three of his decisions came in the last 10 contests, as he lowered his ERA from 4.50 to the final 3.70. The Kentucky native has possibilities.

Year	Team	W	L	SV	ERA	IP	H	BB	K
1986	ChN......	1	2	1	4.56	23.2	24	10	21
1987	ChN......	1	1	0	6.89	32.2	40	14	20
1988	ChN......	1	1	1	7.66	22.1	26	9	22
1989	Tex	2	1	0	3.70	58.1	42	33	45
		5	5	2	5.26	137.0	132	66	108

Erik Hanson

Birth Date: 5/18/65
Throws: Right
1989 Club:
Seattle Mariners
Contest Code #: 751

Rating: 3

The Seattle Mariners' Erik Hanson may well be ready for bigger and better. The former Wake Forest All-American has moved quickly through the M's organization, even after missing all but 3 games of his first pro season (1986) while rehabilitating a right knee injury. Given a late-season shot with Seattle in late 1988 (after a no-hitter for Calgary), Hanson earned a fuller look in 1989 and made it pay off. Hanson made 17 starts for the M's, went 9–5, and rang up a nifty 3.18 ERA. A power pitcher throughout his career, New Jersey native Erik fanned 75 in 113⅓ innings while walking only 32. Not bad. Only once as a pro has Hanson soared beyond the 3's in ERA. In Calgary the numbers read 4.23, but that was the season an 0–5 start turned into a 12–2 finish.

Year	Team	W	L	SV	ERA	IP	H	BB	K
1988	Sea......	2	3	0	3.24	41.2	35	12	36
1989	Sea......	9	5	0	3.18	113.1	103	32	75
		11	8	0	3.19	155.0	138	44	111

Pete Harnisch

Birth Date: 9/23/66
Throws: Right
1989 Club:
Baltimore Orioles
Contest Code #: 752

Rating: 3

Only twenty-three, Pete Harnisch figures big in the Orioles plans for the near—and distant—future. A former Fordham U. star, Pete touched base at Bluefield, Hagerstown, Charlotte, and Rochester over parts of two minor-league seasons before arriving in Baltimore. He didn't do badly in 1989. In 17 big-league starts, he managed 2 complete games, striking out 70 in only 103 ⅓ innings of work. Control was a problem. Pete walked 64.

Our scouts believe the Orioles rushed Harnisch to the big time, which doesn't help. He has excellent arm strength and throws hard. He owns a sharp slider and can be a power pitcher. He's an excellent fielder, too, which helps keep pitchers in the big leagues. He will be a solid first-division pitcher in time. Whether that time is 1990 is a question.

Year	Team	W	L	SV	ERA	IP	H	BB	K
1988	Bal	0	2	0	5.54	13.0	13	9	10
1989	Bal	5	9	0	4.62	103.1	97	64	70
		5	11	0	4.72	116.1	110	73	80

Greg Harris

Birth Date: 11/2/55
Throws: Right
1989 Club:
Philadelphia Phillies &
Boston Red Sox
Contest Code #: 753

Rating: 2

Only world-class trivia buffs (and very old people) remember *Major Bowes' Original Amateur Hour* on the radio. The old major constantly reminded listeners that the wheel of show biz fortune spun around and around "and where it stops, nobody knows."

Sounds a lot like Greg Harris' major-league career. An original Met free-agent selection in 1976, Harris got to the majors with the New York club in 1981 and began spinning around the bigs, with modest results. The 6', 175-pound righthander spent part of 1982 with Cincinnati, parts of 1983 and 1984 with the Padres and Expos, three full seasons (1985–1987) with Texas, and part of 1988 and 1989 with the Phillies. After going 2–2 with Philly last season, he was released on August 1 and signed by the Red Sox on August 7. Another 2–2 record with the Sox (he permitted 7 of 11 runners he inherited to score) leaves him wide open for continued travel.

Year	Team	W	L	SV	ERA	IP	H	BB	K
1981	NYN	3	5	1	4.43	69.0	65	28	54
1982	Cin	2	6	1	4.83	91.1	96	37	67
1983	SD.......	0	0	0	27.00	1.0	2	3	1
1984	SD.......	2	1	1	2.70	36.2	28	18	30
1984	Mon	0	1	2	2.04	17.2	10	7	15
1985	Tex	5	4	11	2.47	113.0	74	43	111
1986	Tex	10	8	20	2.83	111.1	103	42	95

1987	Tex	5	10	0	4.86	140.2	157	56	106
1988	Phi	4	6	1	2.36	107.0	80	52	71
1989	Phi	2	2	1	3.58	75.1	64	43	51
1989	Bos	2	2	0	2.57	28.0	21	15	25
		35	45	38	3.52	791.0	700	344	626

Bryan Harvey

Birth Date: 6/2/63
Throws: Right
1989 Club:
California Angels
Contest Code #: 754

Rating: 3

Here's another of California manager Doug Rader's fine young arms. Harvey isn't quite there yet, but he's coming. Given his tools, his future looks bright. A one-time star at UNC-Charlotte, Harvey has been a winner at every stop in his professional career. At Midland (Texas) in 1987, his 20 saves (and 2.04 ERA) earned him designation as the Angels' "Minor League Player of the Year." In 1988, his first big-league season, he went 7–5 with the Angels in 50 games, picking up 17 saves and a second-place finish in the AL Rookie-of-the-Year balloting. Last year, he went 3–3 (3.44 ERA) with 25 of California's team total of 38 saves.

Rader is never reluctant to hand the ball to Harvey in tough situations. His fastball is a plus, his slider is good, and his forkball is downright nasty. He's just the sort of guy hitters don't want to see late in a game.

The son of one of the nation's top slow-pitch softball players, Harvey is a definite comer.

Year	Team	W	L	SV	ERA	IP	H	BB	K
1987	Cal	0	0	0	0.00	5.0	6	2	3
1988	Cal	7	5	17	2.13	76.0	59	20	67
1989	Cal	3	3	25	3.44	55.0	36	41	78
		10	8	42	2.58	136.0	101	63	148

Andy Hawkins

Birth Date: 1/21/60
Throws: Right
1989 Club:
New York Yankees
Contest Code #: 755

Rating: 3

Andy Hawkins certainly gave the Yankees their money's worth last season. The former seven-year San Diego Padre came to New York via the free-agency route prior to the 1989 season. The Texas native wound up as the Yankees' biggest winner (15), biggest loser (15), and busiest pitcher (208⅓ innings, 95 ahead of runner-up Dave LaPoint). The reliable right-hander put in his fourth 200-plus inning season in the last five years.

Hawkins also led the Yankees with 5 complete games and 2 shutouts. Hawkins doesn't have a lot of power. His fastball is, at best, borderline. He needs to set it up with good stuff, and he often does. Andy's straight change is pretty good, and his slider is first-rate. At age thirty, it's not inconceivable that Hawk could keep cranking out the innings and wins in the 1990s.

Year	Team	W	L	SV	ERA	IP	H	BB	K
1982	SD.......	2	5	0	4.10	63.2	66	27	25
1983	SD.......	5	7	0	2.93	119.2	106	48	59
1984	SD.......	8	9	0	4.68	146.0	143	72	77
1985	SD.......	18	8	0	3.15	228.2	229	65	69
1986	SD.......	10	8	0	4.30	209.1	218	75	117

Year	Team	W	L	SV	ERA	IP	H	BB	K
1987	SD.......	3	10	0	5.05	117.2	131	49	51
1988	SD.......	14	11	0	3.35	217.2	196	76	91
1989	NYA......	15	15	0	4.80	208.1	238	76	98
		75	73	0	4.00	1311.0	1327	488	587

Tom Henke

Birth Date: 12/21/57
Throws: Right
1989 Club:
Toronto Blue Jays
Contest Code #: 756

Rating: 5

Modern baseball axiom: You cannot win without a premier closer. Think about it. Even if a team operates with a "closer by committee," the end-of-game stopper is an absolute must in these days of the 6-inning starter. One key to Toronto's 1989 AL-East pennant was its supercloser, Tom Henke. The big (6'5", 225 pounds) right-hander is the Jays' all-time save leader with 119, including 20 last season. He also won 8 games (and lost 3) along with an impressive and career-best 1.92 ERA.

Unlike many closers, Henke is a 3-pitch pitcher. Both his fastball and slider rate a plus from major-league scouts. His splitter isn't quite in that company, but it isn't bad. The Missouri native got into 41 games for the Texas Rangers between 1982 and 1984 before he was selected by Toronto in the major-league compensation after the Jays lost powerful DH Cliff Johnson.

Year	Team	W	L	SV	ERA	IP	H	BB	K
1982	Tex	1	0	0	1.15	15.2	14	8	9
1983	Tex	1	0	1	3.37	16.0	16	4	17
1984	Tex	1	1	2	6.35	28.1	36	20	25
1985	Tor.......	3	3	13	2.02	40.0	29	8	42
1986	Tor.......	9	5	27	3.35	91.1	63	32	118
1987	Tor.......	0	6	34	2.49	94.0	62	25	128
1988	Tor.......	4	4	25	2.91	68.0	60	24	66
1989	Tor.......	8	3	20	1.92	89.0	66	25	116
		27	22	122	2.81	442.1	346	146	521

Mike Henneman

Birth Date: 12/11/61
Throws: Right
1989 Club:
Detroit Tigers
Contest Code #: 757

Rating: 5

How bad were the 1989 Detroit Tigers? Check this out. Reliever Mike Henneman was the team's top pitcher with a better than .500 record. The bullpen ace went 11–4 for the 59–103 Tigers, finishing 35 of his 60 appearances and picking up 8 saves.

Still, there's concern about the twenty-eight-year-old. His ERA, 1.87 in 1988 and 2.44 overall, zoomed to 3.70. The glitter seemed to disappear, though the Missouri native is still a first-rater as a setup man or short reliever. His fastball ranks at the plus level, and his slider is, at least, decent. His control remains an asset; he always seems to be around the plate. Though Henneman's save line dipped from 22 to 8 last season, the team's poor record was at least in part to blame. If Detroit ever decided to move the 6'4", 195-pounder, the offers would pile up quickly.

Year	Team	W	L	SV	ERA	IP	H	BB	K
1987	Det	11	3	7	2.98	96.2	86	30	75
1988	Det	9	6	22	1.87	91.1	72	24	58
1989	Det	11	4	8	3.70	90.0	84	51	69
		31	13	37	2.85	278.0	242	105	202

Guillermo Hernandez

Birth Date: 11/14/54
Throws: Left
1989 Club:
Detroit Tigers
Contest Code #: 758

Rating: 3

The former Willie Hernandez pitches just as well as a thirty-five-year-old Guillermo Hernandez. The tough lefty has been tidying up others' messes in major-league bullpens since 1977, when he worked in 67 games for the Chicago Cubs. Since then, he has toiled in 742 games for the Phillies and Tigers (since that championship season of 1984), failing to show very much wear and tear. These days, Hernandez gets by on guile and skill as much as power, though he can still throw smoke (30 strikeouts in 31⅓ innings a year ago). The 5.75 ERA (up from a previous career number of 3.31) is cause for alarm. But Señor Hernandez remains a solid member of the Tiger bullpen corps.

Year	Team	W	L	SV	ERA	IP	H	BB	K
1977	ChN......	8	7	4	3.03	110.0	94	28	78
1978	ChN......	8	2	3	3.75	60.0	57	35	38
1979	ChN......	4	4	0	5.01	79.0	85	39	53
1980	ChN......	1	9	0	4.42	108.0	115	45	75
1981	ChN......	0	0	2	3.86	14.0	14	8	13
1982	ChN......	4	6	10	3.00	75.0	74	24	54
1983	ChN......	1	0	1	3.20	19.2	16	6	18
1983	Phi	8	4	7	3.29	95.2	93	26	75
1984	Det	9	3	32	1.92	140.1	96	36	112
1985	Det	8	10	31	2.70	106.2	82	14	76
1986	Det	8	7	24	3.55	88.2	87	21	77
1987	Det	3	4	8	3.67	49.0	53	20	30
1988	Det	6	5	10	3.06	67.2	50	31	59
1989	Det	2	2	15	5.75	31.1	36	16	30
		70	63	147	3.38	1045.0	952	349	788

Eric Hetzel

Birth Date: 9/25/63
Throws: Right
1989 Club:
Boston Red Sox
Contest Code #: 759

Rating: 1

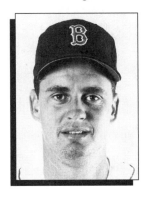

Where does Eric Hetzel go from here? The former LSU star (he was voted the Bengals' Outstanding Pitcher before Ben Jefferson got there) has experienced a checkered career, missing the entire 1986 season because of injury and going 6–10 for AAA Pawtucket in 1988, though the record was no indication of his ability.

Given a brief shot at Boston in 1989, he impressed some folks. In 11 starts and 1 relief appearance, the one-time number-one pick in the nation (secondary draft), averaged only a little over 4-innings-plus per start and walked 28 batters in 50⅓ innings—not a good sign. But he also struck out 33, which helps. A definite power pitcher, Hetzel needs to improve his control to remain in Boston.

Year	Team	W	L	SV	ERA	IP	H	BB	K
1989	Bos......	2	3	0	6.26	50.1	61	28	33
		2	3	0	6.26	50.1	61	28	33

Greg Hibbard

Birth Date: 9/13/64
Throws: Left
1989 Club:
Chicago White Sox
Contest Code #: 760

Rating: 2

Greg Hibbard's major-league debut in 1989 wasn't half bad. The New Orleans–born southpaw made 23 starts for the Chicago White Sox, went 6–7, and racked up a better-than-decent 3.21 ERA and a pair of complete games. Hibbard's performance made some baseball insiders sit up and take notice.

Still, the scouts aren't prepared to certify the career potential of the former Kansas City Royal farmhand. His stuff appears to be a bit short, in scouting parlance, although he changes speeds well. A one-time University of Alabama hurler, Hibbard was a sixteenth-round selection by the Royals in 1986. Greg spent only 2½ seasons in the minors—including three stops in 1987 alone—before getting into the Chisox lineup last season. He does show promise, but for now, rates as a #9 or #10 pitcher.

Year	Team	W	L	SV	ERA	IP	H	BB	K
1989	ChA......	6	7	0	3.21	137.1	142	41	55
		6	7	0	3.21	137.1	142	41	55

Kevin Hickey

Birth Date: 2/25/56
Throws: Left
1989 Club:
Baltimore Orioles
Contest Code #: 761

Rating: 3

Talk about sticking with it. Kevin Hickey hadn't appeared in a major-league game since the Chicago White Sox dropped him at the end of the 1983 season. He traveled the minor-league road thereafter, as property of the Yankees, Phillies, White Sox, and Giants, before finally latching on with the Orioles' system after the 1987 season. For Hickey, the wait was worthwhile. He got into 51 games for the Birds in 1989, picking up a couple of saves along the way.

Basically, he's a situation reliever. Thanks to a pretty decent slider, he's tough on left-handed batters—and that's about all. His fastball comes up a little short. As a result, he simply can't get it done against right-handed hitters.

Year	Team	W	L	SV	ERA	IP	H	BB	K
1981	ChA......	0	2	3	3.68	44.0	38	18	17
1982	ChA......	4	4	6	3.00	78.0	73	30	38
1983	ChA......	1	2	5	5.23	20.2	23	11	8
1989	Bal	2	3	2	2.92	49.1	38	23	28
		7	11	16	3.37	192.0	172	82	91

Teddy Higuera

Birth Date: 11/9/58
Throws: Left
1989 Club:
Milwaukee Brewers
Contest Code #: 762

Rating: 5

What if the Milwaukee Brewers had had Teddy Higuera for the entire 1989 season? No one in the beer-and-bratwurst capital wants to think about it. With Higuera limited to only 22 post-surgery starts, the Brewers fell 8 games short in its aborted attempt to catch the Toronto Blue Jays late last year.

Higuera must be considered one of the premier lefties in the game. Though he only went 9–6 after rushing back from the DL last season, his 3.46 ERA and 91 strikeouts in 135⅓ innings clearly demonstrated his capabilities. Though he has an arsenal of effective pitches, opposing batters simply can't handle his breaking ball, which he sets up well. The Mexican native is a wonderful competitor; the book on Higuera says: Get him early or not at all. With a five-year record of 78–44, Higuera is ready for even better in the 1990s.

Year	Team	W	L	SV	ERA	IP	H	BB	K
1985	Mil	15	8	0	3.90	212.1	186	63	127
1986	Mil	20	11	0	2.79	248.1	226	74	207
1987	Mil	18	10	0	3.85	261.2	236	87	240
1988	Mil	16	9	0	2.45	227.1	168	59	192
1989	Mil	9	6	0	3.46	135.1	125	48	91
		78	44	0	3.28	1085.0	941	331	857

Shawn Hillegas

Birth Date: 8/21/64
Throws: Right
1989 Club:
Chicago White Sox
Contest Code #: 763

Rating: 3

Forget Shawn Hillegas' 7–11 record and 4.74 ERA last year. The experts liked what they saw in the former L.A. Dodger's first full major-league season. They also like his fastball and report that his slider isn't bad. In short, here's a youngster who's just getting started on what should be a fine big-league career.

Hillegas has been around. Born in California, he went to high school in Pennsylvania and junior college in Georgia (he went 11–0 with a 1.73 ERA in 1984), then joined the Dodgers' organization, which had made Hillegas their first-round choice in the January 1984 draft. A 13–5 mark at Albuquerque in 1987 earned him a late-season promotion to Los Angeles. He came to the Chisox in a trade for Rick Horton in late 1988. Hillegas may be a pitch away from stardom in the majors, but there's plenty to build on.

Year	Team	W	L	SV	ERA	IP	H	BB	K
1987	LA.......	4	3	0	3.57	58.0	52	31	51
1988	LA.......	3	4	0	4.13	56.2	54	17	30
1988	ChA......	3	2	0	3.15	40.0	30	18	26
1989	ChA......	7	11	3	4.74	119.2	132	51	76
		17	20	3	4.13	274.1	268	117	183

Brian Holman

Birth Date: 1/25/65
Throws: Right
1989 Club:
Montreal Expos &
Seattle Mariners
Contest Code #: 764

Rating: 3

When the Montreal Expos decided to package a parcel of potential pitchers to purchase a possible pennant, Brian Holman came to Seattle in the Mark Langston deal. The Mariners like what they got. The twenty-five-year-old went 8–10 for the M's in 22 starts and finished what he started 6 times—easily the top figure among Seattle hurlers—and his 2 shutouts tied for club leadership with Scott Bankhead. The 6'4", 185-pound right-hander's 3.44 ERA easily surpassed his W-L record. At Montreal, Holman had been used mainly in relief (he started 3 games) and was 1–2 with a 4.83 ERA before the deal. The scouts feel that Holman's stuff is about average across-the-board, but they like his mound savvy. His control is a problem at times, and he occasionally struggles with his pitch location.

Year	Team	W	L	SV	ERA	IP	H	BB	K
1988	Mon	4	8	0	3.23	100.1	101	34	58
1989	Mon	1	2	0	4.83	31.2	34	15	23
1989	Sea	8	10	0	3.44	159.2	160	62	82
		13	20	0	3.52	291.2	295	111	163

Brian Holton

Birth Date: 11/29/59
Throws: Right
1989 Club:
Baltimore Orioles
Contest Code #: 765

Rating: 3

Once a hot Los Angeles Dodger prospect, Brian Holton came to the Orioles in the Eddie Murray trade. Like most Dodger-schooled pitchers, Holton knows his business. But his limitations may outweigh his assets. He has a fine repertoire of pitches—fastball, curve, cut fastball, and change. Unfortunately, none of them is what you can consider an "out" pitch. Power isn't the name of Brian's game (51 strikeouts in 116⅓ innings). He is basically a breaking-ball pitcher, the curve being his best pitch.

Considering his 1988 Dodger numbers, 1989 was a disappointment. After a 1.70 ERA and only 1 homer in 84⅔ innings, he blew up to 4.02 and 11 homers. He's still tough against righties, but will have to bounce back to keep the faith in Baltimore. An eight-year minor-leaguer, the thirty-year-old may still have the necessary ability.

Year	Team	W	L	SV	ERA	IP	H	BB	K
1985	LA	1	1	0	9.00	4.0	9	1	1
1986	LA	2	3	0	4.44	24.1	28	6	24
1987	LA	3	2	2	3.89	83.1	87	32	58
1988	LA	7	3	1	1.70	84.2	69	26	49
1989	Bal	5	7	0	4.02	116.1	140	39	51
		18	16	3	3.45	312.2	333	104	183

Rick Honeycutt

Birth Date: 6/29/54
Throws: Left
1989 Club:
Oakland Athletics
Contest Code #: 766

Rating: 4

Though left-hander Rick Honeycutt's stuff is a little short these days, he has great mound sense and makes the most of an outstanding ability to change speeds. The one-time Mariner, Ranger, and Dodger knows how to pitch. The thirty-five-year-old has been doing his thing on big-league mounds since 1977, only 1 ½ seasons removed from a standout career at the U. of Tennessee (where he was an All-American first baseman).

A starter for virtually his entire major-league career, Honeycutt moved to the bullpen when he arrived in Oakland in mid-1987. Now he's the left-handed accompaniment to right-handed closer Dennis Eckersley. The 6'1", 191-pounder made a team-high 64 appearances last year, splitting four decisions and picking up 12 saves. His 2.35 ERA was his career best.

It took awhile for Rick to adjust to full-time life in the bullpen when he was dealt to Oakland. Now that he has the hang of it, however, he feels pretty good about it.

Year	Team	W	L	SV	ERA	IP	H	BB	K
1977	Sea	0	1	0	4.34	29.0	26	11	17
1978	Sea	5	11	0	4.90	134.0	150	49	50
1979	Sea	11	12	0	4.04	194.0	201	67	83
1980	Sea	10	17	0	3.95	203.0	221	60	79
1981	Tex	11	6	0	3.30	128.0	120	17	40
1982	Tex	5	17	0	5.27	164.0	201	54	64
1983	Tex	14	8	0	2.42	174.2	168	37	56
1983	LA	2	3	0	5.77	39.0	46	13	18
1984	LA	10	9	0	2.84	183.2	180	51	75
1985	LA	8	12	1	3.42	142.0	141	49	67
1986	LA	11	9	0	3.32	171.0	164	45	100
1987	LA	2	12	0	4.59	115.2	133	45	92
1987	Oak	1	4	0	5.33	23.2	25	9	10
1988	Oak	3	2	7	3.50	79.2	74	25	47
1989	Oak	2	2	12	2.35	76.2	56	26	52
		95	125	20	3.76	1858.0	1906	558	850

Charlie Hough

Birth Date: 1/5/48
Throws: Right
1989 Club:
Texas Rangers
Contest Code #: 767

Rating: 3

Old baseball axiom: Knuckleballers aren't supposed to get sore shoulders. Just as he has disproved all sorts of baseball stories over the years, Charlie disproved that one too last season. The results weren't disastrous. Hough still won 10 games, fourth among Ranger pitchers, though he lost 13. It was his lowest victory total since 1981 (4–1), following seasons of 16, 15, 16, 14, 17, 18, and 15 wins, topping the club in each of those years. You expect knuckleballers to flirt with control problems, yet Hough was the only AL pitcher with more than 162 innings (the minimum qualification) with more walks allowed (95) than strikeouts (94).

At age forty-one, you might be ready to write Charlie off. But the Hawaii native has been amazing folks for years. Besides, knuckleballers have a great history of sticking around long enough to thrill their grandchildren.

Year	Team	W	L	SV	ERA	IP	H	BB	K
1970	LA	0	0	2	5.29	17.0	18	11	8
1971	LA	0	0	0	4.50	4.0	3	3	4
1972	LA	0	0	0	3.00	3.0	2	2	4
1973	LA	4	2	5	2.75	72.0	52	45	70
1974	LA	9	4	1	3.75	96.0	65	40	63
1975	LA	3	7	4	2.95	61.0	43	34	34

1976	LA.......	12	8	18	2.20	143.0	102	77	81
1977	LA.......	6	12	22	3.33	127.0	98	70	105
1978	LA.......	5	5	7	3.29	93.0	69	48	66
1979	LA.......	7	5	0	4.77	151.0	152	66	76
1980	LA.......	1	3	1	5.62	32.0	37	21	25
1980	Tex	2	2	0	3.98	61.0	54	37	47
1981	Tex	4	1	1	2.96	82.0	61	31	69
1982	Tex	16	13	0	3.95	228.0	217	72	128
1983	Tex	15	13	0	3.18	252.0	219	95	152
1984	Tex	16	14	0	3.76	266.0	260	94	164
1985	Tex	14	16	0	3.31	250.1	198	83	141
1986	Tex	17	10	0	3.79	230.1	188	89	146
1987	Tex	18	13	0	3.79	285.1	238	124	223
1988	Tex	15	16	0	3.32	252.0	202	126	174
1989	Tex	10	13	0	4.35	182.0	168	95	94
		174	157	61	3.60	2888.0	2446	1263	1874

Mike Jackson

Birth Date: 12/22/64
Throws: Right
1989 Club:
Seattle Mariners
Contest Code #: 768

Rating: 3

A six-man trade brought Mike Jackson to Seattle from the Philadelphia Phillies in December 1987. Now, he's the only one left with either team. He could hang around for a while. He has an excellent arm and a mean, nasty slurve (slider-curve) that, at times, can be a dominating pitch. At the least, it's very effective.

The weakness in his game is control. When it deserts him, which happens from time to time, it's a real problem. The Houston native was used mostly as a setup man in 1989. He was kept busy, making 65 appearances covering 99 ⅓ innings. His 4–6 record was not indicative of his work, which produced a 3.17 ERA. Despite his setup work, he finished 27 games and picked up 7 saves, giving him a two-year total of 11. To take the next step, he needs to reduce his base-on-balls total (54 last season).

Year	Team	W	L	SV	ERA	IP	H	BB	K
1986	Phi	0	0	0	3.38	13.1	12	4	3
1987	Phi	3	10	1	4.20	109.1	88	56	93
1988	Sea......	6	5	4	2.63	99.1	74	43	76
1989	Sea......	4	6	7	3.17	99.1	81	54	94
		13	21	12	3.36	321.1	255	157	266

Mike Jeffcoat

Birth Date: 8/3/59
Throws: Left
1989 Club:
Texas Rangers
Contest Code #: 769

Rating: 1

An injury to left-hander Jamie Moyer gave former Indian and Giant Mike Jeffcoat one more shot in the big leagues. The lefty from Arkansas has never been more than a borderline player in previous trials and isn't likely ever to do much better. Jeffcoat makes his living with a decent-enough split-fingered fastball and impeccable control. Other than that, his biggest advantage is that he's a left-hander.

Despite not arriving in Texas until May 31 last season, he wound up with his best big-league season, going 9–6 with a 3.58 ERA in 22 starts. He tied for the club lead (with Nolan Ryan—not bad company!) in shutouts with 2 and established career highs in all of those categories as well as in strikeouts (64). In fact, his winning season started out 5–5 until Jeffcoat won 4 of his last 5 decisions with a 2.51 ERA. He may just hang in there.

Year	Team	W	L	SV	ERA	IP	H	BB	K
1983	Cle	1	3	0	3.31	32.2	32	13	9
1984	Cle	5	2	1	2.99	75.1	82	24	41
1985	Cle	0	0	0	2.80	9.2	8	6	4
1985	SF	0	2	0	5.32	22.0	27	6	10
1987	Tex	0	1	0	12.86	7.0	11	4	1
1988	Tex	0	2	0	11.70	10.0	19	5	5
1989	Tex	9	6	0	3.58	130.2	139	33	64
		15	16	1	4.01	287.1	318	91	134

Dave Johnson

Birth Date: 10/24/59
Throws: Right
1989 Club:
Baltimore Orioles
Contest Code #: 770

Rating: 1

Dave Johnson clearly dispels the old rumor that you can't go home again. The Baltimore native is getting along just fine, thank you, in his native city. The 5'11", 177-pound right-hander tossed 4 complete games in his 14 starts for the hometown Birds in 1989, though his 4–7 record and his 4.23 ERA were just about average. So is his stuff. One danger sign is Johnson's walk-strikeout ratio. In 89⅓ innings, Dave walked only 28, but he struck out only 26. He also allowed just about a hit an inning (90 in all, 11 of them round-trippers).

Year	Team	W	L	SV	ERA	IP	H	BB	K
1987	Pit	0	0	0	9.95	6.1	13	2	4
1989	Bal	4	7	0	4.23	89.1	90	28	26
		4	7	0	4.61	95.2	103	30	30

Randy Johnson

Birth Date: 9/10/63
Throws: Left
1989 Club:
Montreal Expos &
Seattle Mariners
Contest Code #: 771

Rating: 3

If Randy Johnson doesn't make it as a pitcher for the Seattle Mariners, the Seattle SuperSonics may be waiting. The tallest baseball player ever, Johnson came to the M's from Montreal in the Mark Langston deal last summer. Now, the 6'10" former Southern Cal basketballer is poised to become a dominating major-league pitcher.

Not surprisingly, power is the name of the big guy's game. His aggressiveness makes him doubly tough; he's never afraid to come at a hitter. Though he makes his living with his fastball, he's working hard on a curve and a slider. Control is the key question. The California native isn't terribly wild, but he's just wild enough (with a 95-mph fastball) to keep hitters loose. Still, he'll need a little more control to move into the ranks of premier pitchers.

Johnson went 7–9 for the M's last summer, walking 70 and allowing 11 homers in 131 innings. The numbers should improve in 1990.

Year	Team	W	L	SV	ERA	IP	H	BB	K
1988	Mon	3	0	0	2.42	26.0	23	7	25
1989	Mon	0	4	0	6.68	29.2	29	26	26
1989	Sea	7	9	0	4.40	131.0	118	70	104
		10	13	0	4.48	186.2	170	103	155

Doug Jones

Birth Date: 6/24/57
Throws: Right
1989 Club:
Cleveland Indians
Contest Code #: 772

Rating: 5

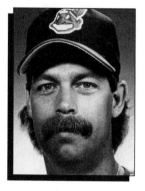

You figure it out. Doug Jones flounders around the Milwaukee organization for seven years, basically as a starter. Released by the Brewers, he hooks on with the Indians, becomes a relief pitcher, and five years later is one of the AL's premier closers. Worth the wait? Sure.

It wasn't until 1987, Jones' tenth year as a pro, that he became a full-time major leaguer. The California native took over as the Indians' closer in 1988 (3–4, 2.27, 37 saves) and kept up the pace in 1989. Taking fullest advantage of his sneaky fastball and superb change of speed, Jones was 7–10 with a 2.34 ERA and 32 saves, easily becoming the Tribe's all-time leading saver. He had a hand in 39 of Cleveland's 73 wins. Always around the plate, the 6'2", 195-pound right-hander fanned 65 enemy batters and walked only 13 in 80⅔ innings.

Year	Team	W	L	SV	ERA	IP	H	BB	K
1986	Cle	1	0	1	2.50	18.0	18	6	12
1987	Cle	6	5	8	3.15	91.1	101	24	87
1988	Cle	3	4	37	2.27	83.1	69	16	72
1989	Cle	7	10	32	2.34	80.2	76	13	65
		17	19	78	2.60	273.1	264	59	236

Jimmy Key

Birth Date: 4/22/61
Throws: Left
1989 Club:
Toronto Blue Jays
Contest Code #: 773

Rating: 4

Toronto fans will always have a warm spot in their hearts for Jimmy Key. When the Alabama native notched his first Blue Jay win on May 1, 1985, he ended a string of nearly four full seasons in which no Jay lefty starter had won a game. Incredible!

Since then, Key has won another 73 games, becoming the team's all-time winning southpaw. His 13–14 record and 3.87 ERA showed signs of inconsistency in 1989, and the scouting report concurs. His fastball velocity comes up a bit short, but he's an artist in terms of location. Fortunately, the rest of his arsenal—curve, slider, change-up—is excellent. If there's a shortcoming in his game, it's control. Occasionally it deserts him, and that's a problem. When he's right, however, he's as tough as they come.

Elbow surgery limited Key to only 131⅓ innings in 1988, but he came back with 216 solid innings last season, making it four seasons out of five with 200 or more.

Year	Team	W	L	SV	ERA	IP	H	BB	K
1984	Tor.......	4	5	10	4.65	62.0	70	32	44
1985	Tor.......	14	6	0	3.00	212.2	188	50	85
1986	Tor.......	14	11	0	3.57	232.0	222	74	141
1987	Tor.......	17	8	0	2.76	261.0	210	66	161
1988	Tor.......	12	5	0	3.29	131.1	127	30	65
1989	Tor.......	13	14	0	3.87	216.0	226	27	118
		74	49	10	3.36	1115.0	1043	279	614

Eric King

Birth Date: 4/10/64
Throws: Right
1989 Club:
Chicago White Sox
Contest Code #: 774

Rating: 2

Back in 1986, a twenty-two-year-old right-hander named Eric King looked like the Detroit Tigers' ace of the future. The Tigers had picked up the California native from the San Francisco Giants (in a deal that also involved Dave LaPoint, Matt Nokes, Juan Berenguer, and Bob Melvin). Detroit promoted the 6'2", 180-pounder from Nashville on May 14 and by season's end, he had shown the American League that he was something special.

Though his control was spotty, he had plenty of pop on his fastball, moved the ball around well, and had the out pitch when he needed it. The result: an 11–4 record, 3 complete games among 16 starts, and 3 saves in 17 relief appearances. Wow! Unfortunately, he has never matched that record. By 1988 he spent a couple of months in Toledo and by 1989 he was dealt to the White Sox. Off his 9–10 record—but with an improved 3.39 ERA—King could do the job for Chicago.

Year	Team	W	L	SV	ERA	IP	H	BB	K
1986	Det	11	4	3	3.51	138.1	108	63	79
1987	Det	6	9	9	4.89	116.0	111	60	89
1988	Det	4	1	3	3.41	68.2	60	34	45
1989	ChA......	9	10	0	3.39	159.1	144	64	72
		30	24	15	3.79	482.1	423	221	285

Mark Knudson

Birth Date: 10/28/60
Throws: Right
1989 Club:
Milwaukee Brewers
Contest Code #: 775

Rating: 3

At age twenty-nine, Mark Knudson has become a proven 3-inning pitcher. Look for the Milwaukee Brewers to use him mainly in long or middle relief, though he did get an occasional spot start (7 of 'em) last season. Knudson is basically a 2-pitch pitcher. Both his fastball and curve rate in the average category. Possibly his biggest asset is his toughness; he's never afraid to challenge the hitters. His problems arise the second time through the lineup.

Knudson, who pitched 16 innings for the Brewers in 1988, got a full year in Milwaukee last season. He actually thrived as a starter, with a 6–1 mark and a 2.23 ERA. One was a 2-hitter against the Mariners in September, keying a second-half comeback (2–3, 4.37 before the All-Star break; 6–2, 2.51 after the break).

Year	Team	W	L	SV	ERA	IP	H	BB	K
1985	Hou......	0	2	0	9.00	11.0	21	3	4
1986	Hou......	1	5	0	4.22	42.2	48	15	20
1986	Mil	0	1	0	7.64	17.2	22	5	9
1987	Mil	4	4	0	5.37	62.0	88	14	26
1988	Mil	0	0	0	1.12	16.0	17	2	7
1989	Mil	8	5	0	3.35	123.2	110	29	47
		13	17	0	4.32	273.0	306	68	113

Bill Krueger

Birth Date: 4/24/58
Throws: Left
1989 Club:
Milwaukee Brewers
Contest Code #: 776

Rating: 2

A Dodger in 1988, a Pirate in spring training 1989, Bill Krueger signed on with the Milwaukee Brewers after being released by the Bucs. It was a good move by the Brew Crew.

Krueger started the season in Denver (1–1, 2.03) and quickly returned to the majors. Used as both a starter and reliever, he wound up going 3–2 for Milwaukee, with a decent 3.84 ERA. By May 3 he had the first of his three saves and his first victory on May 6 (after two innings of scoreless relief). Pressed into duty as a starter in June, the big (6'5", 210-pound) lefty was 2–2 and was even better back in the bullpen in July and August, allowing only five earned runs in 39 innings, a 1.15 ERA.

Though Krueger doesn't figure to have a key role in the Milwaukee pennant drive in 1990, his versatility makes him a decent addition to the staff.

Year	Team	W	L	SV	ERA	IP	H	BB	K
1983	Oak......	7	6	0	3.61	109.2	104	53	58
1984	Oak......	10	10	0	4.75	142.0	156	85	61
1985	Oak......	9	10	0	4.52	151.1	165	69	56
1986	Oak......	1	2	1	6.03	34.1	40	13	10
1987	Oak......	0	3	0	9.54	5.2	9	8	2
1987	LA.......	0	0	0	0.00	2.1	3	1	2
1988	LA.......	0	0	0	11.59	2.1	4	2	1
1989	Mil	3	2	3	3.84	93.2	96	33	72
		30	33	4	4.44	541.1	577	264	262

Dennis Lamp

Birth Date: 9/23/52
Throws: Right
1989 Club:
Boston Red Sox
Contest Code #: 777

Rating: 3

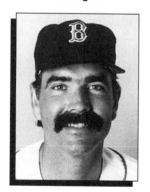

The major-league clock is beginning to run out on Dennis Lamp. A big leaguer since 1977, Lamp has earned the label "well-traveled" after stops in Chicago (NL and AL), Toronto, Oakland, and, now, Boston. He didn't fare badly for the 1989 Bosox, with a 4–2 mark and a 2.32 ERA. But his stuff is awfully limited and he's rapidly earning a new label, "hanging on."

At age thirty-seven, Lamp has benefited from his lengthy stay at the top. He knows how to pitch. His slider is still top-notch, but the rest of his repertoire is just a shade above ordinary. He was sound enough to get into 42 games for the Sox in 1989, pitching 112⅓ innings. The key is his control. He's always around the plate, and he knows how to nibble.

He should have a job in 1990, though he was a free agent after last season. Long range, however, he's still on a year-to-year basis.

Year	Team	W	L	SV	ERA	IP	H	BB	K
1977	ChN......	0	2	0	6.30	30.0	43	8	12
1978	ChN......	7	15	0	3.29	224.0	221	56	73
1979	ChN......	11	10	0	3.51	200.0	223	46	86
1980	ChN......	10	14	0	5.19	203.0	259	82	83
1981	ChA......	7	6	0	2.41	127.0	103	43	71
1982	ChA......	11	8	5	3.99	189.2	206	59	78
1983	ChA......	7	7	15	3.71	116.1	123	29	44
1984	Tor.......	8	8	9	4.55	85.0	97	38	45
1985	Tor.......	11	0	2	3.32	105.2	96	27	68
1986	Tor.......	2	6	2	5.05	73.0	93	23	30
1987	Oak......	1	3	0	5.08	56.2	76	22	36
1988	Bos......	7	6	0	3.48	82.2	92	19	49
1989	Bos......	4	2	2	2.32	112.1	96	27	61
		86	87	35	3.81	1605.1	1728	479	736

Mark Langston

Birth Date: 8/20/60
Throws: Left
1989 Club:
Seattle Mariners &
Montreal Expos
Contest Code #: 778

Rating: 5

Mark Langston, toiling in anonymity for the moribund Seattle Mariners, averaged 14 victories and 204 strikeouts per season. Baseball observers often wondered how good Langston would be on a winning team. The answer should have come last season, when Montreal general manager Dave Dombrowski boldly traded three pitching prospects for Langston, but the Expos played a Seattle-style second half.

By August 15, when the Expos were still in the thick of the Eastern Division race, Langston had won 10 of 13 decisions, with an ERA of 1.90 in 118⅔ innings. At the time, the Expos' offense was tied for fifth in the league in RBI's. Then the roof fell in. The Expos slid to a ninth-place tie in RBI's and Langston, bothered by a sore arm, won only two of his next eight decisions. Over his last 58 innings, Langston allowed 22 earned runs (3.96 ERA), 50 hits, and 37 walks (a combined 1.5 base runners per inning).

Langston's poor performance down the stretch didn't stop big-league teams from offering big bucks when his contract expired following the season. The winners of the Langston sweepstakes were the California Angels, at a cool $3.2 million per year. Over a full season Langston may not be as great as he was from last May to mid-August, but he's still one of the game's best left-handers.

Year	Team	W	L	SV	ERA	IP	H	BB	K
1984	Sea......	17	10	0	3.40	225.0	188	118	204
1985	Sea......	7	14	0	5.47	126.2	122	91	72
1986	Sea......	12	14	0	4.85	239.1	234	123	245
1987	Sea......	19	13	0	3.84	272.0	242	114	262
1988	Sea......	15	11	0	3.34	261.1	222	110	235
1989	Sea......	4	5	0	3.56	73.1	60	19	60
1989	Mon.....	12	9	0	2.39	176.2	138	93	175
		86	76	0	3.80	1374.1	1206	668	1253

Dave LaPoint

Birth Date: 7/29/59
Throws: Left
1989 Club:
New York Yankees
Contest Code #: 779

Rating: 3

If lefty Dave LaPoint kept a uniform from each of his former ball clubs, he'd need an extra closet just to find hanging space. The native of upstate New York has shuffled from league to league and coast to coast since 1980, when he first arrived in the majors with Milwaukee. Late in 1981, he put in his first National League stint with St. Louis, where he stayed through 1984. Then it was on to San Francisco (1985), Detroit and San Diego (1986), back to St. Louis and on to the White Sox (1987), Pittsburgh (1988), and, finally, the Bronx as a free agent (1989).

If his performance last year is any indication, he could move on again. He went 6–9 with a 5.62 ERA for New York, making 20 starts and averaging only 5½ innings per outing. His fastball is somewhat short, though his change-up is decent and his curveball is excellent.

Year	Team	W	L	SV	ERA	IP	H	BB	K
1980	Mil......	1	0	1	6.00	15.0	17	13	5
1981	StL......	1	0	0	4.09	11.0	12	2	4
1982	StL......	9	3	0	3.42	152.2	170	52	81
1983	StL......	12	9	0	3.95	191.1	191	84	113

1984	StL	12	10	0	3.96	193.0	205	77	130
1985	SF	7	17	0	3.57	206.2	215	74	122
1986	Det	3	6	0	5.72	67.2	85	32	36
1986	SD	1	4	0	4.26	61.1	67	24	41
1987	StL	1	1	0	6.75	16.0	26	5	8
1987	ChA	6	3	0	2.94	82.2	69	31	43
1988	ChA	10	11	0	3.40	161.1	151	47	79
1988	Pit	4	2	0	2.77	52.0	54	10	19
1989	NYA	6	9	0	5.62	113.2	146	45	51
		73	75	1	3.96	1324.1	1408	496	732

Terry Leach

Birth Date: 3/13/54
Throws: Right
1989 Club:
New York Mets &
Kansas City Royals
Contest Code #: 780

Rating: 2

Credit Frank Cashen and his staff. The Mets haven't made many personnel mistakes over the years, which explains the fact that the club hasn't finished lower than second in any of the past six seasons. As the Mets slipped farther and farther behind the Cubs last summer, New York fans howled about the Mets' abrupt sale of Terry Leach to the Kansas City Royals. Unfortunately, fan sentiment got in the way of good solid baseball judgment, which is Cashen's strong suit.

Face it, the nice-guy submariner, a Met hero in 1987 when he went when forced into a starting role, 11–1 just isn't a dominating major-league pitcher. The problem is that Leach's fastball simply isn't sinking as it once did, which makes it easier for right-handers to hit him. Left-handed hitters, always a challenge for Leach, now find him fairly easy pickings. After a 5–6 season with a 4.15 ERA and 78 hits in 73⅔ innings, Leach's career is heading nowhere.

Year	Team	W	L	SV	ERA	IP	H	BB	K
1981	NYN	1	1	0	2.57	35.0	26	12	16
1982	NYN	2	1	3	4.17	45.1	46	18	30
1984	Tor.	0	0	0	27.00	1.0	2	2	0
1985	NYN	3	4	1	2.91	55.2	48	14	30
1986	NYN	0	0	0	2.70	6.2	6	3	4
1987	NYN	11	1	0	3.22	131.1	132	29	61
1988	NYN	7	2	3	2.54	92.0	95	24	51
1989	NYN	0	0	0	4.22	21.1	19	4	2
1989	KC	5	6	0	4.15	73.2	78	36	34
		29	15	7	3.33	462.0	452	142	228

Tim Leary

Birth Date: 12/23/58
Throws: Right
1989 Club:
Los Angeles Dodgers &
Cincinnati Reds
Contest Code #: 781

Rating: 3

We sometimes forget how terrible the Mets were during the early 1980s, but Tim Leary never will. In 1980, Leary, billed as the next Tom Seaver, had an exceptional year at Double A Jackson, leading the Texas League in victories (15) and shutouts (6). The following spring, manager Joe Torre convinced the Mets' brass to let Leary break camp with the big club. Leary's first start, against the Cubs, lasted just two innings; he strained a muscle in his right elbow and did not pitch again until August. Then Leary damaged nerves in his throwing shoulder, an injury that took doctors a year to diagnose, and didn't pitch again until 1983.

With the damage done, the Mets shipped Leary to the Brewers in 1985 as part of a six-player, four-team deal. Two years later Leary was traded to the Dodgers. Following a poor 1987 season, Leary learned to throw a split-

fingered fastball during winter ball. His career was reborn.

Leary pitched reasonably well in the first half of last season, winning 6 games with an ERA of 3.38. In July the Dodgers, stuffed to the gills with starters and starved for power hitters, traded Leary to the Reds for outfielder Kal Daniels. Pitching for a team in turmoil, Leary managed only two more wins. And he missed two turns late in the season because of sprained ligaments in his pitching hand, which hampered his ability to throw his splitter. Still, the Yankees thought well enough of Leary to trade for him during the off-season. He should win at least 10 games, and possibly more, in 1990.

Year	Team	W	L	SV	ERA	IP	H	BB	K
1981	NYN	0	0	0	0.00	2.0	0	1	3
1983	NYN	1	1	0	3.38	10.2	15	4	9
1984	NYN	3	3	0	4.03	53.2	61	18	29
1985	Mil	1	4	0	4.05	33.1	40	8	29
1986	Mil	12	12	0	4.21	188.1	216	53	110
1987	LA.......	3	11	1	4.76	107.2	121	36	61
1988	LA.......	17	11	0	2.91	228.2	201	56	180
1989	LA.......	6	7	0	3.38	117.1	107	37	59
1989	Cin	2	7	0	3.71	89.2	98	31	64
		45	56	1	3.71	831.1	859	244	544

Bill Long

Birth Date: 2/29/60
Throws: Right
1989 Club:
Chicago White Sox
Contest Code #: 782

Rating: 2

In Chicago, they'll always refer to the 1984 LaMarr-Hoyt-to-San-Diego trade as the Ozzie Guillen trade. But Bill Long will remember it as the trade that gave him a shot at the major leagues. A one-time San Diego Padres' second-round draft choice, Long spent four years in the Padres' organization before arriving for a brief stay with the Chisox in late 1985. He didn't get there to stay until 1988.

The book on Long emphasizes his good breaking ball, though the rest of his stuff is probably below average. He does move the ball around well, a definite plus. A former Miami of Ohio star—along with Houston second sacker Bill Doran—Long made 8 starts among his 30 appearances with the Sox last year. He went 5–5 with a 3.92 ERA.

Year	Team	W	L	SV	ERA	IP	H	BB	K
1985	ChA......	0	1	0	10.29	14.0	25	5	13
1987	ChA......	8	8	1	4.37	169.0	179	28	72
1988	ChA......	8	11	2	4.03	174.0	187	43	77
1989	ChA......	5	5	1	3.92	98.2	101	37	51
		21	25	4	4.33	455.2	492	113	213

Tom McCarthy

Birth Date: 6/18/61
Throws: Right
1989 Club:
Chicago White Sox
Contest Code #: 783

Rating: 1

It's easy to win the Rookie-of-the-Year Award. Have a couple or three great minor-league years, come to the big club, and knock the cover off the ball (or pitch it well enough to prevent the opponent from doing so). It's a lot harder to win the Oldest-Rookie-of-the-Year Award. That's the special province of Tom McCarthy, who finally got a full season in the majors after ten years of waiting and eighteen innings of major-league action.

Was it worth it? Ask McCarthy. The 6′, 180-pounder spent his first seven years with the Red Sox organization, including 3½ straight seasons at AA Winston-Salem (NC). He finally got a shot at Boston in late 1985, where five innings of work produced nary a major-league decision. Traded to the Mets, he never got to Shea Stadium, spending three seasons at Tidewater. Dealt to the Chisox, he went 2–0 in six games in 1988 and 1–2 in 50 games in 1989. Hang in there, Tom.

Year	Team	W	L	SV	ERA	IP	H	BB	K
1985	Bos......	0	0	0	10.80	5.0	7	4	2
1988	ChA......	2	0	1	1.38	13.0	9	2	5
1989	ChA......	1	2	0	3.51	66.2	72	20	27
		3	2	1	3.61	84.2	88	26	34

Kirk McCaskill

Birth Date: 4/9/61
Throws: Right
1989 Club:
California Angels
Contest Code #: 784

Rating: 4

After two straight seasons marred by trips to the DL, Kirk McCaskill found the secret to good health in 1989 and became a reliable full-season starter (15–10, 2.93 ERA) for the California Angels. Along with Bert Blyleven and Chuck Finley, McCaskill helped get the Angels into the AL-West title hunt.

The solution, say some scouts, was the improved control that the Canadian native discovered last season. Prior to 1989, McCaskill's strikeouts-to-walk ratio generally fell in the 3:2 area. Last year, it was closer to 2:1, which made a difference. If the stamina problem is finally licked, McCaskill could remain a key man on the Angels' staff. He owns an excellent curveball, and the rest of his stuff is good. He's aggressive on the mound and doesn't hesitate to go after hitters. If the 1989 McCaskill is the real McCaskill, the Angels are in fine shape.

Year	Team	W	L	SV	ERA	IP	H	BB	K
1985	Cal	12	12	0	4.70	189.2	189	64	102
1986	Cal	17	10	0	3.36	246.1	207	92	202
1987	Cal	4	6	0	5.67	74.2	84	34	56
1988	Cal	8	6	0	4.31	146.1	155	61	98
1989	Cal	15	10	0	2.93	212.0	202	59	107
		56	44	0	3.90	869.0	837	310	565

Bob McClure

Birth Date: 4/29/53
Throws: Left
1989 Club:
California Angels
Contest Code #: 785

Rating: 4

Bob McClure is amazing. If he were a football player, he'd be the kind of guy who'd go in on obvious passing downs. He's a situation player, whose specialty is getting left-handed hitters. And that's about it. Most of his stuff is below average, yet he still manages to get hitters out most of the time. His fastball isn't much, but his breaking ball is his best pitch.

After twelve full and three partial big-league seasons, the thirty-seven-year-old (in April) left-hander has learned all the tricks of the game—which keeps him in the big leagues. The former Royal, Brewer (ten years), Expo, and Met simply knows how to pitch and changes speeds with the best. Of course, it helps to be in the right place at the right time. Last season, McClure got into 48 games, finished 27 of them, earned 3 saves and—amazingly—had a 6–1 won-lost mark with a sparkling 1.55 ERA in 52⅓ innings of work.

Year	Team	W	L	SV	ERA	IP	H	BB	K
1975	KC.......	1	0	1	0.00	15.0	4	14	15
1976	KC.......	0	0	0	9.00	4.0	3	8	3
1977	Mil	2	1	6	2.54	71.0	64	34	57
1978	Mil	2	6	9	3.74	65.0	53	30	47
1979	Mil	5	2	5	3.88	51.0	53	24	37
1980	Mil	5	8	10	3.07	91.0	83	37	47
1981	Mil	0	0	0	3.37	8.0	7	4	6
1982	Mil	12	7	0	4.22	172.2	160	74	99
1983	Mil	9	9	0	4.50	142.0	152	68	68
1984	Mil	4	8	1	4.38	139.2	154	52	68
1985	Mil	4	1	3	4.31	85.2	91	30	57
1986	Mil	2	1	0	3.86	16.1	18	10	11
1986	Mon	2	5	6	3.02	62.2	53	23	42
1987	Mon	6	1	5	3.44	52.1	47	20	33
1988	Mon	1	3	2	6.16	19.0	23	6	12
1988	NYN	1	0	1	4.09	11.0	12	2	7
1989	Cal	6	1	3	1.55	52.1	39	15	36
		62	53	52	3.77	1058.2	1016	451	645

Lance McCullers

Birth Date: 3/8/64
Throws: Right
1989 Club:
New York Yankees
Contest Code #: 785

Rating: 3

A four-and-a-half-year major leaguer at age twenty-six, Lance McCullers has a lot of the tools and one major problem. Scouts point to McCullers' delivery, which includes one awful head jerk, as the cause of his control difficulties. No one in the Phildelphia, San Diego, or New York organizations has managed to help Lance solve it yet. So his problems continue.

McCullers' best pitch is his fastball. It's his out pitch and enabled him to fan 82 batters in 84⅔ innings last season. And while his 37 walks don't appear to be a cause for alarm, his lack of control forces him to work behind the hitters and make pitches he'd rather not make. The book on McCullers also rates his slider highly.

McCullers spent three-plus seasons with the Padres before coming over to the Yankees, winning 21 and losing 28 with a nifty 2.96 ERA. He came to the Bronx in the Jack Clark deal after the 1988 season.

Year	Team	W	L	SV	ERA	IP	H	BB	K
1985	SD.......	0	2	5	2.31	35.0	23	16	27
1986	SD.......	10	10	5	2.78	136.0	103	58	92
1987	SD.......	8	10	16	3.72	123.1	115	59	126
1988	SD.......	3	6	10	2.49	97.2	70	55	81
1989	NYA......	4	3	3	4.57	84.2	83	37	82
		25	31	39	3.25	476.2	394	225	408

Craig McMurtry

Birth Date: 11/5/59
Throws: Right
1989 Club:
Texas Rangers
Contest Code #: 786

Rating: 2

Craig McMurtry's checkered career became more checkered in 1989. The Texas native hasn't enjoyed a full, healthy season in the majors since he went 9–17 for the Atlanta Braves way back in 1984. Since then, it has been minor-league assignments, injuries, free agency, finally three-and-a-half months on the Texas Rangers' disabled list last year.

The future looks absolutely bleak. McMurtry was lit up virtually every time he took the mound for the Rangers —and that was only 19 times last year. Though he managed 3 scoreless innings against Oakland in his final appearance of the season last September, he had allowed 16 earned runs in his previous 11 innings and finished the year with a decidedly unimpressive 7.43 ERA in only 23 innings.

Year	Team	W	L	SV	ERA	IP	H	BB	K
1983	Atl.......	15	9	0	3.08	224.2	204	88	105
1984	Atl.......	9	17	0	4.32	183.1	184	102	99
1985	Atl.......	0	3	1	6.60	45.0	56	27	28
1986	Atl.......	1	6	0	4.75	79.2	82	43	50
1988	Tex	3	3	3	2.25	60.0	37	24	35
1989	Tex	0	0	0	7.43	23.0	29	13	14
		28	38	4	4.01	615.2	592	297	331

Gary Mielke

Birth Date: 1/28/63
Throws: Right
1989 Club:
Texas Rangers
Contest Code #: 787

Rating: 2

Though he didn't arrive in Texas until May 22 last season, right-hander Gary Mielke wound up making more appearances (43) than all but three other Ranger pitchers. Though he hurled 49⅔ innings in those outings, he managed only one decision—a victory over the Boston Red Sox—and a 3.26 ERA. In addition to his first big-league win, he also rang up his first save— against the world-champion Oakland Athletics. The one-time Mankato (MN) State star had been in only 3 major-league box scores (all in 1987) before last season.

Mielke's biggest plus is a deceptive delivery that gets hitters off balance. Generally, his stuff is a little short— and when he gets the ball up in the strike zone, he gets tattooed.

Year	Team	W	L	SV	ERA	IP	H	BB	K
1987	Tex	0	0	0	6.00	3.0	3	1	3
1989	Tex	1	0	1	3.26	49.2	52	25	26
		1	0	1	3.42	52.2	55	26	29

Bob Milacki

Birth Date: 7/28/64
Throws: Right
1989 Club:
Baltimore Orioles
Contest Code #: 788

Rating: 4

Along with Jeff Ballard, Bob Milacki is the future of the Orioles. Only twenty-five, Ballard is imposing on the mound at 6'4" and 220 pounds. The Trenton (NJ) native spent the better part of five seasons in the Orioles' system before arriving to stay late in 1988. A 2–0 record (only 9 hits allowed in 25 innings) excited Bird watchers. He made 3 starts, the only 3 games Baltimore won after September 11.

They quickly found out in 1989 that the right-hander was worth waiting for. Bob went 14–12 for Baltimore, with 3 complete games, including a team-high 2 shutouts. He was also the club leader in strikeouts with 113 in 243 innings. Our scouts were impressed with the way Milacki came on late in the season. None of his four pitches is awesome, although his change-up is mighty tough. Look for Milacki to get even better in 1990 and maybe even better after that!

Year	Team	W	L	SV	ERA	IP	H	BB	K
1988	Bal	2	0	0	0.72	25.0	9	9	18
1989	Bal	14	12	0	3.74	243.0	233	88	113
		16	12	0	3.46	268.0	242	97	131

Greg Minton

Birth Date: 7/29/51
Throws: Right
1989 Club:
California Angels
Contest Code #: 789

Rating: 4

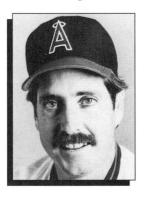

At age thirty-eight, Greg Minton continues to get people out. The right-hander has been in the majors since a short visit in 1975 and seems to have learned a few things along the way.

A San Francisco Giant until released on May 28, 1987, Minton signed with the Angels on June 2 of that year and has proven a pleasant surprise. Although he has been just better than a .500 pitcher for the Angels (including 4–3 last year), he's always available, and his ERA for the last two seasons has dipped to 2.85 in 1988 and 2.20 in 1989. He remains one of the toughest pitchers for enemy batters to take deep.

Greg holds the all-time record for consecutive innings pitched without allowing a home run—269⅓, from 1978 to 1982. The scouts aren't overly impressed with Minton's stuff though, calling it inconsistent. At times, he throws a good hard sinker, which is tough to handle. There has been noise in more than a few major-league dugouts that Minton's 2-strike pitch occasionally arrives at the plate bearing excessive moisture.

Year	Team	W	L	SV	ERA	IP	H	BB	K
1975	SF	1	1	0	6.88	17.0	19	11	6
1976	SF	0	3	0	4.85	26.0	32	12	7
1977	SF	1	1	0	4.50	14.0	14	4	5
1978	SF	0	1	0	7.87	16.0	22	8	6
1979	SF	4	3	4	1.80	80.0	59	27	33
1980	SF	4	6	19	2.47	91.0	81	34	42
1981	SF	4	5	21	2.89	84.0	84	36	29
1982	SF	10	4	30	1.83	123.0	108	42	58
1983	SF	7	11	22	3.54	106.2	117	47	38
1984	SF	4	9	19	3.76	124.1	130	57	48
1985	SF	5	4	4	3.54	96.2	98	54	37
1986	SF	4	4	5	3.93	68.2	63	34	34
1987	SF	1	0	1	3.47	23.1	30	10	9
1987	Cal	5	4	10	3.08	76.0	71	29	35
1988	Cal	4	5	7	2.85	79.0	67	34	46
1989	Cal	4	3	8	2.20	90.0	76	37	42
		58	64	150	3.11	1115.2	1071	476	475

Richard Monteleone

Birth Date: 3/22/63
Throws: Right
1989 Club:
California Angels
Contest Code #: 790

Rating: 2

It's hard to figure out Rich Monteleone. At 6'2" and 217 pounds, he looks like a pitcher. The ingredients seem to be there. His fastball is decent enough, and his straight change can be downright challenging. But he seems to have trouble putting it together to win ball games.

There's hope, of course. The Tampa, FL, native is just twenty-seven, with only 30 major-league appearances under his belt. In his first full shot last year (he pitched three times each for the 1987 Mariners and 1988 Angels), he went 2–2 but with a decent 3.18 ERA in 24 California outings, allowing about a hit an inning (39 in 39⅔ innings of work) and with a 2:1 strikeouts-to-walks ratio (27–13).

Getting over the how-to-win hump is the last hurdle for Monteleone. The one-time Tiger property who was later released by Seattle must learn to do it soon.

Year	Team	W	L	SV	ERA	IP	H	BB	K
1987	Sea......	0	0	0	6.43	7.0	10	4	2
1988	Cal	0	0	0	0.00	4.1	4	1	3
1989	Cal	2	2	0	3.18	39.2	39	13	27
		2	2	0	3.35	51.0	53	18	32

Jeff Montgomery

Birth Date: 1/7/62
Throws: Right
1989 Club:
Kansas City Royals
Contest Code #: 791

Rating: 2

Jeff Montgomery seems to be stuck on 7 wins. He'll take it. After a trade with Cincinnati brought Montgomery to the Royals in mid-1988, he got into 45 games in relief and went 7–2. In 1989, handed a co-closer role with Steve Farr, Montgomery responded with an awesome season: a 7–3 record in 63 games, 18 saves, and a frightening 1.37 ERA.

His pitching arsenal is far from complete. His curveball is excellent and getting better. Scouts rate his fastball and slider only average, so Montgomery has been working hard on his change-up. For a youngster (twenty-eight) with only a season and a half in the big leagues behind him, he has wonderful control (94 strikeouts and only 25 walks in 92 innings last year). Interestingly, despite the fact that Montgomery has made 121 relief appearances and only 1 start (with Cincinnati in 1987) in his short career, at least one scout told us that Montgomery could easily become an effective starter.

Year	Team	W	L	SV	ERA	IP	H	BB	K
1987	Cin	2	2	0	6.52	19.1	25	9	13
1988	KC.......	7	2	1	3.45	62.2	54	30	47
1989	KC.......	7	3	18	1.37	92.0	66	25	94
		16	7	19	2.69	174.0	145	64	154

Mike Moore

Birth Date: 11/26/59
Throws: Right
1989 Club:
Oakland Athletics
Contest Code #: 792

Rating: 5

It took only one winning season (17–10 in 1985) with the Seattle Mariners to convince the Oakland A's and a bunch of other clubs to open the vault to obtain Mike Moore. The A's shelled out $1.25 million last year for the Mariner free agent. He was worth every nickel.

The durable right-hander spent five full and two partial seasons with Seattle before finally bolting to the A's before the 1989 season, pitching from 212 to 266 innings per season. Between 1985 and 1987, he served up 37 complete games—but a 17–10 mark in 1985 marked his only .500-plus season. With a little more support in Oakland, Moore went 19–11 with a nifty 2.61 ERA in 241⅔ innings for the 1989 world champs. His two World Series wins satisfied Moore's dreams in leaving the Kingdome.

The 6'4", 205-pounder throws an outstanding fastball and slider, and his splitter isn't bad either. Now that the A's have given him the support he has always needed, he should be around for awhile.

Year	Team	W	L	SV	ERA	IP	H	BB	K
1982	Sea......	7	14	0	5.36	144.1	159	79	73
1983	Sea......	6	8	0	4.71	128.0	130	60	108
1984	Sea......	7	17	0	4.97	212.0	236	85	158
1985	Sea......	17	10	0	3.46	247.0	230	70	155
1986	Sea......	11	13	1	4.30	266.0	279	94	146
1987	Sea......	9	19	0	4.71	231.0	268	84	115
1988	Sea......	9	15	1	3.78	228.2	196	63	182
1989	Oak......	19	11	0	2.61	241.2	193	83	172
		85	107	2	4.13	1698.2	1691	618	1109

Jack Morris

Birth Date: 5/16/55
Throws: Right
1989 Club:
Detroit Tigers
Contest Code #: 793

Rating: 3

The Detroit Tigers' forgettable 1989 season took an impressive streak down with it. Premier right-hander Jack Morris, the only major-league pitcher with 15 or more wins in each season from 1982 to 1988, slipped to an un-Morrislike 6–14 with a hefty 4.86 ERA. Talk about being in the wrong place at the wrong time. Morris figures to win again, though, especially with a team that wins more than 59 games.

The one-time Brigham Young star has been forced to adjust his game in recent seasons as his fastball has gone back to the average range. These days, his splitter is his out pitch. His slider is fairly decent, too. The thirty-four-year-old, whose 1984 no-hitter remains a career highlight, is a bulldog on the mound. He keeps coming after the hitters. Another 6-victory season seems out of the question, however.

Year	Team	W	L	SV	ERA	IP	H	BB	K
1977	Det	1	1	0	3.72	46.0	38	23	28
1978	Det	3	5	0	4.33	106.0	107	49	48
1979	Det	17	7	0	3.27	198.0	179	59	113
1980	Det	16	15	0	4.18	250.0	252	87	112
1981	Det	14	7	0	3.05	198.0	153	78	97
1982	Det	17	16	0	4.06	266.1	247	96	135
1983	Det	20	13	0	3.34	293.2	257	83	232
1984	Det	19	11	0	3.60	240.1	221	87	148
1985	Det	16	11	0	3.33	257.0	212	110	191
1986	Det	21	8	0	3.27	267.0	229	82	223
1987	Det	18	11	0	3.38	266.0	227	93	208
1988	Det	15	13	0	3.94	235.0	225	83	168
1989	Det	6	14	0	4.86	170.1	189	59	115
		183	132	0	3.66	2793.2	2536	989	1818

Jamie Moyer

Birth Date: 11/18/62
Throws: Left
1989 Club:
Texas Rangers
Contest Code #: 794

Rating: 2

The Rangers are still waiting. There's no doubt that left-hander Jamie Moyer was one of the keys to the deal that sent Mitch Williams to the Chicago Cubs prior to the 1989 season. But shoulder woes shelved Moyer for half of 1989 and limited him to just 15 starts for his new club. Texas hopes that it was the bum shoulder that sent Moyer down to defeat in 9 of his final 10 decisions last year. The one-time St. Joseph's (Philadelphia) star was 3–1 with a 2.28 ERA before his season went south. He was 0–5, 6.66 in his next 6 games, then returned in September to continue downhill. In the final month, Moyer was 1–4 with a 5.96 ERA.

Moyer, with only one over-.500 season to his credit, is a top power pitcher, getting 147 strikeouts in 201 innings in 1987. The Rangers hope that the off-season of rest and good health in 1990 will reverse Moyer's fortunes.

Year	Team	W	L	SV	ERA	IP	H	BB	K
1986	ChN......	7	4	0	5.05	87.1	107	42	45
1987	ChN......	12	15	0	5.10	201.0	210	97	147
1988	ChN......	9	15	0	3.48	202.0	212	55	121
1989	Tex	4	9	0	4.86	76.0	84	33	44
		32	43	0	4.48	566.1	613	227	357

Rob Murphy, Jr.

Birth Date: 5/26/60
Throws: Left
1989 Club:
Boston Red Sox
Contest Code #: 795

Rating: 4

Forget the 5–7 record last year. Rob Murphy is one of the best left-handed relievers in the American League. Look at the rest of the numbers—2.74 ERA, 107 strikeouts in 105 innings. His 9 saves exceeded his three-year total with Cincinnati by 2. That's more like it.

Rob's only problem is his seemingly on-going role as a setup man. In Cincinnati, John Franco did most of the finishing. In Boston, it's Lee Smith (25 saves). An 0–6 record in 1988 moved the Reds to deal Murphy to Boston. (They forgot his 6–0 record in 1986.) Now, the "Sawks" have a near-perfect pair.

Scouts rate Murphy's fastball and curve as plus-pitches. He absolutely eats up left-handed hitters with his sharp breaking ball. His deceptive motion makes his pitches even more effective. Though Murphy would be an excellent lefty closer for most closers, he and Smith should continue to be extremely productive as a tandem for Boston.

Year	Team	W	L	SV	ERA	IP	H	BB	K
1985	Cin	0	0	0	6.00	3.0	2	2	1
1986	Cin	6	0	1	0.72	50.1	26	21	36
1987	Cin	8	5	3	3.04	100.2	91	32	99
1988	Cin	0	6	3	3.08	84.2	69	38	74
1989	Bos......	5	7	9	2.74	105.0	97	41	107
		19	18	16	2.65	343.2	285	134	317

Jaime Navarro

Birth Date: 3/27/67
Throws: Right
1989 Club: Milwaukee Brewers
Contest Code #: 796

Rating: 4

Jaime Navarro is a man in a hurry and, in the long run, that might not be a terrific idea. The Milwaukee Brewers needed someone to shore up their injury-riddled pitching staff in the summer of 1989, and they quickly moved Navarro through their system. Some day, the right-hander is going to be one heckuva pitcher. The 7–8 record wasn't bad, especially when combined with a handsome 3.12 ERA. When you consider that the Brewers only scored 1 run for him (while he was in the game) during all of his losses, it's even more remarkable.

Baseball insiders are high on Navarro, fully believing that he didn't belong in the majors last season. He owns a plus-fastball and a plus-curve ball, and others have survived for years on less. Control, as it is with most pitchers, is a problem for Jaime. It should come with experience, and he figures to get plenty of that. This is a fine young prospect who should become a quality big-league pitcher.

Year	Team	W	L	SV	ERA	IP	H	BB	K
1989	Mil	7	8	0	3.12	109.2	119	32	56
		7	8	0	3.12	109.2	119	32	56

Gene Nelson

Birth Date: 12/3/60
Throws: Right
1989 Club:
Oakland Athletics
Contest Code #: 797

Rating: 3

When Gene Nelson arrived with the New York Yankees in 1981, he looked as if he'd be a super-star. He wasn't. By the following season, he had begun collecting American League uniforms, stopping in Seattle and Chicago before landing in Oakland for the 1987 season.

The inside report on the 6', 174-pound right-hander is extremely favorable. The scouts love his durability. When manager Tony LaRussa needs long relief, Gene is there. A spot starter? Call on Nelson. And he's certainly one of the AL's premier setup men.

Nelson has made 212 appearances in the last four seasons. The Tampa native is extremely tough, challenging every hitter. His plus-curve ball is easily his best pitch, and his slider isn't bad. Despite his 3–5 record last year (3.26 ERA), he's a winner.

Year	Team	W	L	SV	ERA	IP	H	BB	K
1981	NYA......	3	1	0	4.85	39.0	40	23	16
1982	Sea......	6	9	0	4.62	122.2	133	60	71
1983	Sea......	0	3	0	7.87	32.0	38	21	11
1984	ChA......	3	5	1	4.46	74.2	72	17	36
1985	ChA......	10	10	2	4.26	145.2	144	67	101
1986	ChA......	6	6	6	3.85	114.2	118	41	70
1987	Oak......	6	5	3	3.93	123.2	120	35	94
1988	Oak......	9	6	3	3.06	111.2	93	38	67
1989	Oak......	3	5	3	3.26	80.0	60	30	70
		46	50	18	4.14	844.0	818	332	536

Rod Nichols

Birth Date: 12/29/64
Throws: Right
1989 Club:
Cleveland Indians
Contest Code #: 798

Rating: 3

The Cleveland Indians fully expect Rod Nichols to become a first-rate pitcher. The 6'2", 190-pounder has enough tools to win at the major-league level—and while Nichols' 1989 was much better than 1988, it still wasn't as good as the Tribe would like.

The native Iowan, who played his high-school and college ball in New Mexico (and lives in Georgia), has a decent fastball with average velocity. He throws two different curveballs: a standard curve and a slow curve which serves as his change-of-pace. Nichols' control is pretty good. Best of all, he's a tough competitor; he loves to challenge the hitter.

Nichols arrived in the majors in 1988 after two full and two partial years in the Cleveland farm organization. He went 1–7 with a 5.06 ERA his first year, though he pitched better than his record indicates. Last year it was 4–6 and 4.40—better but not good enough.

Year	Team	W	L	SV	ERA	IP	H	BB	K
1988	Cle	1	7	0	5.06	69.1	73	23	31
1989	Cle	4	6	0	4.40	71.2	81	24	42
		5	13	0	4.72	141.0	154	47	73

Tom Niedenfuer

Birth Date: 8/13/59
Throws: Right
1989 Club:
Seattle Mariners
Contest Code #: 799

Rating: 2

After 432 major-league appearances, all out of the bullpen, Tom Niedenfuer may be in trouble. Once one of the game's premier relievers, the former Dodger and Oriole signed with the Mariners in 1989, then proceeded to flop with an 0–3 record, zero saves, and a horrendous 6.69 ERA.

It would be surprising for a thirty-year-old fireman to lose it overnight. Nonetheless, the distress signals are out. Keep in mind that Tom saved 18 games (one shy of his career best) for the 1988 Oriole team that won only 54 games all season. That's why the sudden drop to no wins, no saves, and no ERA is another cause for alarm.

The former Washington State U. star disproved the wisdom of baseball scouts when he broke into pro ball. Bypassed in the 1980 draft, he signed with the Dodgers as a free agent in August 1980 and was in the majors exactly one year later.

Year	Team	W	L	SV	ERA	IP	H	BB	K
1981	LA.......	3	1	2	3.81	26.0	25	6	12
1982	LA.......	3	4	9	2.71	69.2	71	25	60
1983	LA.......	8	3	11	1.90	94.2	55	29	66
1984	LA.......	2	5	11	2.47	47.1	39	23	45
1985	LA.......	7	9	19	2.71	106.1	86	24	102
1986	LA.......	6	6	11	3.71	80.0	86	29	55
1987	LA.......	1	0	1	2.76	16.1	13	9	10
1987	Bal	3	5	13	4.99	52.1	55	22	37
1988	Bal	3	4	18	3.51	59.0	59	19	40
1989	Sea	0	3	0	6.69	36.1	46	15	15
		36	40	95	3.28	588.0	535	201	442

Edwin Nunez

Birth Date: 5/27/63
Throws: Right
1989 Club:
Detroit Tigers
Contest Code #: 800

Rating: 3

Maybe Wayne Fontes should be looking at Edwin Nunez. The Detroit Lions' coach can always find a spot for an athlete who is 6'5" and goes 240. Nunez, his baseball career future in some jeopardy, might like the idea. Perhaps if Nunez had been born in Pennsylvania instead of Puerto Rico, some football coach would have put him in pads and helmet.

Meanwhile, Nunez has been moving his fastball from place to place (three in the last two seasons and counting) better than he has been moving his fastball around the plate. Nunez has been with the Blue Jays, Mets, and Tigers over the past two seasons, compiling a total of 5 wins. Actually, the big, likeable guy didn't do a bad job with Detroit in 1989, going 3–4 in 27 appearances as a setup man. He finished 12 of those games, picking up a save along the way.

Year	Team	W	L	SV	ERA	IP	H	BB	K
1982	Sea......	1	2	0	4.59	35.1	36	16	27
1983	Sea......	0	4	0	4.38	37.0	40	22	35
1984	Sea......	2	2	7	3.19	67.2	55	21	57
1985	Sea......	7	3	16	3.09	90.1	79	34	58
1986	Sea......	1	2	0	5.82	21.2	25	5	17
1987	Sea......	3	4	12	3.80	47.1	45	18	34
1988	Sea......	1	4	0	7.98	29.1	45	14	19
1988	NYN.....	1	0	0	4.50	14.0	21	3	8
1989	Det......	3	4	1	4.17	54.0	49	36	41
		19	25	36	4.15	396.2	395	169	296

Steve Olin

Birth Date: 10/10/65
Throws: Right
1989 Club:
Cleveland Indians
Contest Code #: 801

Rating: 2

A year ago, Steve Olin was so far away from Cleveland that his name appeared in four-point type on page 146 of the Indians' press guide. It made sense. He had been a pro for only two seasons after leaving Portland State U. and hadn't risen past Class A, the lowest minor-league classification.

By the time the 1989 season wrapped up, Olin was in the big time, making 25 appearances for the parent club and even picking up his first major-league save. The Oregon native is the newest member of the submarine club. The sidearmer's fastball has only average velocity, but the bottom usually drops out when it arrives at the plate. He has two types of sliders, which adds to his effectiveness. The 6'2", 185-pounder runs into serious trouble when he gets the ball up, which isn't atypical for sidewinders.

Year	Team	W	L	SV	ERA	IP	H	BB	K
1989	Cle......	1	4	1	3.75	36.0	35	14	24
		1	4	1	3.75	36.0	35	14	24

Gregg Olson

Birth Date: 10/11/66
Throws: Right
1989 Club:
Baltimore Orioles
Contest Code #: 802

Rating: 4

The Orioles' top pick (the fourth overall) in the 1988 draft, Gregg Olson became an instant impact pitcher in 1989 and claimed Rookie-of-the-Year honors, too. A former Auburn U. star, Olson dropped off the 1988 U. S. Olympic squad to start with the Orioles' Hagerstown (MD) farm club in July of 1988. By September, he was in Baltimore and beat Seattle in his debut.

His 1989 performance was surprisingly good. He quickly became the Birds' closer, finishing 52 times in his 64 outings, picking up 27 saves along the way. (No other Oriole reliever hit double figures.) He has great stuff across the board, with a fine fastball and change. But his curveball has folks raving. Scouts compare Olson's "deuce" to Bert Blyleven's or Camilo Pascual's. That's heady stuff. This guy is going to be around for a while—and unless we miss our guess, he'll be one of the game's premier savers.

Year	Team	W	L	SV	ERA	IP	H	BB	K
1988	Bal	1	1	0	3.27	11.0	10	10	9
1989	Bal	5	2	27	1.69	85.0	57	46	90
		6	3	27	1.87	96.0	67	56	99

Jesse Orosco

Birth Date: 4/21/57
Throws: Left
1989 Club:
Cleveland Indians
Contest Code #: 803

Rating: 3

The only guy in the Cleveland Indians' clubhouse with two World Series championship rings, Jesse Orosco may have a long wait for number three.

No New York Met fan will forget the sight of closer Orosco (the Mets' career saves leader) flinging his glove high into the air after finishing both the NLCS and World Series in 1986. By 1988, he was a member of the world-champion L.A. Dodgers, where he won his second hunk of jewelry.

Signed as a free agent by the Indians before the 1989 season, Orosco shocked those who thought he was on a downhill slide. He became Cleveland's premier setup man for closer Doug Jones, appearing in 69 games and running up a 3-4 record and a team-best 2.08 ERA. A one-time Minnesota Twins' farmhand (the Mets got him for Jerry Koosman in 1978), Orosco owns a fastball that's usually above average, a fine curve, and a slider that can be downright nasty. Though he'll be thirty-three in April, Jesse still has the tools to win in the majors.

Year	Team	W	L	SV	ERA	IP	H	BB	K
1979	NYN	1	2	0	4.89	35.0	33	22	22
1981	NYN	0	1	1	1.59	17.0	13	6	18
1982	NYN	4	10	4	2.72	109.1	92	40	89
1983	NYN	13	7	17	1.47	110.0	76	38	84
1984	NYN	10	6	31	2.59	87.0	58	34	85
1985	NYN	8	6	17	2.73	79.0	66	34	68
1986	NYN	8	6	21	2.33	81.0	64	35	62
1987	NYN	3	9	16	4.44	77.0	78	31	78
1988	LA	3	2	9	2.72	53.0	41	30	43
1989	Cle	3	4	3	2.08	78.0	54	26	79
		53	53	119	2.66	726.1	575	296	628

Donn Pall

Birth Date: 1/11/62
Throws: Right
1989 Club:
Chicago White Sox
Contest Code #: 804

Rating: 1

After a two-month shot with the Chisox in 1988, Pall made the most of a full season with the parent club in 1989. Though he's probably not the most talented Chicago pitcher, he showed enough to stay in the big time as a long- and middle-reliever.

Pall, a Chicago native and an unlikely twenty-third-round choice in the June 1985 draft, surprised more than a few scouts when he landed in Chicago after slightly more than 100 minor-league pitching appearances—most of them starts. He became a full-time reliever at AAA Vancouver in 1988 and got to Comiskey Park by the end of July.

Though some scouts believe that Pall is a marginal prospect, most concede that he has made tremendous strides. His fastball is slightly above average, his slider average, and his forkball/splitter is coming. In 53 relief stints in 1989, the 6'1", 180-pound right-hander had a 3.31 ERA along with 6 saves in a 4–5 season.

Year	Team	W	L	SV	ERA	IP	H	BB	K
1988	ChA......	0	2	0	3.45	28.2	39	8	16
1989	ChA......	4	5	6	3.31	87.0	90	19	58
		4	7	6	3.35	115.2	129	27	74

Clay Parker

Birth Date: 12/19/62
Throws: Right
1989 Club:
New York Yankees
Contest Code #: 805

Rating: 3

At the very least, Clay Parker looks good on the mound. He has an excellent feel for the art of pitching. Although most of his stuff right now is just about average, his future looks fairly bright.

The Louisiana native, who started in the Orange Bowl and Sugar Bowl for the LSU Tigers football team, features an excellent slow curve which he uses as a change-up. Parker originally signed with the Seattle Mariners, arriving at the Kingdome after 2½ minor-league seasons. Despite a 10.57 ERA in 3 outings with the M's in 1987, he attracted the attention of the Yanks, who picked him up, along with Lee Guetterman, in a December 1987 deal with Seattle.

After a full season with AAA Columbus, he spent most of 1989 with the Yanks, making 17 starts and pitching 2 complete games. The numbers included a 4–5 record and a not-bad 3.67 ERA.

Year	Team	W	L	SV	ERA	IP	H	BB	K
1987	Sea......	0	0	0	10.57	7.2	15	4	8
1989	NYA......	4	5	0	3.67	120.0	123	31	53
		4	5	0	4.09	127.2	138	35	61

Ken Patterson

Birth Date: 7/8/64
Throws: Left
1989 Club:
Chicago White Sox
Contest Code #: 806

Rating: 2

The White Sox's Ken Patterson got into 50 games last year, after only 9 previous big-league appearances. His ERA was 4.52, and he walked 28 in 65⅔ innings. But when they toted up W's and L's at season's end, there was Patterson atop the Chicago win-percentage standings. The California native, who was selected by the Yankees in the third round of the 1985 draft, went 6-1, completing 18 of his 49 relief appearances (thank goodness for Bobby Thigpen) and making 1 start.

Patterson spent most of 2½ seasons with Yankee farm clubs (Oneonta, Fort Lauderdale, and Albany) before the deal with the White Sox, which brought him a ticket to their AAA club in Hawaii. With his 6-1 1989 record, he now has a 6-3 big-league mark. How many other White Sox pitchers can make that claim?

Year	Team	W	L	SV	ERA	IP	H	BB	K
1988	ChA......	0	2	1	4.79	20.2	25	7	8
1989	ChA......	6	1	0	4.52	65.2	64	28	43
		6	3	1	4.59	86.1	89	35	51

Melido Perez

Birth Date: 2/15/66
Throws: Right
1989 Club:
Chicago White Sox
Contest Code #: 807

Rating: 3

Some pitchers pitch better with their heads than with their arms. The Chicago White Soxs' Melido Perez is right up there with the best. He has borderline stuff—except for a downright mean fork ball, but he flat out knows how to pitch, which makes him a key member of the Soxs' rotation.

Another of the game's Dominican darlings and the brother of the Yankees' Pascual Perez, Melido worked his way through the Royals' chain before arriving in the bigs with Kaycee in September 1987. Dealt to the Sox three months later, he has made 63 starts for Chicago over the past two seasons. The big winner (and loser) on the Chicago staff (11-14) last year, Perez saw his ERA blow up from 3.79 to 5.01 last season. Nonetheless he continues to lead the ball club in strikeouts (141 last year), innings pitched (183⅓ in 1989), among other categories.

Year	Team	W	L	SV	ERA	IP	H	BB	K
1987	KC.......	1	1	0	7.84	10.1	18	5	5
1988	ChA......	12	10	0	3.79	197.0	186	72	138
1989	ChA......	11	14	0	5.01	183.1	187	90	141
		24	25	0	4.47	390.2	391	167	284

Pascual Perez

Birth Date: 5/17/57
Throws: Right
1989 Club:
Montreal Expos
Contest Code #: 808

Rating: 4

Animated, agitated Pascual Perez is one *loco hombre*. When he's in top form, his slider drops like a limbo dancer. He'll clench his fist after a strikeout, leap in the air, and strut around the mound as if he's just won a million-dollar lottery prize.

Opponents have come to accept Perez's on-field antics, but there's a lingering question yet to be answered: Why is there a dark blotch on the front of Perez's uniform just above his left pectoral muscle? Is it caused by an excess of hairstyling gel he uses to keep his ring curls just so, or is it a ready supply of spitball lubricant?

Perez's record with the Expos was unquestionably good, but it's uncertain how he'll fare with the Yankees, who signed him during the off-season. If he gets off to a fast start in 1990, expect more questions about the blotch on his uniform.

Year	Team	W	L	SV	ERA	IP	H	BB	K
1980	Pit.......	0	1	0	3.75	12.0	15	2	7
1981	Pit.......	2	7	0	3.98	86.0	92	34	46
1982	Atl.......	4	4	0	3.06	79.1	85	17	29
1983	Atl.......	15	8	0	3.43	215.1	213	51	144
1984	Atl.......	14	8	0	3.74	211.2	208	51	145
1985	Atl.......	1	13	0	6.14	95.1	115	57	57
1987	Mon	7	0	0	2.30	70.1	52	16	58
1988	Mon	12	8	0	2.44	188.0	133	44	131
1989	Mon	9	13	0	3.31	198.1	178	45	152
		64	62	0	3.48	1156.1	1091	317	769

Jeff Peterek

Birth Date: 9/22/63
Throws: Right
1989 Club:
Milwaukee Brewers
Contest Code #: 809

Rating: 2

What does the future hold for Jeff Peterek? It's much too early to tell. Pressed into the Milwaukee pitching lineup in mid-August last season—due to injuries, the Brewers employed no fewer than twenty pitchers last season—Peterek had 4 relatively ineffective starts before switching to the bullpen in September for 3 relief appearances.

The right-hander went 0–2 with a 4.02 ERA, which reflected his minor-league numbers. At Denver, Peterek was 9–9, including one 12 ⅓-inning stint in a 3–0 Zephyrs' loss to Iowa. His 3.61 ERA was fair. Whether Jeff fits into Milwaukee's 1990 plans is a major question-mark.

Year	Team	W	L	SV	ERA	IP	H	BB	K
1989	Mil	0	2	0	4.02	31.1	31	14	16
		0	2	0	4.02	31.1	31	14	16

Dan Petry

Birth Date: 11/13/58
Throws: Right
1989 Club:
California Angels
Contest Code #: 810

Rating: 3

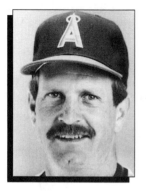

It looks as though it's just about over for Dan Petry. Once one of the mainstays of the Detroit Tigers' staff (including back-to-back 19–11 and 18–8 seasons), the right-hander doesn't seem to have it anymore. A starter throughout his career, Petry has become a middle reliever and spot starter, and his second-straight 3-victory season (3–2) in 1989 gives ample evidence of his decline.

The tip-off is a series of ongoing arm problems that limited him to only 19 appearances and 51 innings a year ago. His ERA soared to 5.47, and his walks (23) outnumbered his strikeouts (21)—another sure sign of trouble. He also allowed a home run every 6.375 innings, and that's just too much. The native Californian knows his craft—but though the spirit and mind are willing, the arm and body are not.

Year	Team	W	L	SV	ERA	IP	H	BB	K
1979	Det	6	5	0	3.95	98.0	90	33	43
1980	Det	10	9	0	3.93	165.0	156	83	88
1981	Det	10	9	0	3.00	141.0	115	57	79
1982	Det	15	9	0	3.22	246.0	220	100	132
1983	Det	19	11	0	3.92	266.1	256	99	122
1984	Det	18	8	0	3.24	233.1	231	66	144
1985	Det	15	13	0	3.36	238.2	190	81	109
1986	Det	5	10	0	4.66	116.0	122	53	56
1987	Det	9	7	0	5.61	134.2	148	76	93
1988	Cal	3	9	0	4.38	139.2	139	59	64
1989	Cal	3	2	0	5.47	51.0	53	23	21
		113	92	0	3.85	1829.2	1720	730	951

Dan Plesac

Birth Date: 2/4/62
Throws: Left
1989 Club:
Milwaukee Brewers
Contest Code #: 811

Rating: 5

It took only four seasons for Dan Plesac to gain the relief pitchers' Century Club. The big (6'5", 210 pounds) left-hander's 33rd and final save last season gave him an even 100 in the 210 appearances he has made for the Brew Crew. That made him Milwaukee's all-time saves leader, passing Rollie Fingers, who had 97. The Indiana native has two basic pitches: an outstanding fastball and a deadly slider. Either can be his out pitches—a rare combination for a starter or reliever.

A first-round draft choice of the Brewers in June 1983, Plesac put in three successful minor-league seasons before reaching the parent club to stay in 1986. His ERA figures offer clear indication of his progress, dropping from 2.97 to 2.61 to 2.41 to last year's 2.35. Plesac is certainly one of the game's premier closers.

Year	Team	W	L	SV	ERA	IP	H	BB	K
1986	Mil	10	7	14	2.97	91.0	81	29	75
1987	Mil	5	6	23	2.61	79.1	63	23	89
1988	Mil	1	2	30	2.41	52.1	46	12	52
1989	Mil	3	4	33	2.35	61.1	47	17	52
		19	19	100	2.63	284.0	237	81	268

Eric Plunk

Birth Date: 9/3/63
Throws: Right
1989 Club:
Oakland Athletics &
New York Yankees
Contest Code #: 812

Rating: 3

Eric Plunk and Rickey Henderson: two names that will go down in baseball history together. Seems that whenever Rickey is traded, Eric goes the other way. A 1981 Yankee draftee, California native Plunk went home when he was dealt to Oakland in a 1984 deal which brought Rickey to the Bronx Bombers. Then, in 1989, when Henderson decided that he was done with Steinbrenner, Plunk was one of the A's who went to New York in exchange for the left-fielder. One-sided trades? Could be. But Plunk is doing what he can do to hold up his end. The right-hander worked in 50 games last season, winning 8 and losing 6, to raise his career W-L mark to 23–21. Though he started 7 times a year ago, Plunk is best suited to setup work. A hard thrower, Eric relies on a solid fastball and an occasionally good slider. Sporadic control is a problem from time to time.

Year	Team	W	L	SV	ERA	IP	H	BB	K
1986	Oak......	4	7	0	5.31	120.1	91	102	98
1987	Oak......	4	6	2	4.74	95.0	91	62	90
1988	Oak......	7	2	5	3.00	78.0	62	39	79
1989	Oak......	1	1	1	2.20	28.2	17	12	24
1989	NYA......	7	5	0	3.69	75.2	65	52	61
		23	21	8	4.19	397.2	326	267	352

Shane Rawley

Birth Date: 7/27/55
Throws: Left
1989 Club:
Minnesota Twins
Contest Code #: 813

Rating: 2

Shane Rawley's heralded return to the American League last year was anything but a cause for celebration. The Wisconsin native must be scratching his head wondering how his career has gone south. One of the Phillies' premier starters from 1984 to 1987 (51–32), he plummeted to 8–16 in 1988 before the deal that brought him to Minnesota for the 1989 campaign.

Then it got worse. The once-powerful lefty made 25 starts for the Twins, with a 5–12 mark and a horrific 5.21 ERA. He was lit up for 19 homers in 145 innings of work. It appears that Rawley's arm simply isn't as strong as it once was. Almost everything in his pitching arsenal is now below average, though his change-up is still pretty decent. So is his control. You have to believe that a pitcher who has been a big winner in the past will figure out a way to win again. Still, it will take a massive comeback for Rawley to approach his Philadelphia success.

Year	Team	W	L	SV	ERA	IP	H	BB	K
1978	Sea......	4	9	4	4.14	111.0	114	51	66
1979	Sea......	5	9	11	3.86	84.0	88	40	48
1980	Sea......	7	7	13	3.32	114.0	103	63	68
1981	Sea......	4	6	8	3.97	68.0	64	38	35
1982	NYA......	11	10	3	4.06	164.0	165	54	111
1983	NYA......	14	14	1	3.78	238.1	246	79	124
1984	NYA......	2	3	0	6.21	42.0	46	27	24
1984	Phi	10	6	0	3.81	120.1	117	27	58
1985	Phi	13	8	0	3.31	198.2	188	81	106
1986	Phi	11	7	0	3.54	157.2	166	50	73
1987	Phi	17	11	0	4.39	229.2	250	86	123
1988	Phi	8	16	0	4.18	198.0	220	78	87
1989	Min......	5	12	0	5.21	145.0	167	60	68
		111	118	40	4.02	1870.2	1934	734	991

Jeff Reardon

Birth Date: 10/1/55
Throws: Right
1989 Club:
Minnesota Twins
Contest Code #: 814

Rating: 4

The baseball numbers game is nearly as fascinating as the game itself. When closer supreme Jeff Reardon led the Twins to the AL West title (and world championship) in 1987, he went 8–8 with a 4.48 ERA and 31 saves. Minnesota sportswriters couldn't find enough adjectives to describe their bullpen savior. In 1989, the ex-Met and Expo was 5–4 with a 4.07 ERA and 31 saves. Yet, outside of the Twin Cities, you hardly knew he was alive.

The imposing (6', 200 pounds) Reardon may have lost a tad off his fastball, but he still gets the job done day in and day out. He worked in 65 Minny games last summer and finished 61 of them. Boston, which signed Reardon in the off-season, is looking for similar numbers. Basically a high ball pitcher, which would seem to be a danger with Fenway's Green Monster, Jeff is blessed with good control. The key to his future hinges on his ability to learn to pitch, not merely throw.

Year	Team	W	L	SV	ERA	IP	H	BB	K
1979	NYN	1	2	2	1.71	21.0	12	9	10
1980	NYN	8	7	6	2.62	110.0	96	47	101
1981	NYN	1	0	2	3.45	28.2	27	12	28
1981	Mon	2	0	6	1.30	41.2	21	9	21
1982	Mon	7	4	26	2.06	109.0	87	36	86
1983	Mon	7	9	21	3.03	92.0	87	44	78
1984	Mon	7	7	23	2.90	87.0	70	37	79
1985	Mon	2	8	41	3.18	87.2	68	26	67
1986	Mon	7	9	35	3.94	89.0	83	26	67
1987	Min	8	8	31	4.48	80.1	70	28	83
1988	Min	2	4	42	2.47	73.0	68	15	56
1989	Min	5	4	31	4.07	73.0	68	12	46
		57	62	266	3.03	892.1	757	301	722

Jerry Reed

Birth Date: 10/8/55
Throws: Right
1989 Club:
Seattle Mariners
Contest Code #: 815

Rating: 3

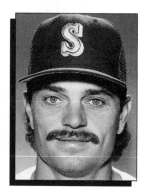

Jerry Reed will never be the kind of pitcher a manager discusses with the media at spring training. But when the team breaks camp, Reed is likely to make the trip. Over the last eight seasons, the 6'1", 190-pound Reed has spent about four-and-a-half years in the majors—with Philadelphia, Cleveland, and Seattle. None of his stuff is overpowering. His slider is probably his best pitch.

His greatest asset, however, is his durability. From 1981 to 1988, Reed made 153 big-league appearances but was involved in only 21 decisions. That made 1989 his biggest year. In 52 Mariner games, the former Western Carolina star was 7–7 with a decent 3.19 ERA. Walking 43 in only 101⅔ innings is probably his biggest problem. Though Reed will probably never be more than the number-nine or number-ten pitcher on any staff, his everyday availability makes him a good man to have around.

Year	Team	W	L	SV	ERA	IP	H	BB	K
1981	Phi	0	1	0	7.20	5.0	7	6	5
1982	Phi	1	0	0	5.20	8.2	11	3	1
1982	Cle	1	1	0	3.45	15.2	15	3	10
1983	Cle	0	0	0	7.17	21.1	26	9	11
1985	Cle	3	5	8	4.11	72.1	67	19	37
1986	Sea	4	0	0	3.12	34.2	38	13	16
1987	Sea	1	2	7	3.42	81.2	79	24	51
1988	Sea	1	1	1	3.96	86.1	82	33	48
1989	Sea	7	7	0	3.19	101.2	89	43	50
		18	17	16	3.83	427.1	414	153	229

Dave Righetti

Birth Date: 11/28/56
Throws: Left
1989 Club:
New York Yankees
Contest Code #: 816

Rating: 4

When Yankee fans get together, the debate almost always focuses on the future of Rags Righetti. A starter? A reliever? For now, it's Bucky Dent's call, though George Steinbrenner seems to make all the decisions in the Bronx. "Starter" advocates always remind you of Righetti's July 4, 1983, no-hitter. Those who opt for "relief" point to his 187 saves since 1984.

The problem with switching the California native's role lies in the fact that he's basically a two-pitch pitcher. His fastball and slider are still both excellent, but that's just about his entire arsenal. As a starter, he'll need another good pitch—and that's easier said than done.

Rags' control is still good, though he's not quite as overpowering as he has been in the past. Like most thirty-three-year-old power pitchers, he'll have to learn to be more of a pitcher. Meanwhile, his 25 saves and 3.00 ERA last year indicate that he should still be a successful closer.

Year	Team	W	L	SV	ERA	IP	H	BB	K
1979	NYA......	0	1	0	3.71	17.0	10	10	13
1981	NYA......	8	4	0	2.06	105.0	75	38	89
1982	NYA......	11	10	1	3.79	183.0	155	108	163
1983	NYA......	14	8	0	3.44	217.0	194	67	169
1984	NYA......	5	6	31	2.34	96.1	79	37	90
1985	NYA......	12	7	29	2.78	107.0	96	45	92
1986	NYA......	8	8	46	2.45	106.2	88	35	83
1987	NYA......	8	6	31	3.51	95.0	95	44	77
1988	NYA......	5	4	25	3.52	87.0	86	37	70
1989	NYA......	2	6	25	3.00	69.0	73	26	51
		73	60	188	3.09	1083.0	951	447	897

Kevin Ritz

Birth Date: 6/8/65
Throws: Right
1989 Club:
Detroit Tigers
Contest Code #: 817

Rating: 2

A year after tossing shutouts at such Eastern League powers as Vermont and Reading, Kevin Ritz found himself in Detroit, where he ranks as one of the Tigers' brightest young prospects. On a staff populated by graybeards, a twenty-four-year-old who can bring the ball with decent velocity is a valuable commodity.

A native New Jerseyan who grew up in Iowa, the 6'4", 195-pound right-hander got to Tiger Stadium in time to make 12 starts, including 1 complete game. His 4.38 ERA was respectable on a team led by Frank Tanana's 3.58. His 4–6 record was likewise respectable and his control, though still erratic, was better than it had been in the minors. (At Lakeland in 1986, for example, Ritz walked 45 and struck out only 39.) If he can control his control, he has a great shot to stick with the Tigers in 1990 and beyond.

Year	Team	W	L	SV	ERA	IP	H	BB	K
1989	Det	4	6	0	4.38	74.0	75	44	56
		4	6	0	4.38	74.0	75	44	56

Jeff Robinson

Birth Date: 12/13/60
Throws: Right
1989 Club:
Pittsburgh Pirates
Contest Code #: 818

Rating: 2

Jeff Robinson has been a streaky pitcher through most of his career. No matter how well he's pitching, he always encounters a three-week slump, then rebounds. In past seasons Robinson's clubs could turn to another reliever during one of his lulls, but last season, with Jim Gott sidelined for the entire campaign, the blond-haired Californian had to go it alone.

When the slump hit, manager Jim Leyland put Robinson in the starting rotation. After some early successes, Robinson struggled upon his return to the bullpen. So Robinson became a starter once more. This time, he could barely sustain his good performances beyond a game or two.

The reality is that Robinson is a setup man. He has a good split-fingered fastball that bores down and in on right-handed batters. With a good closer behind him, Robinson is capable of 10 victories and 10 saves a season.

Year	Team	W	L	SV	ERA	IP	H	BB	K
1984	SF......	7	15	0	4.56	171.2	195	52	102
1985	SF......	0	0	0	5.11	12.1	16	10	8
1986	SF......	6	3	8	3.36	104.1	92	32	90
1987	SF......	6	8	10	2.79	96.2	69	48	82
1987	Pit......	2	1	4	3.04	26.2	20	6	19
1988	Pit......	11	5	9	3.03	124.2	113	39	87
1989	Pit......	7	13	4	4.59	141.1	161	59	95
		39	45	35	3.80	677.2	666	246	483

Jeff Mark Robinson

Birth Date: 12/14/61
Throws: Right
1989 Club:
Detroit Tigers
Contest Code #: 819

Rating: 2

A healthy Jeff Robinson figures to be one of the keys to a return to the pennant race by the Detroit Tigers. When he's sound, Robinson has everything he needs to become a top-flight major leaguer.

In his first two seasons in Detroit, the impressive-looking 6'6", 210-pound right-hander made 44 starts (and 9 relief appearances), winning 22 and losing only 12. His fastball, which ranks anywhere from average to plus, has a boring action—the kind that saws off enemy bats. Although his slider is just about average, his splitter or fork ball can be downright nasty at times.

A two-sport star (baseball and basketball) at Azusa Pacific, Robinson was a number-three selection in the June 1983 draft. A 10–7 mark at Nashville in 1986 won him a promotion to the Tiger roster. After averaging 150 innings in each of his first two years, he was limited to only 78 in 1989. Better times lie ahead.

Year	Team	W	L	SV	ERA	IP	H	BB	K
1987	Det	9	6	0	5.37	127.1	132	54	98
1988	Det	13	6	0	2.98	172.0	121	72	114
1989	Det	4	5	0	4.73	78.0	76	46	40
		26	17	0	4.15	377.1	329	172	252

Kenny Rogers

Birth Date: 11/19/64
Throws: Left
1989 Club:
Texas Rangers
Contest Code #: 820

Rating: 3

Like his bearded namesake, the Texas Rangers' Kenny Rogers makes beautiful music—in the Arlington Stadium bullpen. The rookie lefty wound up the 1989 season as his team's busiest pitcher with 73 appearances, third highest in the American League. No other rookie hurler got into as many games as the 6'1", 200-pound left-hander.

Insiders are impressed with most of his pitches, featuring a good slider and fastball, and they like his innate athleticism. Like most youngsters, he occasionally runs into control probems—which should be alleviated with more experience. A homegrown product, Rogers was selected by the Rangers in the thirty-eighth round of the 1982 draft and spent seven full seasons in the minors before arriving with the Rangers last spring. His 2.93 ERA trailed only that of super-closer Jeff Russell. Rogers allowed only 60 hits and 2 homers in 73⅔ innings.

Year	Team	W	L	SV	ERA	IP	H	BB	K
1989	Tex	3	4	2	2.93	73.2	60	42	63
		3	4	2	2.93	73.2	60	42	63

Steve Rosenberg

Birth Date: 10/31/64
Throws: Left
1989 Club:
Chicago White Sox
Contest Code #: 821

Rating: 3

Would you believe that a pitcher with a 4–13 record as a starter and reliever would be called a "comer" by scouts? That's our report on Chicago lefty Steve Rosenberg. The experts think Rosenberg may only be a pitch or so away from becoming a first-rate big leaguer.

The one-time U. of Florida standout came to the big leagues with the Chisox in mid-1988, after a stint in the Yankees' minor-league system. The 6', 185-pounder came to the Sox in a five-man deal with the Yanks in November 1987 and arrived in Chicago in mid-1988. Insiders praise Rosenberg's fastball as "sneaky," reporting that it gets up on the hitters. His slider is decent at times, though it tends to be inconsistent, but his change-up is coming along well. Patience is the watchword for this twenty-five-year-old.

Year	Team	W	L	SV	ERA	IP	H	BB	K
1988	ChA......	0	1	1	4.30	46.0	53	19	28
1989	ChA......	4	13	0	4.94	142.0	148	58	77
		4	14	1	4.79	188.0	201	77	105

Jeff Russell

Birth Date: 9/2/61
Throws: Right
1989 Club:
Texas Rangers
Contest Code #: 822

Rating: 4

List baseball's best closers and you won't have to go very far before you find Texas' Jeff Russell. Big and strong at 6'3" and 210 pounds, Russell has one of the best arms in the game. Only Mark Davis rang up more saves (44) than Russell's 38—the sixth-highest total in AL history. Russell also led the AL in games finished with a club-record 66.

The pressure of Mitch Williams' departure fell squarely upon Russell's broad shoulders last spring. He was more than up to it. Depending largely on a nasty fastball and tricky slider, the Ohio native became the second Ranger ever to win the AL Rolaids Relief Man competition. (Jim Kern was the first, in 1979.) Not only does he have excellent stuff, but his control ranges up into the "good" area, a combination that enemy batters find deadly. Only Dennis Eckersley (.162) had a lower batting-average-allowed mark than Russell's (.182).

Year	Team	W	L	SV	ERA	IP	H	BB	K
1983	Cin	4	5	0	3.03	68.1	58	22	40
1984	Cin	6	18	0	4.26	181.2	186	65	101
1985	Tex	3	6	0	7.55	62.0	85	27	44
1986	Tex	5	2	2	3.40	82.0	74	31	54
1987	Tex	5	4	3	4.44	97.1	109	52	56
1988	Tex	10	9	0	3.82	188.2	183	66	88
1989	Tex	6	4	38	1.98	72.2	45	24	77
		39	48	43	4.02	752.2	740	287	460

Nolan Ryan

Birth Date: 1/31/47
Throws: Right
1989 Club:
Texas Rangers
Contest Code #: 823

Rating: 5

There aren't enough adjectives in our vocabulary to describe the athletic marvel that is Nolan Ryan. The 6'2", 210-pounder, who started pitching professionally while another Texan, Lyndon Johnson, was in the White House, seems to get better and better every year. Can anyone understand how a forty-two-year-old could punch out 301 enemy batters last year, 66 more than anyone else in the majors, and throw 2 complete-game 1-hitters?

Though Ryan teased the media about his future plans, there was little doubt that he'd be back at age forty-three for his twenty-third full season in the big time. Why not? He led his club with 16 wins in 1989, had his best strikeout total since he fanned 341 in 1977, averaged 11.32 Ks per nine innings—the third-highest total in history, behind Ryan himself and Doc Gooden. When Detroit's Mickey Lolich crossed the 300-strikeout barrier in 1971, he set an age-group record at age 31. Ryan blasted that record by eleven years last season.

The fastball is still outstanding, the change-up is most effective, and the arm looks absolutely sound. Eleven wins short of the magic 300, Nolan Ryan will continue to challenge every hitter every time up, just as he has done since he struck out 116 batters in 78 innings for the Mets' Marion farm club in 1965!

Year	Team	W	L	SV	ERA	IP	H	BB	K
1966	NYN	0	1	0	15.00	3.0	5	3	6
1968	NYN	6	9	0	3.09	134.0	93	75	133
1969	NYN	6	3	1	3.54	89.0	60	53	92

1970	NYN	7	11	1	3.41	132.0	86	97	125
1971	NYN	10	14	0	3.97	152.0	125	116	137
1972	Cal	19	16	0	2.28	284.0	166	157	329
1973	Cal	21	16	1	2.87	326.0	238	162	383
1974	Cal	22	16	0	2.89	333.0	221	202	367
1975	Cal	14	12	0	3.45	198.0	152	132	186
1976	Cal	17	18	0	3.36	284.0	193	183	327
1977	Cal	19	16	0	2.77	299.0	198	204	341
1978	Cal	10	13	0	3.71	235.0	183	148	260
1979	Cal	16	14	0	3.59	223.0	169	114	223
1980	Hou......	11	10	0	3.35	234.0	205	98	200
1981	Hou......	11	5	0	1.69	149.0	99	68	140
1982	Hou......	16	12	0	3.16	250.1	196	109	245
1983	Hou......	14	9	0	2.98	196.1	134	101	183
1984	Hou......	12	11	0	3.04	183.2	143	69	197
1985	Hou......	10	12	0	3.80	232.0	205	95	209
1986	Hou......	12	8	0	3.34	178.0	119	82	194
1987	Hou......	8	16	0	2.76	211.2	154	87	270
1988	Hou......	12	11	0	3.52	220.0	186	87	228
1989	Tex	16	10	0	3.20	239.1	162	98	301
		289	263	3	3.15	4786.1	3492	2540	5076

Bret Saberhagen

Birth Date: 4/11/64
Throws: Right
1989 Club:
Kansas City Royals
Contest Code #: 824

Rating: 5

Since this is an even-numbered year, Bret Saberhagen figures to fall flat on his face. If you subscribe to the lessons of history, it could happen, but it won't. In his rookie year, 1984, at age twenty, the Royal righty ace went 10–11 with a not-bad 3.48 ERA. Still, it wasn't the kind of year that made you sit up and take notice. But 1985 did. Saberhagen led the Royals to the world championship with a sparkling 20–6 record (and 2 more World Series victories) and a 2.87 ERA. Too much off-season partying spoiled 1986 (7–12, 4.15), but in odd-numbered 1987, it was back to the top (18–10). Naturally 1988 was a bummer (14–16) before rising to the top with a super 1989 (a major-league leading 23–6, 2.16 ERA, 193 strikeouts, 12 complete games, 4 shutouts)—enough to win the Cy Young Award. It doesn't get much better than that.

So why should 1990 be different from past even-numbered years? Because, at age twenty-six, the six-year veteran has matured. He has great stuff across the board, has total command of all his pitches, owns excellent control (only 43 walks in 262⅓ innings a year ago), and goes after hitters. We're convinced.

Year	Team	W	L	SV	ERA	IP	H	BB	K
1984	KC.......	10	11	1	3.48	157.2	138	36	73
1985	KC.......	20	6	0	2.87	235.1	211	38	158
1986	KC.......	7	12	0	4.15	156.0	165	29	112
1987	KC.......	18	10	0	3.36	257.0	246	53	163
1988	KC.......	14	16	0	3.80	260.2	271	59	171
1989	KC.......	23	6	0	2.16	262.1	209	43	193
		92	61	1	3.23	1329.0	1240	258	870

Scott Sanderson

Birth Date: 7/22/56
Throws: Right
1989 Club:
Chicago Cubs
Contest Code #: 825

Rating: 1

Since joining the Cubs in 1984, Scott Sanderson has had the body of a twig. He's been on the disabled list in 1984 (back spasms), 1985 (a partial tear of the medial collateral ligament in his right knee), 1987 (tenderness of the right shoulder), and 1988 (removal of a disc in his back). This did not deter the Oakland A's, who signed Sanderson in the off-season.

When healthy, Sanderson has been quite hittable. In 737⅔ innings since 1984 he's given up 312 earned runs (3.8 per 9 innings). Last season Sanderson became a forgotten man on the Cubs' staff when manager Don Zimmer excluded him from the three-man rotation he used the last two months of 1989. Sanderson, who'd hurled 92⅓ innings before the All-Star break, pitched only 54 innings over the second half.

Sanderson needs pinpoint control in the lower half of the strike zone to be effective. Whenever his pitches are waist-level or higher, hitters bang them out of the park.

Year	Team	W	L	SV	ERA	IP	H	BB	K
1978	Mon	4	2	0	2.51	61.0	52	21	50
1979	Mon	9	8	1	3.43	168.0	148	54	138
1980	Mon	16	11	0	3.11	211.0	206	56	125
1981	Mon	9	7	0	2.96	137.0	122	31	77
1982	Mon	12	12	0	3.46	224.0	212	58	158
1983	Mon	6	7	1	4.65	81.1	98	20	55
1984	ChN......	8	5	0	3.14	140.2	140	24	76
1985	ChN......	5	6	0	3.12	121.0	100	27	80
1986	ChN......	9	11	1	4.19	169.2	165	37	124
1987	ChN......	8	9	2	4.29	144.2	156	50	106
1988	ChN......	1	2	0	5.28	15.1	13	3	6
1989	ChN......	11	9	0	3.94	146.1	155	31	86
		98	89	5	3.55	1620.0	1567	412	1081

Dave Schmidt

Birth Date: 4/22/57
Throws: Right
1989 Club:
Baltimore Orioles
Contest Code #: 826

Rating: 3

A former Texas Ranger and Chicago White Sox, righty Dave Schmidt is a decent-enough major-league pitcher, though he's no world-beater. Schmidt played out his option with the Chisox in 1986, then signed as a free agent with the Birds in January 1987.

Control is the key for Schmidt. With it, he can be extremely tough. Without it, he's just another thrower. Dave is a three-pitch worker: fastball, slider, palmball. The last, which looks like a split-finger fastball, is easily his best pitch.

Schmidt got 26 starts for the Birds in 1989, in addition to 12 relief appearances. What's disturbing is that his career 3.33 ERA blew up to 5.69. In 156⅔ innings of work, he struck out 46 and walked 36. Not good enough. Neither was his 10–13 record. It also didn't do Dave any good that 1989 was the "walk" year of his contract.

Year	Team	W	L	SV	ERA	IP	H	BB	K
1981	Tex	0	1	1	3.09	32.0	31	11	13
1982	Tex	4	6	6	3.20	109.2	118	25	69
1983	Tex	3	3	2	3.89	46.1	42	14	29
1984	Tex	6	6	12	2.56	70.1	69	20	46
1985	Tex	7	6	5	3.15	85.2	81	22	46
1986	ChA......	3	6	8	3.31	92.1	94	27	67
1987	Bal	10	5	1	3.77	124.0	128	26	70
1988	Bal	8	5	2	3.40	129.2	129	38	67
1989	Bal	10	13	0	5.69	156.2	196	36	46
		51	51	37	3.76	846.2	888	219	453

Mike Schooler

Birth Date: 8/10/62
Throws: Right
1989 Club:
Seattle Mariners
Contest Code #: 827

Rating: 2

Mike Schooler seems to be walking around under a cloud. The twenty-seven-year-old from Cal State-Fullerton gave up 27 runs (24 earned) in 67 appearances last season and yet lost 7 decisions.

Despite his 1–7 won-lost record, Schooler is rapidly becoming one of the AL's top closers. The 6'3", 220-pound powerman is blessed with a good arm and a nasty slider. Lack of control, long a key weakness for Schooler, is no longer. He walked only 19 in 77 innings in 1989. That was a key in Mike's 33 saves, which puts him right in the thick of the AL relief man's race.

The big right-hander was Seattle's second-round selection in the 1985 draft. He spent three-and-a-half seasons in the M's farm system, starting 64 straight games before moving to the bullpen with Calgary in 1988. Twenty appearances later he was in Seattle, where after 107 relief outings, he has become the bullpen's main man.

Year	Team	W	L	SV	ERA	IP	H	BB	K
1988	Sea......	5	8	15	3.54	48.1	45	24	54
1989	Sea......	1	7	33	2.81	77.0	81	19	69
		6	15	48	3.09	125.1	126	43	123

Steve Searcy

Birth Date: 6/4/64
Throws: Left
1989 Club:
Detroit Tigers
Contest Code #: 828

Rating: 2

The Detroit Tigers keep hoping that Steve Searcy makes it. Their third selection in the June 1985 draft, the 6'1", 185-pound left-hander has done it all at the minor-league level, but his major-league cups of coffee have been unsatisfying.

The ex-Tennessee Vol was superb at AA Glens Falls in 1986, where league managers praised his curve ball and pick-off moves as the loop's best. Then he was voted the AAA International League's MVP following a 13–7 season in 1988, complete with a stingy 2.59 ERA and 167 league-leading strikeouts in 170 innings.

To date, it hasn't happened for the Knoxville (TN) native at Detroit. He was 0–2 with a 5.62 ERA in two 1988 starts, then came back to go 1–1 (but with a 6.05 ERA) in 2 starts and 6 relief appearances in 1989. Searcy seems to have the tools, however. Patience, Detroit.

Year	Team	W	L	SV	ERA	IP	H	BB	K
1988	Det	0	2	0	5.62	8.0	8	4	5
1989	Det	1	1	0	6.05	22.1	27	12	11
		1	3	0	5.93	30.1	35	16	16

Lee Smith, Jr.

Birth Date: 12/4/57
Throws: Right
1989 Club:
Boston Red Sox
Contest Code #: 829

Rating: 4

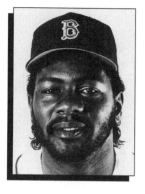

The numbers can be deceptive. Last season looked like Lee Smith's best in years—and it wasn't bad. He went 6–1, picked up 25 team-leading saves, and fanned 96 batters in 70⅔ innings. Terrific. But his ERA (3.57) was his worst since 1984, and the changes in his game plan became noticeable.

The long-time Chicago Cub closer was supposed to bring a pennant to Boston. He hasn't. The blazing, overpowering fastball came up a foot or two short, and that's death to a power pitcher. He can still bring it in at times, but it's beginning to go. The massive (6'6", 250 pounds) Smith now relies more and more on a fine slider. But that's not Lee Smith. The weight and the aching knees are beginning to take their toll. Still, there might be another couple of great years in the strong right arm of the thirty-two-year-old.

Year	Team	W	L	SV	ERA	IP	H	BB	K
1980	ChN......	2	0	0	2.86	22.0	21	14	17
1981	ChN......	3	6	1	3.49	67.0	57	31	50
1982	ChN......	2	5	17	2.69	117.0	105	37	99
1983	ChN......	4	10	29	1.65	103.1	70	41	91
1984	ChN......	9	7	33	3.65	101.0	98	35	86
1985	ChN......	7	4	33	3.04	97.2	87	32	112
1986	ChN......	9	9	31	3.09	90.1	69	42	93
1987	ChN......	4	10	36	3.12	83.2	84	32	96
1988	Bos......	4	5	29	2.80	83.2	72	37	96
1989	Bos......	6	1	25	3.57	70.2	53	33	96
		50	57	234	2.96	836.1	716	334	836

Roy Smith

Birth Date: 9/6/961
Throws: Right
1989 Club:
Minnesota Twins
Contest Code #: 830

Rating: 3

Roy Smith may have finally found his major-league niche. From 1984 to 1988, Smith did split seasons, first with Cleveland, then with Minnesota, and their AAA affiliates. Now, it looks as though he can finally send out his laundry. Fact is, over the past three years, his record with the Twins (two cups of coffee and one full year) is 14–6. Not bad. In fact, he worked 172⅓ innings for Minny in 1989, with decent numbers (10–6, 3.92 ERA).

Still, Smith may find it increasingly difficult to keep his role with the Twins. The acquisition of five ex-Met arms in the Frank Viola trade hurts the future of a relatively inexperienced twenty-eight-year-old. Though Smith's stuff is strictly average, he knows how to change speeds very effectively. Though he'll never be a front-line big-league pitcher, his bus-riding, AAA days seem to be over.

Year	Team	W	L	SV	ERA	IP	H	BB	K
1984	Cle	5	5	0	4.59	86.1	91	40	55
1985	Cle	1	4	0	5.34	62.1	84	17	28
1986	Min......	0	2	0	6.97	10.1	13	5	8
1987	Min......	1	0	0	4.96	16.1	20	6	8
1988	Min......	3	0	0	2.68	37.0	29	12	17
1989	Min......	10	6	1	3.92	172.1	180	51	92
		20	17	1	4.31	384.2	417	131	208

Mike Smithson

Birth Date: 1/21/55
Throws: Right
1989 Club:
Boston Red Sox
Contest Code #: 831

Rating: 3

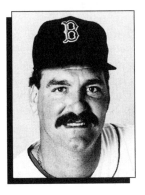

Mike Smithson is one tough cookie. He's a tough competitor who isn't afraid of anyone. And he's not a bad pitcher, although you might not believe it after glancing at Mike's 1989 record with Boston. He went 7–14 in 40 appearances, 19 of them starts. His ERA was an unhealthy 4.95, and he gave up a team-high 21 homers.

Still, the scouts think he can pitch. A one-time Red Sox farmhand, he didn't get to Fenway Park until the 1988 season. He had other stopovers at Texas and Minnesota along the way, winning 43 games for the Twins in three sparkling years (1984–86). He'll likely concentrate on middle and long relief in 1990, with a spot start a real possibility. He's not a power pitcher (61 strikeouts in 143⅔ innings last year). He's a junkman, using a sinker and slider with great effect. Better still, he's always around the plate, which means he doesn't get himself into trouble very often.

Year	Team	W	L	SV	ERA	IP	H	BB	K
1982	Tex	3	4	0	5.01	46.2	51	13	24
1983	Tex	10	14	0	3.91	223.1	233	71	135
1984	Min	15	13	0	3.68	252.0	246	54	144
1985	Min	15	14	0	4.34	257.0	264	78	127
1986	Min	13	14	0	4.77	198.0	234	57	114
1987	Min	4	7	0	5.94	109.0	126	38	53
1988	Bos	9	6	0	5.97	126.2	149	37	73
1989	Bos	7	14	2	4.95	143.2	170	35	61
		76	86	2	4.58	1356.1	1473	383	731

Dave Stewart

Birth Date: 2/19/57
Throws: Right
1989 Club:
Oakland Athletics
Contest Code #: 832

Rating: 5

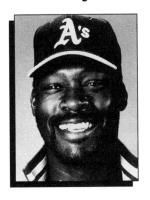

Baseball people often compare Dave Stewart to Rodney Dangerfield. They say he doesn't get any respect. Wrong! He gets plenty of respect; he just doesn't get many awards. The winningest pitcher in the game the last three years (20–13, 21–12, 21–9), Stewie is still looking for his first Cy Young Award. He did, however, win MVP honors for his two victories in the 1989 World Series.

There probably isn't a better money pitcher in the game today. Pressure never rattles the nine-year big-league veteran. It wasn't too long ago (1986) that Stewart was unemployed. Released by the Phillies, the 6'2", 200-pounder with the little, squeaky voice wondered what his next stop would be. When his hometown A's called, Dave ran. It was the team's most valuable phone call ever.

Stew's entire arsenal is first-rate. Both his fastball and slider are at the "plus" level, and his splitter is right up there, too. Bottom line: Stewart's a winner!

Year	Team	W	L	SV	ERA	IP	H	BB	K
1978	LA	0	0	0	0.00	2.0	1	0	1
1981	LA	4	3	6	2.51	43.0	40	14	29
1982	LA	9	8	1	3.81	146.1	137	49	80
1983	Tex	5	2	0	2.14	59.0	50	17	24
1983	LA	5	2	8	2.96	76.0	67	33	54
1984	Tex	7	14	0	4.73	192.1	193	87	119
1985	Tex	0	6	4	5.42	81.1	86	37	64
1985	Phi	0	0	0	6.24	4.1	5	4	2
1986	Phi	0	0	0	6.57	12.1	15	4	9
1986	Oak	9	5	0	3.74	149.1	137	65	102

1987	Oak......	20	13	0	3.68	261.1	224	105	205
1988	Oak......	21	12	0	3.23	275.2	240	110	192
1989	Oak......	21	9	0	3.32	257.2	260	69	155
		101	74	19	3.68	1560.2	1455	594	1036

Dave Stieb

Birth Date: 7/22/57
Throws: Right
1989 Club:
Toronto Blue Jays
Contest Code #: 833

Rating: 5

Toronto's premier starter (he got the ball for Game 1 of last year's AL Championship Series), Dave Stieb can be overpowering at times. In his last 23 starts in 1989, he allowed 3 earned runs or less 17 times. An above-average fastball and slider plus a curve that Stieb uses as a change-up gives him an impressive array of pitches. Hard-luck Dave has lost 3 no-hitters with two men out in the ninth.

About the only weakness in his game is control. It deserts him at times, which can leave him dangling precariously. Otherwise, the native Californian has it all. Toronto's all-time winner (148–117) is the key to a second straight visit to the ALCS.

Year	Team	W	L	SV	ERA	IP	H	BB	K
1979	Tor.......	8	8	0	4.33	129.0	139	48	52
1980	Tor.......	12	15	0	3.70	243.0	232	83	108
1981	Tor.......	11	10	0	3.18	184.0	148	61	89
1982	Tor.......	17	14	0	3.25	288.1	271	75	141
1983	Tor.......	17	12	0	3.04	278.0	223	93	187
1984	Tor.......	16	8	0	2.83	267.0	215	88	198
1985	Tor.......	14	13	0	2.48	265.0	206	96	167
1986	Tor.......	7	12	1	4.74	205.0	239	87	127
1987	Tor.......	13	9	0	4.09	185.0	164	87	115
1988	Tor.......	16	8	0	3.04	207.1	157	79	147
1989	Tor.......	17	8	0	3.35	206.2	164	76	101
		148	117	1	3.37	2458.1	2158	873	1432

Todd Stottlemyre

Birth Date: 5/20/65
Throws: Right
1989 Club:
Toronto Blue Jays
Contest Code #: 834

Rating: 3

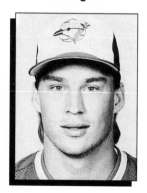

When Todd Stottlemyre made his major-league debut in 1988, he had a perfect game going against the Seattle Mariners for 6⅓. It hasn't exactly been downhill since then, but where can you go from there?

Developing consistency is the key to Todd's future. The son of former Yankee ace and current Met pitching coach Mel Stottlemyre owns an above-average fastball which sometimes fails to move. Even the game's hardest throwers know how dangerous that is. His slider tends to be on the nasty side, but that pitch too is inconsistent.

Whether or not he's getting off-season help from his dad, he is developing a change-up that will help his game. Todd was 7–7 with a 3.88 ERA in 1989, making 18 starts among his 27 game appearances. Scouts rate the 6'3", 190-pound right-hander "a comer."

Year	Team	W	L	SV	ERA	IP	H	BB	K
1988	Tor.......	4	8	0	5.69	98.0	109	46	67
1989	Tor.......	7	7	0	3.88	127.2	137	44	63
		11	15	0	4.67	225.2	246	90	130

Bill Swift

Birth Date: 10/27/61
Throws: Right
1989 Club:
Seattle Mariners
Contest Code #: 835

Rating: 2

On the surface, nothing about Bill Swift will excite you. The Seattle Mariners' right-hander has average stuff all across the board, but there's an unusual sinking action on his fastball which makes it very good indeed at times.

Swift had been a starter for much of his career, which now spans 3½ big-league seasons. Then M's manager, Jim Lefebvre, switched the Maine native to a setup role out of the bullpen. Overall, he made 16 starts and 21 relief appearances in 1989, going 7–3 with a 4.43 ERA. It was the culmination of an excellent comeback for the one-time U. of Maine and 1984 U. S. Olympic Team star, who was 8–19 for Seattle in 1985 and 1986 before spending the entire 1987 season at AAA Calgary of the Pacific Coast League. He returned to the majors in 1988 to go 8–12 for the M's.

Year	Team	W	L	SV	ERA	IP	H	BB	K
1985	Sea......	6	10	0	4.77	120.2	131	48	55
1986	Sea......	2	9	0	5.46	115.1	148	55	55
1988	Sea......	8	12	0	4.59	174.2	199	65	47
1989	Sea......	7	3	1	4.43	130.0	140	38	45
		23	34	1	4.78	540.2	618	206	202

Greg Swindell

Birth Date: 1/2/65
Throws: Left
1989 Club:
Cleveland Indians
Contest Code #: 836

Rating: 4

After three-plus major-league seasons, Greg Swindell has become Cleveland's premier starter. His 13–6 record and 3.37 ERA stuck out for the 73–89 Tribe in 1989.

If Penn State is "Linebacker U.," then the U. of Texas is "Pitcher U.," and Swindell is one of the all-time Longhorns (43–8, 1.92 ERA). He was also the youngest member of the 1984 U. S. Olympic baseball team. The second player chosen in the 1986 draft, the 6'3", 225-pound lefty made only 3 starts in the minors, then moved to Cleveland to stay.

Over the past two seasons, he has won 31 games, pitched 17 complete games and 6 shutouts, and led the club in strikeouts twice. His fastball is above average in velocity and has great movement. His hard slider rates above average as well, and his curveball is decent. Best of all, he's always around the plate. With more support from his teammates, there's no telling how good he can be.

Year	Team	W	L	SV	ERA	IP	H	BB	K
1986	Cle	5	2	0	4.23	61.2	57	15	46
1987	Cle	3	8	0	5.10	102.1	112	37	97
1988	Cle	18	14	0	3.20	242.0	234	45	180
1989	Cle	13	6	0	3.37	184.1	170	51	129
		39	30	0	3.69	590.1	573	148	452

Frank Tanana

Birth Date: 7/3/53
Throws: Left
1989 Club:
Detroit Tigers
Contest Code #: 837

Rating: 4

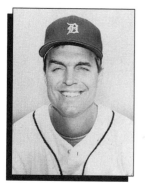

To give you an idea of how tough things were in Detroit last summer, consider this. Frank Tanana produced 10 victories (and 14 defeats) to lead all Tiger starters. And his 3.58 ERA was the best on the club. It was the thirty-six-year-old lefty's first losing season in Detroit, after a four-year mark of 51-37.

A first-round selection of the California Angels in the 1971 draft, Tanana got to the big leagues late in 1973 and has remained in the American League (visiting Boston and Texas between his California and Detroit days) ever since. Tanana makes his living with his curveball. That pitch sets up his fastball, which is especially sneaky when the batter is looking for the breaking pitch. The seventeen-year veteran is one of the great masters of the change of speeds and, unlike too many young pitchers, isn't afraid to come inside on the hitter. Great control completes the Tanana assortment, which produced a hefty new contract and should produce an improved performance in 1990.

Year	Team	W	L	SV	ERA	IP	H	BB	K
1973	Cal	2	2	0	3.12	26.0	20	8	22
1974	Cal	14	19	0	3.11	269.0	262	77	180
1975	Cal	16	9	0	2.63	257.0	211	73	269
1976	Cal	19	10	0	2.44	288.0	212	73	261
1977	Cal	15	9	0	2.54	241.0	201	61	205
1978	Cal	18	12	0	3.65	239.0	239	60	137
1979	Cal	7	5	0	3.90	90.0	93	25	46
1980	Cal	11	12	0	4.15	204.0	223	45	113
1981	Bos	4	10	0	4.02	141.0	142	43	78
1982	Tex	7	18	0	4.21	194.1	199	55	87
1983	Tex	7	9	0	3.16	159.1	144	49	108
1984	Tex	15	15	0	3.25	246.1	234	81	141
1985	Det	10	7	0	3.34	137.1	131	34	107
1985	Tex	2	7	0	5.91	77.2	89	23	52
1986	Det	12	9	0	4.16	188.1	196	65	119
1987	Det	15	10	0	3.91	218.2	216	56	146
1988	Det	14	11	0	4.21	203.0	213	64	127
1989	Det	10	14	0	3.58	223.2	227	74	147
		198	188	0	3.49	3403.2	3252	966	2345

Walt Terrell

Birth Date: 5/11/58
Throws: Right
1989 Club:
San Diego Padres &
New York Yankees
Contest Code #: 838

Rating: 3

Walt Terrell begins the 1990s with his third different opening-day address. The one-time New York Met phenom has lost the label and some of his stuff as well. (The Mets got All-Star third sacker Howard Johnson when they dealt Terrell to Detroit!) Terrell returned to New York with the Yankees last summer, hoping that some of that old Gotham magic will rub off in the Bronx.

It'll have to be powerful. The 6'2", 205-pound Terrell struggles with his control, which gets him into hot water at times. His forkball, which he uses as a change-up, is, perhaps, his best pitch. The rest of his stuff is basically borderline. Terrell made 13 starts for the Bombers last summer, getting decisions in all but 2 of them (6–5). He had been 5–13 (ugh!) in San Diego before the trade.

Year	Team	W	L	SV	ERA	IP	H	BB	K
1982	NYN	0	3	0	3.43	21.0	22	14	8
1983	NYN	8	8	0	3.57	133.2	123	55	59
1984	NYN	11	12	0	3.52	215.0	232	80	114
1985	Det	15	10	0	3.85	229.0	221	95	130
1986	Det	15	12	0	4.56	217.1	199	98	93

		W	L	SV	ERA	IP	H	BB	K
1987	Det	17	10	0	4.05	244.2	254	94	143
1988	Det	7	16	0	3.97	206.1	199	78	84
1989	SD	5	13	0	4.01	123.1	134	26	63
1989	NYA	6	5	0	5.20	83.0	102	24	30
		84	89	0	4.01	1473.1	1486	564	724

Bobby Thigpen

Birth Date: 7/17/63
Throws: Right
1989 Club:
Chicago White Sox
Contest Code #: 839

Rating: 5

When major-league general managers go shopping (fishing?) at Comiskey Park, they usually begin with Bobby Thigpen. The Chisox premier closer is arguably the team's best pitcher, which might be faint praise, but isn't intended to be. The 6′3″, 195-pound fireman has outstanding stuff. Both his fastball and slider are outstanding and his control, once his biggest bugaboo, is rapidly improving.

A big leaguer for only three seasons and a couple of days, Thigpen made only 54 minor-league appearances (the last 25 were starts) before coming to Chicago in 1986. In fact, Thigpen lacked pitching experience coming out of college. (He was primarily an outfielder at Mississippi State, except for an occasional spot start.) So gaining experience is the key to Thigpen's future development.

Year	Team	W	L	SV	ERA	IP	H	BB	K
1986	ChA	2	0	7	1.77	35.2	26	12	20
1987	ChA	7	5	16	2.73	89.0	86	24	52
1988	ChA	5	8	34	3.30	90.0	96	33	62
1989	ChA	2	6	34	3.76	79.0	62	40	47
		16	19	91	3.06	293.2	270	109	181

Mark Thurmond

Birth Date: 9/12/56
Throws: Left
1989 Club:
Baltimore Orioles
Contest Code #: 840

Rating: 4

Mark Thurmond made a comeback of sorts a year ago. After losing his major-league job with a 1–8 mark for the awful 1988 Orioles (with a subsequent demotion to Rochester), the thirty-three-year-old lefty bounced back with a 2–4 mark and 3.90 ERA in 49 appearances with the Birds. The native Texan burst into the big time with San Diego back in 1983, going 7–3 and 14–8 with the Padres his first two years. He hasn't had a winning season since, bouncing from San Diego to Detroit and on to Baltimore. Walking only 17 in 90 innings of work, Thurmond showed he still has control. Trouble is, despite a four-pitch repertoire (fastball, curve, slider, change), none of them is overwhelming. Worse still, the 6′, 193-pounder has a tough time getting right-handed batters out. That means middle relief and special-situation relief—which isn't good news for an eleven-year pro who has been bouncing around of late.

Year	Team	W	L	SV	ERA	IP	H	BB	K
1983	SD	7	3	0	2.65	115.1	104	33	49
1984	SD	14	8	0	2.97	178.2	174	55	57
1985	SD	7	11	2	3.97	138.1	154	44	57
1986	SD	3	7	0	6.50	70.2	96	27	32
1986	Det	4	1	3	1.92	51.2	44	17	17

1987	Det	0	1	5	4.23	61.2	83	24	21
1988	Bal	1	8	3	4.58	74.2	80	27	29
1989	Bal	2	4	4	3.90	90.0	102	17	34
		38	43	17	3.71	781.0	837	244	296

Duane Ward

Birth Date: 5/28/64
Throws: Right
1989 Club:
Toronto Blue Jays
Contest Code #: 841

Rating: 2

Power is the name of Duane Ward's game. In 1989, the hefty 6'4", 205-pounder led his club in the two power categories: strikeouts (122) and wild pitches. There has never been a doubt about Ward's heat. He can really bring it to the plate. On occasion, the plate moves around on the right-hander. On other occasions, the fastball doesn't move, which can be hazardous to a power pitcher's health.

The New Mexico native came to the Jays in the middle of the 1986 season, after a single decision (a loss) as a member of the Atlanta Braves. His first full season in Toronto was 1988 (9–3, 3.30 ERA, 15 saves). As half of the Jays' closing crew in 1989, he went 4–10 with a 3.77 ERA and another 15 saves. If Ward can increase the control and movement on his fastball and improve an already effective slider, Toronto will be that much stronger.

Year	Team	W	L	SV	ERA	IP	H	BB	K
1986	Atl.......	0	1	0	7.31	16.0	22	8	8
1986	Tor......	0	1	0	13.50	2.0	3	4	1
1987	Tor......	1	0	0	6.95	11.2	14	12	10
1988	Tor......	9	3	15	3.30	111.2	101	60	91
1989	Tor......	4	10	15	3.77	114.2	94	58	122
		14	15	30	4.01	256.0	234	142	232

Gary Wayne

Birth Date: 11/30/62
Throws: Left
1989 Club:
Minnesota Twins
Contest Code #: 842

Rating: 2

Gary Wayne has the perfect background for a relief pitcher. He majored in math at the U. of Michigan. All the better for him to compute his numbers. The long, lean lefty enjoyed a decent rookie year after the Twins acquired him from the Expos' farm system after the 1988 season. Montreal let him go after a series of foot fractures and re-fractures sidelined him for all but 7⅓ innings of that season.

Thanks to a tricky delivery that the scouts call "funky", Wayne was an effective setup man for Jeff Reardon. He worked 71 innings in 60 games, finishing 21 times and recording one save. The scouts aren't impressed with Wayne's stuff, though his motion enables him to get as much as possible out of it. What will keep him in action is the fact that he's a left-hander. Southpaws remain valuable commodities.

Year	Team	W	L	SV	ERA	IP	H	BB	K
1989	Min......	3	4	1	3.30	71.0	55	36	41
		3	4	1	3.30	71.0	55	36	41

Bill Wegman

Birth Date: 12/19/62
Throws: Right
1989 Club:
Milwaukee Brewers
Contest Code #: 843

Rating: 3

Bill Wegman must have loved New Year's Day. He couldn't wait to see the new decade roll in. Except for bad luck, the 6'5", 200-pound Milwaukee Brewer hurler didn't have any luck at all in 1989. First, he struggled against anything the American League could offer. His 2–6 record was something he'd like to forget, but the month of May was even worse. Wegman went 1–3 with a highly inelegant 10.35 ERA. The Brew Crew went 2–9 in the games he worked. By June 1, he was on the DL with right-shoulder tendinitis, finally winding up on the surgeon's table on July 7. Word out of the Arizona Instructional League last fall indicated that Wegman had a shot to come back strong in 1990.

Year	Team	W	L	SV	ERA	IP	H	BB	K
1985	Mil	2	0	0	3.57	17.2	17	3	6
1986	Mil	5	12	0	5.13	198.1	217	43	82
1987	Mil	12	11	0	4.24	225.0	229	53	102
1988	Mil	13	13	0	4.12	199.0	207	50	84
1989	Mil	2	6	0	6.71	51.0	69	21	27
		34	42	0	4.62	691.0	739	170	301

Bob Welch

Birth Date: 11/3/56
Throws: Right
1989 Club:
Oakland Athletics
Contest Code #: 844

Rating: 5

Bob Welch seems to be getting better and better. A lifetime 115–86 (3.14 ERA) in 10 NL years with Los Angeles, Welch came to Oakland in the well-documented three-way deal before the 1988 season, and has proceeded to put together a pair of 17-win seasons (17–9, 17–8) for his new employers.

Baseball folks love Welch because of his tremendous work habits and his totally competitive nature. He combines a plus-fastball with a mean curve to baffle AL hitters. He comes after the hitters and has that unique ability to make the big pitch when he needs to. The lanky 6'3", 193-pound right-hander was an All-American at Eastern Michigan U. before spending two seasons in the Dodgers' minor-league system. Welch's 209⅔ innings pitched in 1989 marked his fourth straight year over 200 since a sprained elbow sidelined him in 1985.

Year	Team	W	L	SV	ERA	IP	H	BB	K
1978	LA	7	4	3	2.03	111.0	92	26	66
1979	LA	5	6	5	4.00	81.0	82	32	64
1980	LA	14	9	0	3.28	214.0	190	79	141
1981	LA	9	5	0	3.45	141.0	141	41	88
1982	LA	16	11	0	3.36	235.2	199	81	176
1983	LA	15	12	0	2.65	204.0	164	72	156
1984	LA	13	13	0	3.78	178.2	191	58	126
1985	LA	14	4	0	2.31	167.1	141	35	96
1986	LA	7	13	0	3.28	235.2	227	55	183
1987	LA	15	9	0	3.22	251.2	204	86	196
1988	Oak	17	9	0	3.64	244.2	237	81	158
1989	Oak	17	8	0	3.00	209.2	191	78	137
		149	103	8	3.18	2274.1	2059	724	1587

David Wells

Birth Date: 5/20/63
Throws: Left
1989 Club:
Toronto Blue Jays
Contest Code #: 845

Rating: 2

Big-league scouts are mighty impressed with line-backer-sized lefty David Wells. The California native started in the Toronto Blue Jays organization in 1982, saw his first big-league action late in the 1987 season, and had his busiest year in 1989. The 6'4", 225-pounder got into 54 Toronto games (all in relief) last year, running up a 7–4 record and a healthy 2.40 ERA. He got credit for 2 saves, despite finishing 19 games.

The book on Wells points to a plus-fastball and a plus-slider (at least most of the time). The weakness in his game to this point is his inability to change speeds. He was working on a split-fingered fastball late last year, which could fill that function for him. The future for a big left-hander who can throw hard, hit the corners, and change speeds is tremendous.

Year	Team	W	L	SV	ERA	IP	H	BB	K
1987	Tor.......	4	3	1	3.99	29.1	37	12	32
1988	Tor.......	3	5	4	4.62	64.1	65	31	56
1989	Tor.......	7	4	2	2.40	86.1	66	28	78
		14	12	7	3.45	180.0	168	71	166

David West

Birth Date: 9/1/64
Throws: Left
1989 Club:
New York Mets &
Minnesota Twins
Contest Code #: 846

Rating: 3

Last spring, the only question about left-hander David West was when he would arrive with the New York Mets. Off three straight sub-3.00 ERA years in the minors (including a spectacular 1.80 and a 12–4 record with Tidewater in 1988), West carried the "can't miss" label with pride. There were a few eyebrows raised when the Mets returned the 6'6", 220-pounder to Tidewater to open 1989. Then when he finally arrived in June, wise heads nodded—well, wisely.

The can't-miss superstar missed at Shea. He was rocked, running up a hefty 7.40 ERA and an 0–2 record. The debut prompted the Mets to include West in the deal which brought Frank Viola home to Flushing. Meanwhile, the Twins hope that West will recover the poise, command, and curveball that made him a AAA superstar. His 6.41 ERA in 10 games (5 starts) with Minnesota leaves some doubts.

Year	Team	W	L	SV	ERA	IP	H	BB	K
1988	NYN	1	0	0	3.00	6.0	6	3	3
1989	NYN	0	2	0	7.40	24.1	25	14	19
1989	Min......	3	2	0	6.41	39.1	48	19	31
		4	4	0	6.46	69.2	79	36	53

Frank Williams

Birth Date: 2/13/58
Throws: Right
1989 Club:
Detroit Tigers
Contest Code #: 847

Rating: 2

A sore right elbow threw Frank Williams' 1989 season into disarray. In his first American League season after signing as a free agent, the right-hander had an unremarkable 3–3 season and a 3.64 ERA, even 1 save, in 42 relief appearances for the Detroit Tigers. The elbow, however, sent Williams to the disabled list twice (once in June on the 15-day DL and again in July on the 21-day list). Williams was fairly effective, stranding 25 of 36 inherited runners.

Year	Team	W	L	SV	ERA	IP	H	BB	K
1984	SF.......	9	4	3	3.55	106.1	88	51	91
1985	SF.......	2	4	0	4.19	73.0	65	35	54
1986	SF.......	3	1	1	1.20	52.1	35	21	33
1987	Cin	4	0	2	2.30	105.2	101	39	60
1988	Cin	3	2	1	2.59	62.2	59	35	43
1989	Det	3	3	1	3.64	71.2	70	46	33
		24	14	8	3.00	471.2	418	227	314

Mark Williamson

Birth Date: 7/21/59
Throws: Right
1989 Club:
Baltimore Orioles
Contest Code #: 848

Rating: 3

Mark Williamson is a superb addition to any pitching staff. A tough competitor, he challenges hitters. The payoff last season was his first winning record in the big leagues. Williamson went 8–9 (4.03) and 5–8 (4.90) in his first two trips to Baltimore. In 1989, he got into 65 games for the Birds, going 10–5 with a sparkling 2.93 ERA. He added 9 saves, second only to Gregg Olson among Oriole relievers. Williamson's fastball is far from overpowering. He also throws a sinker, slider, and palmball. The last is his best pitch.

The Californian originally signed with the Padres and came to the Orioles at the end of the 1986 season. He spent parts of the following two seasons with Rochester in addition to time with the O's. But now the minors seem behind him, especially if manager Frank Robinson can get him a spot as a setup man for Olson.

Year	Team	W	L	SV	ERA	IP	H	BB	K
1987	Bal	8	9	3	4.03	125.0	122	41	73
1988	Bal	5	8	2	4.90	117.2	125	40	69
1989	Bal	10	5	9	2.93	107.1	105	30	55
		23	22	14	3.99	350.0	352	111	197

Bobby Witt

Birth Date: 5/11/64
Throws: Right
1989 Club:
Texas Rangers
Contest Code #: 849

Rating: 4

Former Oklahoma Sooner star Bobby Witt continues to show major-league stuff and continues to struggle with control and his won-loss record. One encouraging sign: Witt stayed healthy throughout 1989. The 6'2", 205-pound right-hander had been disabled in each of his previous two seasons. Last year, he was second among Ranger starters in starts (31), innings (194⅓), and strikeouts (166). Still, the record was only 12–13 and the ERA was a hefty 5.14.

Scouts are beginning to scrutinize Witt's fastball, which may have gone just a little backward. These days, Bobby's slider is his most effective pitch. He's working diligently at perfecting his change of speeds. When he runs into control problems, he really struggles. In fact,

Witt led the majors with 114 walks—the third time in his four AL years that he has owned that dubious title.

Year	Team	W	L	SV	ERA	IP	H	BB	K
1986	Tex	11	9	0	5.48	157.2	130	143	174
1987	Tex	8	10	0	4.91	143.0	114	140	160
1988	Tex	8	10	0	3.92	174.1	134	101	148
1989	Tex	12	13	0	5.14	194.1	182	114	166
		39	42	0	4.85	669.1	560	498	648

Mike Witt

Birth Date: 7/20/60
Throws: Right
1989 Club:
California Angels
Contest Code #: 850

Rating: 4

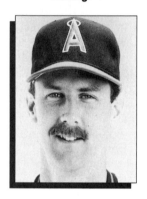

Mike Witt would just like to forget 1989. A season-ending perfect game in 1984, the thirteenth in major-league history, started Witt on a ride to the top of the roller coaster. He led the Angels in victories from 1984 to 1988, averaging 15.4 wins each year. The fastball was overpowering, the curve ball was tricky. Now, after a 9–15 1989 campaign, worst among Angel starters, questions are being asked.

Witt's problems begin with the fastball, which seems to have lost a little of its zip. As a result, Mike goes to the curve ball too often—and enemy hitters are all over it. That has to be a concern for Angel management. Still, Witt was out there 33 times and put in 220 innings. Though not overpowering, Witt has power, as his 123 strikeouts (only 48 walks) indicate. But he had only 5 complete games after years of 14, 10 and 12. At age twenty-nine, however, Mike is too young to give up on.

Year	Team	W	L	SV	ERA	IP	H	BB	K
1981	Cal	8	9	0	3.28	129.0	123	47	75
1982	Cal	8	6	0	3.51	179.2	177	47	85
1983	Cal	7	14	5	4.91	154.0	173	75	77
1984	Cal	15	11	0	3.47	246.2	227	84	196
1985	Cal	15	9	0	3.56	250.0	228	98	180
1986	Cal	18	10	0	2.84	269.0	218	73	208
1987	Cal	16	14	0	4.01	247.0	252	84	192
1988	Cal	13	16	0	4.15	249.2	263	87	133
1989	Cal	9	15	0	4.54	220.0	252	48	123
		109	104	5	3.78	1945.0	1913	643	1269

Ed Wojna

Birth Date: 8/20/60
Throws: Right
1989 Club:
Cleveland Indians
Contest Code #: 851

Rating: 3

The question is not about Ed Wojna's pitching. The itinerant right-hander started in the Philadelphia Phillies' organization in 1981, drifted to the San Diego Padres (for whom he pitched 27 times in 1985–1987), strayed to the Chicago White Sox, and arrived in Cleveland in January 1989. Wojna, who was 4–9 in the NL, is now 0–1 in the AL, after 9 appearances (3 starts) for the Tribe last year.

Year	Team	W	L	SV	ERA	IP	H	BB	K
1985	SD.......	2	4	0	5.79	42.0	53	19	18
1986	SD.......	2	2	0	3.23	39.0	42	16	19
1987	SD.......	0	3	0	5.89	18.1	25	6	13
1989	Cle	0	1	0	4.09	33.0	31	14	10
		4	10	0	4.62	132.1	151	55	60

Rich Yett

Birth Date: 10/6/62
Throws: Right
1989 Club:
Cleveland Indians
Contest Code #: 852

Rating: 3

No one seems to be able to figure out Rich Yett—yet. Velocity? He still throws hard enough. Variety? His stuff is decent enough, and his split-fingered fastball is pretty good. Yet Yett can't seem to put it all together. Control is a problem. In 99 innings last year he struck out 47 and walked 47. As a long reliever and spot starter, he went 5–6 with an unimpressive 5.00 ERA.

The good news for 1990 is that the California native seems to pitch better in even-numbered years. He followed a 5–3 1986 with a 3–9 1987. He bounced back to 9–6 (despite a series of injuries) in 1988 before flopping again in 1989. Possibly the most disturbing statistical fact is his 4.98 career ERA. You simply cannot win consistently in the majors allowing 5 earned runs every 9 innings.

Year	Team	W	L	SV	ERA	IP	H	BB	K
1985	Min......	0	0	0	27.26	0.1	1	2	0
1986	Cle	5	3	1	5.15	78.2	84	37	50
1987	Cle	3	9	1	5.25	97.2	96	49	59
1988	Cle	9	6	0	4.62	134.1	146	55	71
1989	Cle	5	6	0	5.00	99.0	111	47	47
		22	24	2	4.98	410.0	438	190	227

Curt Young

Birth Date: 4/16/60
Throws: Left
1989 Club:
Oakland Athletics
Contest Code #: 853

Rating: 3

One of the few homegrown pitchers on the Oakland roster, Curt Young relies on a sharp breaking ball along with a reasonable fastball and a straight change to make him a valuable member of the Athletics' staff. While most of the A's hurlers, like Dennis Eckersley, Dave Stewart, Bob Welch, and Mike Moore, among others, got their grounding in other big-league organizations, Young has been Oakland property since leaving Central Michigan U. in 1981. The 6'1", 180-pounder spent the better part of three seasons on the Oakland farm before arriving at the Coliseum last in 1983, though he didn't stay full-time until 1987.

For the 1989 world champs, the southpaw went 5–9 with a 3.73 ERA in 20 starts and 5 relief appearances. His 47 walks (only 55 strikeouts) in 111 innings offer proof of sporadic control, which limits Young's overall effectiveness.

Year	Team	W	L	SV	ERA	IP	H	BB	K
1983	Oak......	0	1	0	16.00	9.0	17	5	5
1984	Oak......	9	4	0	4.06	108.2	118	31	41
1985	Oak......	0	4	0	7.24	46.0	57	22	19
1986	Oak......	13	9	0	3.45	198.0	176	57	116
1987	Oak......	13	7	0	4.08	203.0	194	44	124
1988	Oak......	11	8	0	4.15	156.1	162	50	69
1989	Oak......	5	9	0	3.73	111.0	117	47	55
		51	42	0	4.20	832.0	841	256	429

Matt Young

Birth Date: 8/9/58
Throws: Left
1989 Club:
Oakland Athletics
Contest Code #: 854

Rating: 3

On the pitching-rich Athletics, Matt Young is just another arm, and not exactly a healthy one. The big (6'3", 205-pounds) left-hander has a history of arm problems—one that kept him out for the entire 1988 season, before reconstructive elbow surgery (the Tommy John operation) got him back in action in 1989. Young put in four years with Seattle and one with the Los Angeles Dodgers (1987) before arriving in Oakland as part of the multi-team deal involving Alfredo Griffin and Bob Welch. He'll be back in Seattle in 1990.

A starter for the first half of his career, the California native moved to the bullpen in 1986 and has made only 9 starts and 129 relief appearances since then. The scouting reports indicate that Young's stuff remains effective, though sporadic control problems create difficulties.

Year	Team	W	L	SV	ERA	IP	H	BB	K
1983	Sea......	11	15	0	3.27	203.2	178	79	130
1984	Sea......	6	8	0	5.72	113.1	141	57	73
1985	Sea......	12	19	1	4.91	218.1	242	76	136
1986	Sea......	8	6	13	3.82	103.2	108	46	82
1987	LA......	5	8	11	4.47	54.1	62	17	42
1989	Oak......	1	4	0	6.75	37.1	42	31	27
		43	60	25	4.48	730.2	773	306	490

OFFICIAL RULES

NO PURCHASE NECESSARY TO ENTER

1. In the spaces provided on an official entry form, hand print your name, address, and the names and code numbers of the 24 players from the American League whom you have selected for your roster. Only those players profiled in this book may be selected. You must select 6 outfielders, 1 first baseman, 1 second baseman, 1 third baseman, 1 shortstop, 2 additional infielders, 2 catchers, and 10 pitchers. The positions assigned to the players in this book are the positions you must use in choosing your team. Each player profiled in this book has been assigned rating points. Your team's combined rating point total must not exceed 75. You must choose at least one player from at least 7 of the 14 American League teams.

2. Mail your completed entry to: Baseball Contest 1990: American League, P.O. Box 4803, Blair, NE 68009. All entries must be received by the day of the All-Star Game, July 10, 1990. Not responsible for lost, late or misdirected mail.

Additional official entry forms and a complete listing of the American League players profiled in this book can be obtained by sending a self-addressed, stamped (state of WA residents need not affix return postage), #10 envelope by June 20, 1990 to: American League Baseball Entry Form, P.O. Box 4821, Blair, NE 68009. Limit one request per envelope.

3. One $10,000 prize will be awarded to the individual who has selected the roster with the highest combined actual statistics at the end of the 1990 regular season. Points will be based on actual player performance in 1990 and will be tabulated as follows:

Batting Average = 1 point for each .001
Number of Home Runs × 10
Number of Runs Batted In × 3
Number of Runs Scored × 3
Earned Run Average = 1 point for each .01 below 6.00
Number of Wins × 30
Number of Losses × − 10
Number of Saves × 10

A batter must have at least 100 at bats to earn Batting Average points; a pitcher must pitch at least 20 innings to earn Earned Run Average points. In the event of a tie, the prize will be divided in equal shares among the winners.

Changes to an entrant's roster will not be permitted once mailed. If a chosen player is traded to the American League, sent to the minors, injured or retires during the season, the entrant will only earn points for the player's performance before he left the American League during the 1990 regular season.

4. Prizewinner selection will be under the supervision of the D. L. Blair Corporation, an independent judging organization whose decisions are final. Potential winners must respond to any required Affidavit of Eligibility/Prize Acceptance Form within 21 days of attempted delivery of same. Noncompliance within this time period will result in disqualification and an alternate will be selected. Winners will be notified by mail. Taxes on prize are the sole responsibility of the winner(s). No substitution or transfer of prize permitted. Chances of winning are determined by the total number of entries received.

5. Sweepstakes participation open to U.S. citizens residing in the U.S., except employees of Cloverdale Press Inc., Little, Brown & Co., their subsidiaries, affiliates, advertising and promotion agencies and their immediate family members. Offer is subject to all federal, state and local laws and regulations and is void in Puerto Rico and wherever prohibited by law. Winner's entry and acceptance of prize offered constitute permission to use name of winner(s), photograph, or other likeness for purposes of advertising and promotion on behalf of Cloverdale Press Inc. and/or Little, Brown & Co., without further compensation to the winner.

6. For the name of the winner(s), available after March 15, 1991, send a separate, self-addressed, stamped, #10 envelope to: Baseball Winner: American League, P. 0. Box 4846, Blair, NE 68009.

BASEBALL CONTEST 1990: AMERICAN LEAGUE PLAYERS

OFFICIAL ENTRY FORM

NO PURCHASE NECESSARY TO ENTER

Please Print Clearly:

Name _____

Address _____

City _____ State _____ Zip _____

Clearly print the 3-digit codes (see player profiles for the correct codes) and names of the 24 players you have selected for your American League Roster. You must select 6 outfielders, 1 first baseman, 1 second baseman, 1 third baseman, 1 shortstop, 2 additional infielders, 2 catchers and 10 pitchers. (All players selected must be profiled in this book.) You have a total of 75 rating points to spend on your team, based on the ratings for each player in this book. Entries with more than 75 total rating points will be disqualified. You must choose one player from at least 7 of the 14 American League teams.

	Outfielders:	3-Digit Code:		Infielders:	3-Digit Code:
1.	_____	_____	11.	_____	_____
2.	_____	_____	12.	_____	_____
3.	_____	_____		**Catchers:**	
4.	_____	_____	13.	_____	_____
5.	_____	_____	14.	_____	_____
6.	_____	_____		**Pitchers:**	
	First Baseman:		15.	_____	_____
7.	_____	_____	16.	_____	_____
	Second Baseman:		17.	_____	_____
8.	_____	_____	18.	_____	_____
			19.	_____	_____
	Third Baseman:		20.	_____	_____
9.	_____	_____	21.	_____	_____
			22.	_____	_____
	Shortstop:		23.	_____	_____
10.	_____	_____	24.	_____	_____

Mail your completed entry to:

Baseball Contest 1990:
American League Players
P.O. Box 4803
Blair, NE 68009

Entries must be received by the day of the All-Star Game, July 10, 1990. Entrants will receive 10 bonus points per day for each day their entry is received prior to the All-Star Game.

See Official Rules for complete details and to obtain an additional official entry form and complete listing of eligible players profiled in this book.

All federal, state and local laws and regulations apply. Offer void in Puerto Rico and wherever prohibited by law.